A SURVIVAL GUIDE FOR THE PRESCHOOL TEACHER

Jean R. Feldman, Ph.D.

Illustrated by Rebecca Feldman

THE CENTER FOR APPLIED
RESEARCH IN EDUCATION
West Nyack, New York 10995

Library of Congress Cataloging-in-Publication Data

Feldman, Jean R.
    A survival guide for the preschool teacher / Jean R. Feldman
illustrated by Rebecca Feldman.
      p. cm.
    Includes bibliographical references.
    ISBN 0-87628-884-0
    1. Education, Preschool—Handbooks, manuals, etc. 2. Preschool
teaching—Handbooks, manuals, etc. 3. Nursery schools—
Administration—Handbooks, manuals, etc. I. Title.
LB1140.2.F43   1990
372.21—dc20

Printed in the United States of America

20 19 18 17 16

C8840-5

ISBN 0-87628-884-0

**THE CENTER FOR APPLIED RESEARCH
IN EDUCATION**
West Nyack, NY 10994

On the World Wide Web at http://www.phdirect.com

This book is dedicated to
ALL MY CHILDREN

About the Author

Jean Feldman has been teaching young children in the Atlanta area for the past 20 years. Currently she is an instructor in the Early Childhood Department at DeKalb Technical Institute. Dr. Feldman has a B.A. from the University of Georgia, a D.A.S.T. from Emory University, and an M.A. and Ph.D. from Georgia State University. She is a member of the National Association for the Education of Young Children, American Vocational Association, and the Georgia Preschool Association. Dr. Feldman is a frequent presenter to community and professional groups, as well as contributing editor to *Atlanta Parent Newspaper.*

About This Survival Guide

Teaching is both "heart" and "science." The "heart" of teaching lies in the personal characteristics that bring you to the job. The "science" involves your teaching skills and the knowledge you have about children. *A Survival Guide for the Preschool Teacher* is an all-in-one resource that gives you guidelines and step-by-step suggestions for making the most of both the "heart" and "science" of preschool teaching.

Developed for both new and experienced preschool teachers and administrators, this multipurpose book combines essential child development theory with practical application to give you the tools for making the preschool environment a successful and special place for children. Included are scores of easy-to-use activities, games, projects, and lessons—many reproducible—that will help you create a more meaningful, exciting, and challenging preschool program. You will find the following to be some of the special features of this guide:

** Activities, techniques, and strategies can be adapted across the preschool through primary levels.
** Time-saving reproducibles are included throughout.
** Practical, easily accessible materials are suggested for all activities, games, and projects.
** All activities are classroom-tested.
** Language is direct and easy to follow.
** Specific strategies and guidelines for working with staff members are provided.

For ease of use, the book is organized into 15 sections, each one focusing on a critical aspect of preschool education:

CHILDREN, the first section, focuses on basic principles of child development and provides information on age characteristics and their implications for teachers.
CLASSROOM MANAGEMENT AND GUIDANCE includes practical suggestions for establishing classroom rules, developing schedules, communicating with your class, and dealing with discipline problems.
THE LEARNING ENVIRONMENT provides recommendations for organizing and arranging your classroom and creating 12 different kinds of learning centers, as well as an outdoor play area.
CURRICULUM includes strategies for planning and implementing lessons and activities in the major curriculum areas on a daily and yearly basis.
LANGUAGE DEVELOPMENT AND READING READINESS highlights whole

language experiences with activities and games for developing reading, writing, speaking, and listening skills.

MATHEMATICS features manipulatives and hands-on learning experiences to make math more meaningful. Included is a section on computers in the classroom.

SCIENCE provides strategies for motivating children to think and learn about the world around them. Topics include the human body, plants, animals, weather, the earth, the solar system, and ecology.

STORYTIME MAGIC offers creative suggestions, for choosing, introducing, and telling a story.

CREATIVE ARTS features over 100 simple art projects you can do in your classroom. Materials and projects suggested include crayons, chalk, paint, collage, molding, mobiles, and puppets.

MUSIC AND MOVEMENT highlights favorite songs, fingerplays, and suggestions for creative movement. Directions for making homemade instruments are included.

SMALL MOTOR SKILLS features activities that develop small muscles. Prewriting experiences are emphasized.

LARGE MOTOR SKILLS focuses on the importance of physical fitness and offers suggestions for indoor and outdoor games and activities, and ideas for homemade equipment.

NUTRITION AND COOKING provides nutrition tips for children, activities for learning while cooking, and simple recipes for children that include fruits and vegetables, milk and milk products, breads and cereals, and meats.

PUTTING IT ALL TOGETHER WITH A TEACHING THEME provides suggested topics for unit themes. A sample unit on bears is included.

THE PROFESSIONAL TEACHER offers tips for dealing with stress, working with parents, and conducting conferences. A list of professional early childhood organizations is provided.

In addition, at the end of the book you'll find two helpful appendices. *Appendix A* provides games and activity patterns for letter sounds and various monthly activities. *Appendix B* presents a listing of commercial resources and suppliers of educational materials.

A Survival Guide for the Preschool Teacher addresses the many varied roles and responsibilities of the preschool educator—teacher, friend, manager, coach, salesperson, nurse, housekeeper, guide. While trying to fulfill these diverse roles can be challenging, you will know that you have made a difference in the lives of young children. We all have our own personal reasons for choosing to work with children; perhaps yours is a special teacher you had long ago. I hope this book will inspire you and help you in your attempt to be that special teacher for the children in your class.

Jean R. Feldman

Contents

1

CHILDREN

Helping each child develop to his or her full potential physically, socially, emotionally, and intellectually is a tremendous responsibility. Include the elements described in this section in your program, and you'll be well on your way to providing children with the kind of environment that will encourage them to learn, grow, and be happy.

Why Study Child Growth and Development?

Knowledge of child growth and development will enable you to know what behavior and characteristics you can expect in children at different ages. You can use this information to help you decide how to set up the room and how to offer children challenging learning opportunities. Above all, a foundation in child development will help you answer the most important question, "What is *best* for children?"

These principles of development will guide you in making decisions that are developmentally appropriate:

1. Development follows predictable patterns. Children develop in stages and the sequence of these stages is the same.
2. There are large differences in the rate at which children develop. Even when children are the same chronological age, their level of knowledge and skills will vary widely.
3. Development is often uneven. Children may develop more quickly in some areas than others.
4. Development proceeds from simple to complex and from general to specific. Each skill is built on a simpler one until the child learns more refined skills and concepts.
5. Learning proceeds from the concrete to the abstract. Children need real-life experiences interacting with concrete objects in order to construct knowledge.
6. Development cannot be "taught" or hurried. If children are forced to perform beyond their abilities, it may damage their self-concept or cause negative attitudes about school.
7. Children have different styles of learning, as well as different interests, needs, and motivations.
8. Intellectual, social, emotional, and physical development are intricately interwoven. It is important to develop a well-rounded child with experiences in all the domains.

When you understand how children think and behave at different ages, you will know how to guide them, motivate them, and how to provide optimum learning environment and experiences for them. An understanding of child development will also improve your confidence and will enable you to adjust your program to the individual needs of the children in your classroom. Your school library, public library, or a college library are all good sources for material on child growth and development.

What Are the Major Areas of Development?

From the moment of birth, children learn and grow in many ways. These are the major areas in which development will occur:

- *Physical Development*—This involves the way children use their large and small muscles. Large muscles are used for activities such as walking, running, and throwing; small muscles are used for drawing, writing, feeding, and dressing.
- *Social Development*—Social development refers to how children interact with other children and adults in their lives. Social skills include sharing, cooperating, and following rules.

- *Emotional Development*—Emotional development includes children's feelings about themselves, their self-esteem, and their ability to express their feelings.
- *Language Development*—Language development refers to children's ability to listen, understand, speak, and eventually to read and write.
- *Cognitive or Intellectual Development*—Intellectual development involves children's ability to think, reason, and solve problems. It includes forming concepts, remembering ideas, and recognizing objects.

What Should You Know About Two-Year-Olds?

Two-year-olds can be terrific, and sometimes troublesome! They are full of energy and curiosity, so they need teachers who are alert, understanding, flexible, and creative.

What Are Two-Year-Olds Like?		*How Can We Teach Them?*
Very active.	P	Give many opportunities for indoor
Can walk, run, jump on 2 feet, tip-toe, and climb.	H	and outdoor running and climbing.
	Y	Offer children a wide variety of
Can scribble, work a 3- or 4-piece	S	material to work with.
puzzle, string large beads, stack	I	
blocks, mold play dough, and paint.	C	Give children opportunities to
Can feed self, clean-up, and is	A	dress, feed self, and care for toys.
learning to use bathroom.	L	Praise efforts at toileting.
Generally plays alone, but beginning	S	Blocks and housekeeping areas en-
parallel play.	O	courage children to play with others.
Doesn't share well.	C	Have duplicates of toys.
May be aggressive with other	I	Watch children closely and be a
children.	A	good model.
	L	Encourage children to use words to
		express their feelings.

Becoming independent and aware of "self."

Favorite words are "no" and "me do it."

Easily frustrated when cannot do something.

Doesn't like changes.

Emotional swings—laughing or crying.

E M O T I O N A L

Allow children choices and to do as much as they can for themselves.

Have age-appropriate toys and activities.

Provide a secure environment and follow a regular schedule.

Be reassuring and sensitive.

Says 200–600 words.

Understands more than he or she says.

Likes repetition.

Uses language to express ideas.

L A N G U A G E

Encourage children to talk, talk, talk.

Describe what you are doing and what the children are doing.

Sing songs, say rhymes, and reread favorite books.

Expect and encourage children to express their wants and needs.

Short attention span.

Learns through senses.

Can match colors and like pictures.

Can identify body parts.

I N T E L L E C T U A L

Keep activities short. Provide different activities and toys children can choose from.

Let children touch, smell, taste, see, and hear.

Use matching games and sorting activities.

Sing songs and play games with body parts.

What Are the Characteristics of Three-Year-Olds?

Three-year-olds are cooperative, cheerful, and eager to please. They enjoy new experiences, their friends, and are becoming increasingly independent.

What Are Three-Year-Olds Like?

Can walk backwards, run, (swinging arms), balance on 1 foot, climb stairs alternating feet, ride a tricycle, and throw.

Has greater control of hands. Colors, cuts straight line, draws lines and circles.
Can pour juice, use a spoon and fork, dress and undress self.
Brushes teeth, washes hands, and has bladder and bowel control (most of the time!)

Likes friends.

Beginning to share toys and take turns.
Wants to help and please.

Enjoys imaginary play.

More confident of self.

Enjoys laughing.

May go through a difficult stage around 3½.

Can speak most words clearly and make simple sentences.
Vocabulary is expanding.
Uses words to express feelings.

How Can We Teach Them?

P H Y S I C A L
Provide a variety of indoor and outdoor activities with riding toys, balls, a balance beam, and climbing apparatus.
Children will also enjoy creative movement.
Offer crayons, markers, pencils, scissors, play dough, blocks, puzzles, etc.
Encourage children to serve themselves and dress themselves.
Have easy access to bathroom, sink, and soap.

S O C I A L
Provide a large amount of time for informal play.
Reinforce children when they do share.
Give opportunities to help in classroom, such as set table, feed pets, etc.
Dress-up clothes in housekeeping and props in blocks will encourage imaginary play.

E M O T I O N A L
Praise often and use materials and activities where child will experience success.
Read silly stories and do funny stunts.
Have clear rules and be firm, yet loving.

L A N G
Sing songs, say rhymes and finger plays, read books, and describe objects and experiences.
Model ways to express wants and

Can follow simple directions.

U	needs. Help threes work out
A	problems with words.
G	Give children one or two directions
E	at a time to follow.

Curious about world.

Names colors.

Recognizes name.

Counts to 10.

Can compare objects.

Beginning to recognize some shapes, letters, and numerals. Attention span is increasing.

I	Share excitement about learning.
N	Play color games and matching
T	games.
E	Label cubby, chair, pictures, and
L	other possessions.
L	Say counting finger plays, songs,
E	and play counting games.
C	Use sorting games and manipulatives.
T	Do not push children, but give
U	them hands-on experiences with a
A	variety of materials.
L	Plan longer activities.

What Should You Know About Four-Year-Olds?

Four-year-olds are fun, silly, imaginative, excitable, and often a little "wild." Teachers should be enthusiastic and sensitive to meet the changing needs of fours.

What Are Four-Year-Olds Like?

Can run, jump, gallop, hop on 1 foot, swing, and bounce and catch a ball.

Can print name, cut on a line, and draw simple objects.

How Can We Teach Them?

P	Give fours lots of time outside with
H	a variety of equipment to release
Y	all of their energy and excitement.
S	Offer plenty of activities for using
I	small motor skills, with paper,
C	pencils, puzzles, clay, etc.

Dresses self—buttons, snaps, zips, laces, buckles.	**A** **L**	Encourage independence in dressing and undressing.

Loves other children.

Shares toys and plays cooperatively.
Shows concern for feelings of others.

"Out of bounds" behavior at times.

S O C I A L

Schedule large amounts of time for play indoors and outdoors.
Plan for small group projects and cooperative learning.
Call attention to others.
Talk about how their behavior impacts others.
Set clear limits and follow-through on rules.

Shows emotional extremes.
"Loves" one minute and "hates" the next.
May show fears.
Is bold, adventurous, and sure of self.
Highly imaginative.

E M O T I O N A L

Be understanding and patient.

Be reassuring.
Offer new challenges and praise their efforts.
Use creative movement and encourage children to make up "pretend" stories.

Is very silly.

High interest in words.

Asks many questions.
"Why" and "how" are favorite words.
Can repeat songs, finger plays, and stories.
Chatters continually.

L A N G U A G E

Have a good sense of humor and laugh with them. Read funny books.
Make up nonsense words and rhymes.
Answer questions when you can.
Turn questions around and ask, "What do you think?"
Sing and read frequently.

Shows curiosity about the world and other people.

Can make sets.

Names simple shapes.

Beginning to recognize letters and numerals.

Can attend for longer periods of time.

I N T E L L E C T U A L

Go on field trips, invite visitors to speak to your class, and give children many real-life experiences.
Encourage children to work with math manipulatives.
Play shape games and have children trace shapes.
Introduce letters and sounds with games and sensory experiences.
Plan more group activities.

What Are the Characteristics of Five-Year-Olds?

Five is a wonderful age when children love themselves and everyone around them. They are fun, creative, and eager to learn and please.

What Are Five-Year-Olds Like?		How Can We Teach Them?
Can hop, skip, gallop, throw, and kick.	P	Offer physical challenges with a
Writes name and copies simple shapes.	H	variety of equipment.
	Y	Provide children with ample
Handedness is established.	S	writing activities and supplies.
Draws recognizable figures, cuts, sews.	I	Have many art supplies and
	C	manipulatives available.
Ties shoes, combs hair, and cares for self.	A	Praise children for their
	L	independence.
Conforms to group and follows rules.	S	Have children develop class rules.
	O	Play simple games.
Imaginative play is more elaborate.	C	Add prop boxes, costumes, hats, and
	I	other objects to housekeeping,
Is eager to please adults.	A	blocks, and outdoor play.
	L	Encourage children to help in the classroom and at home.
Has a good sense of self.	E	Praise enthusiastically. Encourage
	M	children to talk about themselves.
Shows pride in work.	O	Display work and encourage them
	T	to share their work.
Wants to give and receive affection.	I	Give lots of hugs, kisses, and pats
	O	on the back.
Gets angry when he or she "can't do."	N	Plan activities where they will be

	A	successful. Do not frustrate
	L	children by asking them to think abstractly or do too much academic work.
Communicates well. Uses correct tense and speech patterns.	L	Provide many opportunities for
	A	children to use language. Be an
Can tell full name, address, phone number, and birthday.	N	interested listener.
	G	Play games where children must
Enjoys books.	U	say their name, address, etc.
Can retell a story in sequence.	A	Expose children to a wide variety
	G	of literature.
	E	Let children act out stories or put sequence pictures in order.
Can identify letters and sounds.	I	Make games and use real objects to
	N	reinforce letters and sounds.
Can match numerals and sets (1–10).	T	Give children manipulatives to
	E	make sets.
Can count to 20.	L	Count the children in the room and
	L	other objects in the school.
Knows prepositions; opposites.	E	Let children act out prepositions
Has a much longer attention span.	C	and opposites.
	T	Plan longer group activities.
	U	
	A	
	L	

Should You Rush or Push Children?

NO! NO! NO! There is a tendency in early childhood education these days to do too much, too soon, too fast. Many parents and teachers are falling into the competitive trap of hurrying children, and the long-term effects may be devastating. Children who are pressured may feel stress and may become burned-out by middle school. Further, if one area of development is sacrificed for another, such as academic skills over creativity, children may suffer the consequences in the future and other gifts may remain neglected.

One of the best reasons for not pushing children is that it doesn't always work. No matter how hard you try, there is very little you can do to force a three-year-old to read or ride a two-wheeler. There is an optimum time for learning various tasks, and children will learn them in their own way at their own time if we provide them with the appropriate environment and experiences.

Children have a lifetime to be adults, so let them enjoy their childhood with playful, interesting, and developmentally appropriate activities. Stimulate children and open doors for them, but do not push or rush them. Keep in mind that growth and development are unique to the individual, and try to be sensitive to each child's time clock.

How Do Children Learn?

Children are natural learners—they are curious, interested, and enthusiastic about learning new things. The best way to teach children is to build on play and their natural learning styles.

CHILDREN LEARN THROUGH PLAY. Play is what children do best and enjoy the most. For children, play is their work. Play fosters total development and should be integrated into everything children do.

CHILDREN LEARN BY DOING. Children learn through active involvement with concrete objects. They need many firsthand experiences with real things, such as science experiments, construction, art projects, dramatic play, and field trips.

I HEAR AND I FORGET.
I SEE AND I REMEMBER.
I DO AND I UNDERSTAND.

Chinese Proverb

CHILDREN LEARN THROUGH THEIR SENSES. Children learn by seeing, hearing, touching, tasting, and smelling. Think of each of the senses as a pathway to the brain; the more senses or pathways involved, the more likely learning will occur. Sensory learning also emphasizes the need for a variety of media and materials to stimulate children's senses.

CHILDREN LEARN THROUGH LANGUAGE. Children need to talk about their experiences and to verbalize what they are thinking. Teachers can foster language by describing what they are doing, labeling objects, clarifying children's thoughts, and asking and answering their questions.

CHILDREN LEARN BY MOVING. Children seem to be in constant motion. They have a limited attention span and cannot learn sitting quietly pushing a pencil. Direct their energy with whole body experiences where they can move and use their hands, feet, heads, and bodies to learn.

CHILDREN LEARN BY BEING MOTIVATED. Motivation is a key ingredient to learning. Interesting materials and a stimulating environment will spark children's curiosity and inspire them to learn. Pleasing parents, teachers, praise, rewards, and other personal reasons further motivate children to learn.

CHILDREN LEARN ON THEIR OWN LEVEL. Assess each child's background and skills so you can build on their past experiences. If activities are too easy, children will be bored, but if they are too difficult, children will be frustrated. Break down difficult activities into small steps so each child can succeed and move from simple to more complex activities.

CHILDREN LEARN THROUGH PRAISE AND REINFORCEMENT. "Nothing succeeds like success." Positive experiences and praise encourage children to learn more while building their confidence. Give children constant reinforcement with smiles, pats, and verbal encouragement.

CHILDREN LEARN THROUGH IMITATION. Children learn by observing others and then imitating what they see and hear. Children also imitate values and attitudes that they see in parents, teachers, and peers.

CHILDREN LEARN THROUGH REPETITION. Children build knowledge through repetition and through accumulated experience. The amount of time that is spent on activities is another significant factor in learning.

CHILDREN LEARN BY EXPERIMENTING. Children need the freedom to experiment, explore, try things out, and to make choices. Since they learn through trial and error, accept their mistakes and offer feedback and support.

CHILDREN LEARN THROUGH EXPOSURE. Children are like sponges, learning more in the preschool years than any other period. They need to be stimulated with a wide variety of materials, activities, and subject matter.

CHILDREN LEARN THROUGH INTERACTING WITH FRIENDS. It is amazing how much children learn through talking, watching, and playing with their friends, siblings, and others. Peer teaching is a meaningful way of learning that should not be overlooked.

CHILDREN LEARN IN A POSITIVE ENVIRONMENT. Children need to feel loved, safe, and secure in order to learn. An atmosphere of warmth and acceptance is much more conducive than one that is competitive or threatening.

CHILDREN LEARN WHEN THEIR PHYSICAL NEEDS ARE MET. Children who are hungry, sleepy, or under stress will have a difficult time learning. Make sure children receive good nutrition, proper rest, and emotional support.

CHILDREN LEARN THROUGH WHOLENESS. Learning is not isolated, but should be connected and integrated in all areas of the curriculum. Learning should also focus on the whole child by meeting their physical, social, emotional, and intellectual needs.

When the above guidelines are followed, children will become independent learners who are excited about school and are enthusiastic about learning. They will have a strong foundation, confidence in their abilities, and lifelong skills that will help them continue to learn.

How Do You Nurture a Positive Self-Concept in Children?

Self-concept incorporates all the feelings and perceptions that children have about themselves. Children are not born with a self-concept; it develops from the way people talk to them, respond to them, and treat them. In addition to parents, teachers have a strong impact on children's sense of self.

Sometimes teachers create barriers for children and chip away at their self-esteem without even realizing it. How do you think stereotypes and labels such as "baby," "lazy," and "trouble" make children feel? Put-downs, comparisons, criticisms, and over-protection can further handicap children.

Here are some simple strategies to help children in your classroom feel good and develop a positive self-concept:

1. Accept children for *who* they are and *what* they are. Your acceptance will lead to feelings of self-acceptance in the child.
2. Set clear, reasonable rules and expectations of behavior. When children have boundaries and know what behavior is expected of them, they tend to develop higher self-esteem.
3. Encourage autonomy and independence in children. Know when to "let go."
4. Give children freedom to enjoy themselves—to explore, to be creative, and to laugh.
5. Allow your students to make decisions and accept responsibility.
6. Provide a secure environment where children can feel safe and freely express their feelings and opinions.
7. Show respect for all children in your classroom, regardless of their race, sex, religion, or ethnic background.
8. Try to provide as many experiences as possible in which children can be successful.
9. Encourage children to try new things and to take risks.
10. Have realistic expectations for your students. Know what they are developmentally capable of doing.
11. Replace discouraging remarks and criticism with encouragement and compliments.
12. Help the children you teach see how they are unique and special. Discuss different physical attributes, personality traits, talents, and interests.
13. Talk to your students about being multi-dimensional. For example, "I'm pretty good at singing, but I still need to work on my writing." Point out the things that children do well.
14. Don't expect children to be perfect. Show them it is O.K. to fail and help them learn how to deal with their mistakes and learn from failure.
15. Do not make insulting or negative remarks about children in their presence, and don't allow them to downgrade themselves or others.
16. Be enthusiastic and optimistic about life. Think positive thoughts about yourself, your children, and your situation.
17. Praise and reinforce children to let them know that you recognize their worth. These are some words and phrases to help you:

fantastic	super
great	terrific
wonderful	good try
thank you for. . .	fabulous
much better	all right

great effort	I'm proud of...
Wow!	you're doing better.
I knew you could...	neat
that's right	way to go
very good	perfect

18. Give children lots of smiles and positive reinforcement.

These activities will also encourage a positive self-esteem:

- Ask children to look in a mirror and say one thing they like about themselves.
- Have a "star student" each week. Make a poster about the child with their picture, favorite activities, pets, etc.
- Let each person in the room tell you one positive comment about the special friend and write it on the poster.
- Frequently tell children to hug themselves and tell themselves how nice they are.
- Encourage children to draw pictures and dictate stories about their feelings.
- Take photographs of children and save them in a "class book."
- Let each child make an "All About Me" book. Have them draw pictures of their family, home, friends, school, likes, dislikes, etc.
- Ask children to complete this sentence, "I'm special because. . ."
- Have children dictate words that describe themselves.
- Make "I Can" posters. Let children draw pictures or dictate sentences about all the things they can do.
- Line children up in two rows facing each other. One at a time let a child walk down the aisle as the others gently touch them and say positive things to them.
- Make copies of the notes on page 15 and give them to your students. Personalize them with the child's name and a specific positive comment.

In a supportive environment where there is warmth, respect, and positive reinforcement, children will feel lovable and worthy. A positive self-concept may be one of the most lasting gifts you can give the children you teach!

ABCs for Happy Children

CHILDREN NEED:

A – Acceptance
B – Balance of activities
C – Creative experiences in art, music, drama
D – Desire to learn and positive attitudes about school
E – Exercise and nutritional food to eat
F – Fun! Play!
G – Group experiences
H – Hands-on learning
I – Independence
J – Jobs and responsibility
K – Kindness

World's Greatest Child

Three cheers for_____

yea!

for_____

You are WONDERFUL!

#1
_____

You're a SUPER STAR!

L – Limits and rules
M – Manipulatives and tools
N – Nature exploration
O – Outings and field trips
P – Praise and positive reinforcement
Q – Questions and language
R – Rest and relaxation
S – Stories, stories, stories
T – Time to talk, explore, discover
U – Understanding adults
V – Variety of materials and experiences
W – Work that is meaningful
X – Xylophones and music
Y – "Yes" environment where they can be successful
Z – Zat's not all! What else can you add to this list?

2

CLASSROOM MANAGEMENT AND GUIDANCE

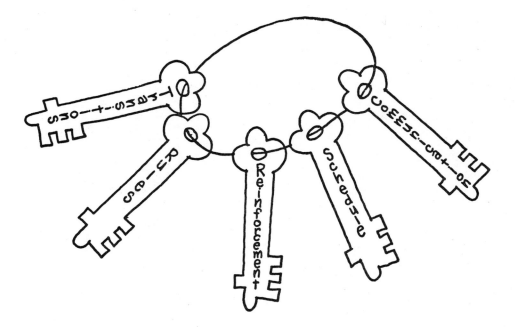

Rules, constructive communciation, positive reinforcement, gentle guidance, schedules, and transitions are key aspects of classroom management. When you follow the guidelines in this section, children will behave appropriately and the classroom will be a peaceful and positive place.

How Do You Develop Good Classroom Management?

Classroom management is something that is difficult to describe, but is vital to good preschool programs. Classroom management is everything the teacher does to assure that he or she will have a well-organized classroom where children can be successful. Consider these guidelines in making decisions, planning, and organizing your classroom:

1. Be prepared! It is better to plan too much than to not have enough planned. Know where you are going and what you want to accomplish each day, and have all your centers, materials, and visual aids prepared ahead of time.

2. Start each day in a positive way. A smile on your face, sincere greeting, and enthusiasm will set you on the course for a good day. Tell the children all the special things you have planned for them each morning and get them excited about different activities.

3. Follow a schedule and routine. Develop a schedule that works well, then consistently follow it. Teach children routines and habits so they will know what is expected of them on a daily basis.

4. Set goals and expectations that are high, yet realistic. Expect children to be good and to do the "right thing."

5. Know as much as you can about the development of the children you teach. Know where they are, where they have come from, and where they are going. Also, be sensitive to the individual backgrounds of children and try to understand their home situations.

6. Model the kind of behavior you expect from your students. If you are kind, consistent, and positive, your students probably will be, too.

7. Encourage children to accept responsibility. It's amazing what little children are capable of if we only give them the opportunity. Hold children responsible for their own behavior and assign them to many jobs in the classroom.

8. Keep your classroom orderly, attractive, and clean. There should be a place for everything, and children should be taught how to put things back in their place. An organized classroom will also help children feel secure and comfortable.

9. Accentuate the positive and ignore minor incidents. Rather than focusing on what children do wrong, look for good behavior and praise children for doing the right thing.

10. An ounce of prevention is worth a pound of cure! Be perceptive and prevent problems whenever possible. Redirect misbehavior, distract children, or remove tempting objects or toys that cause problems.

11. Disperse children when there is a conflict. If tempers start to sizzle, separate children before they blow up. There will also be certain combinations of children who disturb others when they are together. Give these children an assigned seat, have one sit on either side of you, and arrange it so they can focus their attention in a positive way.

12. Teach an interesting lesson. If you are enthusiastic, prepared, have stimulating visuals and materials, and are "tuned in" to your children, they will want to listen to you, participate, and learn.
13. Give children the opportunity to vent their energy. Sitting still or doing activities that are too difficult or inappropriate will increase behavior problems. Make sure children have ample time to play both indoors and outdoors.
14. Establish classroom rules and enforce them consistently and fairly.
15. Communicate clearly and constructively.

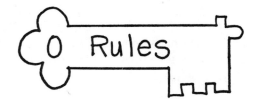

Why Are Classroom Rules Important?

Classroom rules are a positive way to guide children and help them learn acceptable behavior. Rules give children limits and encourage them to develop self-control. Rules should be few, simple, and stated in a positive way. Involve children in making your classroom rules and give them reasons for why rules are important. Write rules on chart paper or poster board and display them in your room, then review them daily until children are familiar with them and the behaviors are established.

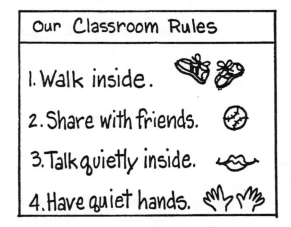

There will also be informal rules that you will need to teach your children throughout the year. For example, when you put out the scissors, there will be rules about what you can cut, where scissors can be used, etc. Say, "Scissors are for cutting paper. They stay at the table and need to be put back in the rack when you are finished using them." Ask children to repeat the rules to you to insure they know exactly what behavior is expected of them.

How Do You Communicate Constructively with Children?

Constructive communication is another key factor in classroom management and guidance. These principles will enable you to communicate more effectively with children:

- *Use positive speech.* Use positive commands and state exactly what you expect from children. Say, "Walk" rather than, "Don't run." Say, "Feet on the floor," rather than, "Get your feet out of the chair." Positive speech will also foster a more pleasant classroom atmosphere.

- *Keep it simple.* Say what you mean and mean what you say as clearly and concisely as you can. Say, "Sit down for a story," rather than, "Don't run around the room because I want to tell you a story, and I can't tell you a story if you're talking and all over the room."

- *Be specific with praise and criticism.* Helpful praise includes describing what the child did right. "Janie, thank you for sitting down and looking at me. I can tell you're ready to hear our story." When a child needs to be criticized, separate the child from the deed. Describe exactly what the child did wrong and what should have been done. "Franco, you forgot to push in your chair and someone could trip over it. Next time please remember to push your chair in under the table."

- *Accept children's feelings.* Listen to children without being critical or judgmental. Respect their thoughts and feelings, even if they are angry or negative. It is better that they use words to get those feelings out, rather than to hit or bite.

- *Listen attentively.* One of the best ways to improve communication is by putting more effort into listening. Get down on the child's eye level and give them your full attention. Sometimes it helps to repeat what they are saying to you for clarification.

- *Talk with your face, body, and tone.* Researchers suggest that 70% to 80% of a person's message is sent by body language and tone of voice. Make your tone compatible with your message, use good eye contact, and have a relaxed body posture.

- *Control your voice.* Use a pleasant and controlled voice in talking with children. Never yell or talk across the room. If a child is over 10 feet away from you, get up and go directly to the child and speak to him or her.

- *Time and reassurance are important.* Good communication takes time, so plan opportunities every day when you can talk and listen to children informally. When children arrive in the morning, centers, outdoor play, snack, and lunch offer opportunities for interacting verbally with children in small groups or individually. And don't forget the importance of reassurance.

How Do You Use Positive Reinforcement?

Reinforcement is one of the most powerful ways teachers can encourage good behavior. When a child's behavior is immediately followed by a positive reinforcer (praise, recognition, reward, etc.) that behavior is "stamped in" and occurs more often. However, when a child's behavior is followed by negative reinforcement (not pleasant or desired), that behavior is "stamped out."

Research has repeatedly shown that positive reinforcement is much more effective than negative reinforcement or punishment. While negative reinforcement may stop the behavior, it does not teach the child the correct behavior. Furthermore, negative reinforcement can create a mood of hostility and can destroy the child's self-esteem. Positive reinforcement tends to increase the occurrence of a desirable behavior, enhances the child's self-concept, and gives the child a feeling of independence and accomplishment. Positive reinforcement should not be used to bribe or manipulate children. However, when used effectively, positive reinforcement will help children see the relationship between their behavior and consequences so they can learn to make good choices and develop self-control.

Patience, persistence, and consistency are the keys to making positive reinforcement work for you. Try to ignore inappropriate behavior as much as possible and "catch them being good." Also, be specific and state exactly what the child has done that you approve of. "Good boy" and "good girl" mean little to children. "I like the way you put up the crayons," or "Thank you for sharing the ball," are much more effective. Above all, praise should always be sincere, meaningful, and deserved.

The type of reinforcement you should use will vary based on the age of the child, the situation, and the value to the child receiving it. There are three major ways to reinforce appropriate behavior in children:

OXOX   *Social Reinforcers*—Smiles and verbal praise are the best and most frequently used ways to reinforce children.

Activity Reinforcers—These include special privileges, such as choosing the story, carrying the ball outside, sitting next to the teacher at lunch, or another favorite activity.

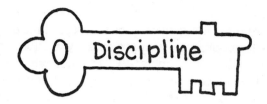

Primary Reinforcers—Stickers, stars, balloons, chips (tokens that can be exchanged for a prize), peanuts, dry cereal, or paper badges may also be used as rewards.

What Is Discipline?

Discipline is not punishment; discipline is guidance; discipline is learning; and discipline is a training process that takes a great deal of time and patience.

DO NOT:

scream
use physical punishment
get in a power struggle
take away food
expect perfection
belittle or embarrass a child in front of the group
compare children
threaten or make empty promises
argue
procrastinate in handling a problem
punish the entire group

DO:

give clear rules and limits
discipline in private
be fair and firm
be consistent
give lots of praise
prevent problems
act promptly
give choices
do something different if what you're doing doesn't work
use developmentally appropriate activities
respect children
listen to children
encourage children to verbalize feelings and frustrations
be affectionate (hug, cuddle, love)
follow through

handle your own discipline problems (asking the school administrator or parent to handle your classroom problems can foster bad feelings)
make each child feel special

What Should You Do When a Child Misbehaves?

If you follow the previous suggestions for classroom management and discipline, and if your program is developmentally appropriate, you should have very few discipline problems. If a child does act inappropriately, consider why the child is misbehaving. Children are trying to tell you something by their behavior! Is the child angry, frustrated, insecure, tired, or does the child need more attention? Is something going on at home you need to be aware of? Observe the child's behavior and record data to see if you can determine a pattern or cause for the problem. Ask yourself, "What can I change or what can I do to help the child do the right thing?"

These are other techniques frequently used by preschool teachers for discipline problems:

1. *Distraction*—Try to distract the child's attention to another toy or activity. If a child is crying, take them to look out the window. If a child starts to grab a toy from a friend, hand them another toy to play with.

2. *Positive Redirection*—Redirect the child's unacceptable behavior into a parallel acceptable behavior. For example, "Crayons aren't for throwing. Color on this paper with the crayons." "It hurts when you hit people. Come over here and hit the pillow if you're angry." Give children alternative behaviors and teach them socially acceptable ways of dealing with their feelings.

3. *"Say It!"*—Verbalization of feelings is a valuable skill to teach children. You will need to remind them often to "use your words," "say how you're feeling," and "tell them with words instead of hitting them."

4. *Natural Consequences*—Natural consequences suggest that what happens should naturally follow the behavior. For example, if the child throws sand, they must leave the sandbox. If they knock over someone's block structure, they should build it back. Natural consequences help children make the connection between their behavior and its impact on others.

5. *Choices*—Choices encourage children to feel responsible for their own behavior. The trick is to give the child two choices, both of which lead to the same desired behavior. For example, if you want the child to clean up blocks say, "Do you want to pick up the large blocks or the small blocks?" "Do you want to walk down the hall alone quietly or do you want to hold my hand?" "Do you want to look at a book before you take your nap, or do you prefer to just lay down?"

6. *Touching*—Physically guide the child to the table for a snack; gently take their hand and pick up a block and return it to the shelf; pat their back if they are tense or upset.

7. *Eye Contact*—Many times if you look directly at the child, he or she will cease the negative behavior.

8. *Time Out*—Time out should be used *sparingly.* The amount of time a child sits in time out should not be more than their age in minutes. (For example, a three-

year-old should not stay in time out for more than 3 minutes, or a four-year-old should not stay more than 4 minutes.) State what the child did wrong so they can think about why they are there, then give them a replacement behavior, such as "next time remember to _____ ." Praise the child for their good behavior within one minute after returning to the group.

How Do You Deal with Common Behavior Problems in Your Classroom?

If a child bites, pull the child aside and very firmly say that biting hurts and is not allowed. Tell them to use words to let others know how they are feeling. Give them an outlet for their anger and frustration, such as a rag to chew on.

If a child is shy, do not force them to do things. Be patient and focus on the child's positive points. Try to offer the child activities and objects that will interest them, involve them in small group work, draw them into conversations, and give them lots of love and praise.

If a child has a temper tantrum, remove the child from the group and ignore them if possible. After the child has quit crying and screaming, pat their back and talk to them about what happened. Encourage them to use words next time and give them an emotional outlet for their feelings, such as playing in water, pounding clay, or running outside.

If a child hits or kicks, tell the child you understand that he or she is angry, but they may not hit because it hurts others. Give them an alternative, such as "you may hit the pillow," "kick the ball," "spit in the toilet," or "pinch the sponge." Keep them busy with large motor activities and opportunities for physical release.

If a child does not participate in group time, ask yourself if your activities are developmentally appropriate and interesting. Have the child sit next to you, pat their back, give them something to hold or something to do, and give them lots of praise for participating.

If a child sucks a finger or has a nervous habit, try to understand why the child is worried or under stress. Give them something to hold or something to do to keep their hands busy.

If a child is a tattle-tale, ignore the tattling and give them attention for the positive things they do.

If a child is too noisy in the classroom, remind the child to use a quiet indoor voice so they don't bother their friends. Preschool classrooms should NOT be silent, but there should be a busy hum.

If a child steals, have them return the object to its rightful owner or place. Ask, "How would you feel if someone took something that belonged to you?"

If a child uses dirty words, tell them you do not like to hear bad words and they may not say them at school.

If a child whines, ignore them and say, "I can't understand you when you use that voice. Tell me again please with your nice voice."

You don't have to handle it alone! Seek help from your school administrators, parents, and outside professionals when you have a special problem.

How Do You Develop a Schedule for Young Children?

A good schedule will help your day flow smoothly and will keep children active and moving in a positive direction. Further, a schedule will give children security and will help them know what to expect. Children's ages, their developmental needs, interests, attention span, and natural body times should be considered in developing a schedule. Although your schedule should follow the same sequence each day, do not pressure yourself or your class by sticking to strict time limits. For this reason, many teachers use time blocks, which are large amounts of time that are set aside for various activities. Time blocks offer greater flexibility and allow you to adjust the schedule to the children's natural interests. If the children are absorbed in an activity, then give them extra time; if they are bored or restless, then move on to the next activity.

In developing a schedule, provide for a variety of activities and balance with:

active and quiet experiences
small group, large group, and independent activities
free choice and structured times
indoor and outdoor play
independent and group experiences
transition times (arrival, departure, toileting, etc.)
ample time for snacks, meals, naps

The most important thing to remember in scheduling is to be *consistent!*

Example of a Full-Day Schedule for Preschoolers

7:00–9:00	Arrival, greet children Open activities—individual choice (dramatics, blocks, art, manipulatives, listening)
9:00–9:30	Circle time (songs, finger plays, roll call, date, weather, count children, review rules) Group lesson
9:30–10:30	Learning centers and activities

language	art
math	dramatics
science	blocks
small motor	library & listening

10:30–10:45	Snack
10:45–11:15	Outdoor play

11:15–11:45	Creative activities—music, movement, art
11:45–12:00	Story
12:00–12:30	Lunch
12:30–12:45	Prepare for nap
12:45–2:30	Nap
2:30–3:00	Wake-up, snack
3:00–4:00	Outdoor play
4:00–4:30	Afternoon activity
4:30–5:00	Story, songs, finger plays
5:00–6:00	Independent activities

Example of a Half-Day Schedule for Preschoolers
Using Time Blocks

Arrival, greet children, open activities
Circle time
Group lesson
Learning centers and activities

language	art
math	dramatics
science	blocks
small motor	library and listening

Music and movement
Snack
Outdoor play
Story
Prepare to go home

Transitions

What Transition Activities Can Be Used to Guide Children?

Transitions are all those "in between" times in your school day, such as when the children arrive, change activities, or move from place to place. By planning for transitions, you can improve classroom management, decrease discipline problems, create learning opportunities, and prepare children for the next activity.

These transition "tricks" will help you guide children throughout the day:

ARRIVAL—Greet children at the door with a smile. Have a sign-in board or a job chart where children can "check in."

Place art materials, toys, manipulatives, and games that will entice children on the floor, tables, and around the room.

CLEAN-UP—Sing a song, play a record, and use positive reinforcement to turn clean-up into a game. (The chapter on "Music and Movement" has some great tunes for this.)

GAINING CONTROL—If you want to quiet children and gain control use one of these tricks.

Turn off the lights.

Ring a bell.

Give directions with sign language.

Lower your voice or whisper.

Give a quiet sign.

Say, "1-2-3—eyes on me."

Play "Simon Says."

Blow bubbles and challenge children to be quiet before they pop.

Count backwards from 10.

Play a music box.

Use a puppet to give children directions.

Use a stop-and-go paddle.

Tell children to squat down on the floor.

Clap your hands and ask children to repeat the pattern.

Say a finger play or sing a song.

red   green

LINE-UP—Use these games to line children up or to dismiss them for different activities.

Tell children to line up if they have on red...blue...yellow...etc; if their eyes are brown...blue...etc.; or if they are wearing pants...a sweater... tennis shoes, etc.

Have children listen for the letter that their name starts with, such as A...B...C...etc. (Start at the end of the alphabet sometimes, too.)

Hold up flashcards, and ask the children to tell you the color, shape, letter, numeral, or word before they are dismissed.

Say birthdays, phone numbers, or addresses. The children may line up when they recognize theirs.

Ask creative thinking questions. "How old would you like to be and why?" "What animal would you like to be?" "Who would you like to change places with?"

Whisper a special message in each child's ear to dismiss them.

Draw a letter or shape on each child's back or hand and ask them to identify it.

Play an echo game where children repeat a phrase or clapping pattern to be dismissed.

Have children line-up like a train with their arms on each other's shoulders.

Change a jump rope into a caterpillar, dinosaur, or merry-go-round that little ones can hold onto as they make a line to move to another location.

NAPTIME—Children need to follow routines at naptime, just as they do at bedtime. Have them go to the bathroom, get water, and slowly relax them. Some schools allow children to bring a sleepy-time friend (stuffed animal) from home to rest with. Turn off the lights, play soft music, read a story, or let children look at books. Calm children by having them blow up like a balloon, then slowly let the air out; tell them to wiggle various parts of their body, then put it to sleep; or ask children to get on a cloud and ride to a place where they are happy. Provide for a gradual wake-up with puzzles, coloring, tapes, and quiet activities for those who get up early.

FIVE-MINUTE IDEAS—Keep a "bag of tricks" in your pocket for when you have to wait, if you finish an activity early, or anytime you have a few extra minutes. Stories, group games, songs, finger plays, and records will focus children's attention in a positive direction. You can also make these teachable times by working on flashcards, playing learning games, having children look at books with a friend, or asking children to write in their journals.

CLOSING—Before children depart, it is important to bring them together and give closure to their day. Review the day in sequential order. "What did you like best?" "What is one new thing you learned today?" Give children something to look forward to at school the following day, such as a cooking experience, art project, or nature outing. Older children will enjoy a "homework" assignment every night. Keep it simple, fun, and relevant to concepts you're working on at school. "Look for all the circles around your home," "Bring in something from your room that starts with 'F'," or "Count all the trees in your yard," are examples of homework children would enjoy.

3

THE LEARNING ENVIRONMENT

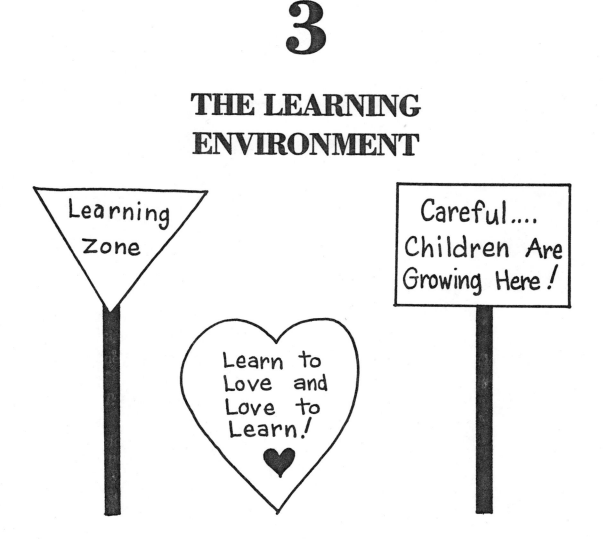

Creating a learning environment where children can play, eat, sleep, explore, and grow presents a great challenge for preschool teachers. Learning centers can provide the kind of variety and stimulation children need in areas such as language, math, science, art, music, dramatics, and large and small motor skills. Outdoor play areas offer additional learning opportunities for children.

How Do You Create a Positive Learning Environment for Children?

Classroom organization and arrangement has a powerful impact on children, their behavior, and their learning. Since children learn by interacting with their environment, the materials and equipment you provide them with is of utmost importance. Key factors to consider are the size of the room, the number of children, their ages, abilities, needs, and interests. Following these suggestions, you can create an attractive, safe, and pleasant environment for children:

1. Draw a floor plan of your room. Mark the windows, doors, sink, lighting, carpeting, washable flooring, etc. Consider how different areas and materials will be used, then sketch the practical location for each center. Art should be near the sink, eating should be on washable flooring, science should be near a window, blocks should be on carpeting, etc.
2. Think about the normal flow of traffic in designing your classroom. For example, don't block the path from the bathroom to the sink, put the trash can near the eating area for easy clean-up, cubbies should be near the door, etc.
3. Avoid large, open spaces, for these cause children to run and be rambunctious. Use shelves, storage units, play units, and divider screens to break down space. In addition, you will have fewer conflicts and children will be less distracted with separate interest areas.
4. Organize the furniture and centers so that the teacher can keep an eye on the children and supervise them at all times.
5. Divide noisy areas from quiet ones. For example, blocks and dramatics should be in one part of the room, while the library and manipulatives should be in another location.
6. Establish rules that limit the number of children in each area, how materials are used, how to take turns, etc.
7. Select safe and durable equipment. Furniture should be child-sized, have rounded corners, be made of non-toxic materials, etc.
8. Choose materials that fit your goals and purpose. Are they challenging, can they be adapted for different purposes, will children enjoy them?
9. Provide doubles of some toys like dolls and cars. This will encourage interaction and prevent fighting.
10. Have enough toys to stimulate and challenge children, but don't overwhelm them with too many materials at once.
11. Rotate materials and toys to keep children interested. Share toys with other teachers, add props to centers, and vary arrangements.
12. Organize your room so like toys are together. For example, puzzles, sewing cards, and manipulatives should be together, writing materials should be grouped, art supplies should be in another area, construction toys together, and so on.
13. Store materials so children can reach them and put them back. Teach children how to care for materials, clean up, and how to return toys where they got them from when they are finished playing with them.
14. To help children with clean-up, label interest areas, shelves, and storage containers. Use words, symbols, illustrations, or pictures of the objects from catalogs.

15. Store teacher supplies, cleaning materials, and anything you don't want the children to play with on a high shelf or locked closet.
16. Avoid being a "pack rat" and having "junk" all around the room. Store what is not being used in cabinets, a storage room, or other out-of-sight area.
17. Add softness to your room with curtains, pillows, plants, foam sculptures, etc.
18. Use soft background colors, then highlight special materials and interest areas with brighter colors.
19. Provide space for large group, small group, and individual learning.
20. Create one open space where you can sing, tell stories, and have circle time and large group experiences.
21. Involve children in making decisions about how the room is arranged. Display their work and help them feel like they are really a part of the room.
22. Crawl around on your hands and knees to see what the room looks like from a child's view. (Don't laugh—it's very enlightening!)
23. Feel free to move your room around until you get an arrangement that works for you and your children.

What Is a Learning Center?

Learning centers are the most natural way to organize your classroom and encourage active learning by children. Terms such as activity areas, interest areas, and discovery centers are often used interchangeably in describing learning centers. A learning center can be an area in your classroom, such as blocks or dramatics, or a learning center can refer to a particular game or activity that will teach a specific skill. Some centers are long term and will remain the whole year, such as the library and computer center; others are concept or skill centers that correlate to a skill or unit you are working on, such as transportation or magnets.

Why Use Learning Centers?

Learning centers allow children to make choices, encourage active learning and hands-on experiences, and provide for individual learning styles. Learning centers will also foster the following:

- Children will develop social skills as they interact cooperatively with others, share materials, and teach each other.
- Centers encourage communication because children can talk and verbalize freely.
- Children can move and be active, so there will be fewer discipline problems and disruptions.

A floor plan similar to the one below would work well with four- or five-year-olds.

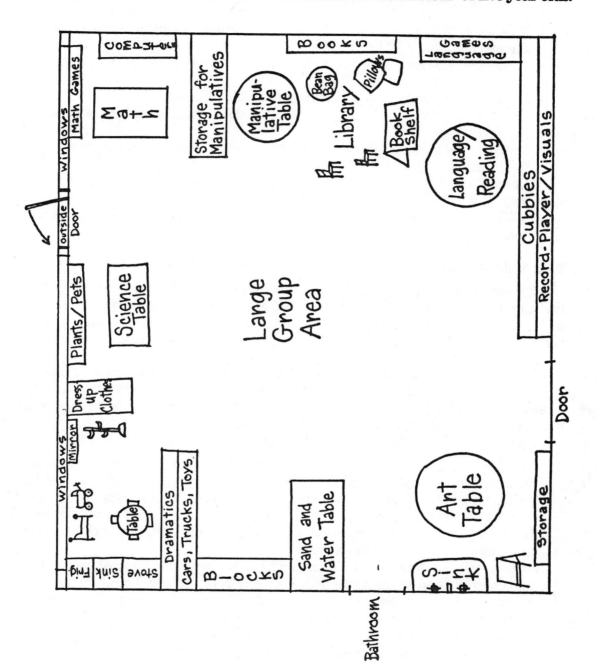

- Learning centers involve a greater use of the senses.
- Centers encourage children to learn in ways that are natural to them.
- They allow children to work independently, in small groups, or one-on-one with the teacher.
- Centers provide for a wide range of abilities and interests because children can progress at their own rate.
- Creativity, curiosity, and experimentation are fostered.
- Centers encourage children to be independent, make decisions, and solve problems.
- Learning centers are a better use of children's time and classroom space and materials.
- Centers offer diversity and flexibility in terms of materials and learning activities.
- With learning centers, children can repeat an activity for pleasure or for reinforcement.

What Is the Role of the Teacher in a Classroom with Learning Centers?

The teacher's role is to plan, develop, and manage learning centers that will be inviting to children. Centers should be based on the children's level of development and should relate to skills and concepts that you are working on. The teacher also needs to guide children, give them positive reinforcement, and keep individual records on their progress.

Start your day with a planning meeting where you explain the centers, demonstrate what is to be done, and show children how to care for materials. Hold a similar conference at the end of the day where children can tell their classmates what they have learned, can show what they have made, or can discuss future plans.

These ideas will assist you in the management of your centers:

Necklaces—Make 2, 3, or 4 color-coded necklaces for each center. For example, you could make 2 red necklaces for the computer center, 4 green necklaces for blocks, 3 yellow necklaces for art, and so on. Hang the necklaces by the appropriate center, then ask children to put on a necklace when they want to play in that particular center. When they are finished, they should hang the necklace back up so another child can have a turn.

Pockets—Give each child an index card with his or her name on it. At each learning center make a small poster with 3 or 4 library pockets. The child puts his or her name card in the pocket when they wish to participate in that center.

Clothespins—Use color-coded clothespins for the different centers you want children to experience each day. You might have red clothespins for manipulatives, orange for math, purple for science, etc. Make each child a necklace from a ribbon or piece of yarn, then hang the clothespins on their necklace. The child places the color-coded clothespin in the appropriate container after they have completed each center.

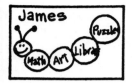

Individual Progress Record—Make a check-sheet for each child. As they complete a center, they may color in the appropriate box.

Activity Chart—Make an activity chart where children can look and see what centers they are to work in each day.

What Should I Do?

Beverly 1. (Listen) 2. (Sand) 3. (Science)

Thomas 1. (Art) 2. (Math) 3. (Library)

Center Cards—Make the number of cards you desire for each center, writing the name of the center on the card and putting a picture or illustration of the center on it. Let children take turns picking a card, then going to the center on their card.

Storage—Use plastic tubs, lunchroom trays, shoe boxes, shirt boxes, large ziplock bags, brown envelopes, or lunch sacks to store activities. Tubs, trays, and boxes can be stored on shelves; bags and envelopes can be hung on a clothesline, attached to a bulletin board, or hung on a pegboard.

What Learning Centers Should Be Provided for Young Children?

There are many different types of learning centers you can create that children will enjoy and that will help you accomplish your goals and objectives. On the following pages you will find some general learning centers and their purpose, as well as materials and equipment that could be used in each area. These centers are included:

Language Arts
Math
Library
Science
Art
Music
Small Motor

Large Motor
Dramatics
Blocks
Sand/Water
The Quiet Place
Outdoor Play Area

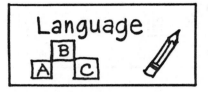

Language Arts Center
(Speaking, Listening, Writing, and Reading)

Purpose: Through the language arts center children can develop oral language, listening skills, vocabulary, letter recognition, rhymes, phonics, reading readiness skills, social skills, sight vocabulary, writing skills, and a positive attitude about reading.

Materials: books
magnetic letters
tactile letters
letter puzzles
picture file
puppets
flannel board
reading readiness games
concentration
alphabet Bingo
lotto
match-up games
same and different games
Lego letter board
typewriter
rebus pictures
chalkboard
paper and pencils
blank books
sequence cards
folder games
wipe-off cards
tape recorder
listening station and tapes
computer and printer

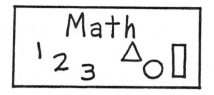

Math Center

Purpose: Through the math center children learn counting, grouping, comparisons, patterns, time, money, measurement, addition, subtraction, geometric shapes, small motor skills, problem-solving, and social skills.

Materials: toy clock
pennies
play money
rulers
balance scale
flannel board
objects to count (shells, rocks, buttons, etc.)
popsicle sticks
toys
geometric shapes
tactile numerals
puzzles
measuring cups and spoons
Cuisenaire rods
dominoes
counting cubes
geoboard
attribute blocks
paper, pencils
chalkboard
computer

Library

Purpose: In the library area children can improve oral language, listening skills, reading readiness skills, and can learn new concepts and develop a love of books.

Materials: books (all sizes, shapes, subjects)

book rack
comfortable seating (pillows, bean bag chair, small rocking chairs, etc.)
homemade books
magazines
flannel board and figures
puppets
sensory books
picture books
dictionary
pictures and posters
listening station

Science Center

Purpose: Through the science center children are able to experiment, solve problems, make decisions, develop concepts about science and nature, improve language, interact socially, as well as develop sensory skills and math concepts.

Materials: magnifying glass
magnets
plants
prisms
animal and cage
aquarium
balance scale
experiments
exhibits (nature collections of rocks, shells, insects, butterflies, etc.)
science books, magazines
pictures and posters
thermometer
color paddles
feely box
terrarium
seeds, nuts, leaves, flowers
bird nests, feathers
sensory activities

Art Center

Purpose: The art center enhances creative expression in children, social skills, oral language, small motor skills, cooperative skills, imagination, and concepts about size, shape, texture, and color. Further, children can release their feelings and can find aesthetic pleasure through art experiences.

Materials: paints
brushes
paper
crayons
newspaper
tissue paper
glue
easel
junk scraps
yarn
finger paint
chalk
clay
play dough
hole punch
scissors
paper sacks
paper cups
paper plates
material scraps
stapler
tape
cotton
magazines
wall paper book
brads
paper clips
popsicle sticks

Music

Purpose: Through music children can improve auditory discrimination and auditory memory, verbal expression, motor skills, creativity, can learn about beat, rhythm, tempo, melody, and can derive personal enjoyment.

Materials: musical instruments
homemade instruments
record player
records
keyboard
autoharp
tone bells
xylophone
tape recorder
piano
musical toys
music box
radio
listening station
visuals for songs

Small Motor Center
(Manipulatives)

Purpose: In the small motor center children develop small muscles, eye-hand coordination, increase their attention span, improve social skills, and build concepts about size, shape, color, and pattern.

Materials: puzzles
puzzle rack
beads

sewing cards
lacing activities
pegboard
Etch-a-Sketch
dressing toys
stacking toys
locks and keys
nuts and bolts
take-apart toys
scissors
hole punch
clay
play dough
pattern cards
parquetry blocks
snap toys
paper and pencils

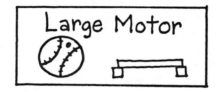

Large Motor

Purpose: Through the large motor center children develop coordination, strength, large muscles, physical fitness, social skills, and can release feelings and frustrations.

Materials: balls
balance beam
bean bags
climbing equipment
hula hoops
tumbling mats
play gym
slide
record player
parachute
jump ropes
balloons
riding toys

Dramatics Center
(Housekeeping)

Purpose: Through the dramatics center children learn cooperative play, social skills, and sex roles while they release emotions, practice language skills, and express creatively.

Materials: kitchen equipment (stove, refrigerator, sink)
pots, pans, dishes, toy broom, sweeper, mop
dress-up clothes (children's, men's, ladies')
pocket books, shoes, hats, ties
full-length mirror
table and chairs
dolls and doll clothes (multi-ethnic dolls of both sexes)
stuffed animals
puppets
doll bed, blankets, pillows
baby carriage
ironing board and iron
food boxes and containers
telephones
old jewelry
paper, pencils
large box for puppet theater, grocery front, fast food restaurant, etc.

Creative dramatics can easily be changed to accommodate different units of study or to spark new interest. Here are some suggestions for centers that will delight children:

Grocery Store: empty food boxes and cans, grocery sacks, grocery cart or wagon, shelves, cash register, play money, cardboard boxes, paper and pencils, dress-up clothes, purses, billfolds

Post Office: envelopes, paper, pencils and pens, rubber stamps, stamp pad, stickers, partitioned box, cash register, play money, bag or sack for carrying mail, old hat, wagon for mail truck

Pet Shop: stuffed animals, puppets, cardboard boxes for cages, plastic bowls, brush, towel, grooming supplies, cash register

Restaurant: paper plates, napkins, plastic cups, silverware, tray, notepad, pencils, apron, menus, cash register, play food, food pictures glued on paper plates, telephone, carry-out food containers

Doctor's Office/ Hospital:	stethoscope, tongue depressors, cotton, bandaids, eye chart, scale, empty medicine bottles, dolls, notepad and pencils, nurse cap, wagon for ambulance, phone, scrub suit and mask
Hat Shop/ Shoe Store:	old shoes (men's, women's, babies', children's, etc.), hats (make in art), purses, mirror, register, play money, hat rack, shoe shine kit
Travel Agency:	travel posters, brochures, pamphlets, books on other countries, tickets, desk, chairs, phone, calendar, notepad and pencils, souvenirs from other countries, dress-up clothes
Beauty Parlor/ Barber Shop:	desk, chairs, calendar, magazines, combs, brushes, mirrors, empty shampoo bottles, rollers, ribbons, barretes, empty make-up containers, towels, dolls, cash register, play sink, phone
Construction:	blueprints, hammer, nails, woodscraps, tape measure, paint brushes, hard hats, lunch box, safety glasses, carpenter's apron, gloves, toy trucks, blocks, cardboard boxes
Theater:	tickets, cash register, chairs, empty food boxes and cups for refreshments, dress-up clothes, puppets, puppet theater, old costumes, mirror, jewelry, hats, glasses, masks
Camp Site:	sleeping bag, back pack, canteen, stones and sticks for fire, blanket to make a tent, play fishing pole
Airport/ Train Station:	phone, tickets, cash register, play money, paper and pencils, travel brochures, suitcase, dress-up clothes, chairs, food trays and paper goods, cardboard boxes to make a train
Fire or Police Station:	paper badges, whistle, helmet or hat, phone, stamp pad, paper and pencils, riding toys, ticket book, map, piece of hose, air tank made from empty plastic liter bottles
School:	desk for teacher, bell, calendar, paper, crayons, pencils, grading stamps, books, chairs, dress-up clothes, glasses, chalkboard
Office:	typewriter, cash register, calculator, paper, pencils, envelopes, phone, calendar, dress-up clothes (adapt to make a bank, newspaper office, etc.)
Windy House:	make several different rooms in your house, such as a bedroom, living room, and kitchen, use contact paper for wallpaper, make a picture window from a poster decorated with a paper window frame and curtains, add props to act out stories, for example, a doll and three bears for "Goldilocks"

Other dramatic play centers that children would enjoy are a farm, circus, bakery, zoo, TV station, rocket ship, toy shop, library, ice cream store, costume shop, or filling station.

Block Center
(Construction)

Purpose: Through playing with blocks children develop concepts of number, size, shape, space, and weight. They also improve manipulative skills, language, social skills, self-confidence, and derive personal satisfaction.

Materials: unit blocks—various shapes and sizes
shelf
carpeted floor
Legos
cardboard boxes
alphabet blocks
foam blocks
wooden cars and trucks
toy street signs
Lincoln Logs
Tinker toys
Bristle blocks
hollow blocks
wooden dollhouse and furniture
wooden barn and animals
plastic dinosaurs or zoo animals
wooden train set
small toys and figures
plastic bins or boxes for accessories
homemade signs and labels for buildings; such as, "hospital," "airport," etc.

Hint: Trace the shape of different blocks on the shelf so children will know where to store them.
Use an area rug or mark a space on the floor with tape so children will know where to play with blocks.
Stuff empty diaper boxes with crumpled newspaper, then cover with contact paper to make giant blocks.
Roll up newspaper into tubes and tape them together to make forts or log houses.
Use masking tape to make roads or highways on the floor.
Use shoe boxes and milk cartons for houses and garages.

Sand/Water

Purpose: Sand and water experiences give children sensory pleasure while developing math concepts, small motor skills, social skills, and language.

Materials: sand or water table (you can use your classroom sink, plastic tubs, or a wading pool)
toy dishes
spoons, shovels, pots, pails
plastic containers
measuring cups, funnel
sponges
soap bubbles
sifter, strainer
plastic boats and toys
smocks
towel
piece of hose
plastic cars and trucks

*rotate sand or water with rice, beans, grits, cornmeal, or snow

The Quiet Place

Purpose: There will be times when children need to be alone to think, relax, release emotions, or gain self-control. The "Quiet Place" provides children with an area where they can have the privacy they need.

Materials: large box lined with pillows or carpet squares
wooden loft
bean bag chair
stuffed chair
plastic cube lined with pillows
small tent (drape a blanket over a table)
cloth tunnel

Outdoor Play Area

Purpose: Learning takes place outdoors as well as indoors. In an outdoor learning area children can develop motor skills, language, social skills, self-confidence, group camaraderie, and can have fun. Consider using your outdoor area for snacks and picnics, nature study, music, art, story time, and other learning experiences.

Materials: climbing apparatus
tricycles and riding toys
wagon
trike path
balls (various sizes)
jump ropes
slide
swings
balance beam
sandbox and toys
woodworking area and materials
painting easel
playhouse or fort
gardening spot and tools
water toys
parachute
hula hoops
bean bags
frisbies
plastic cones
picnic tables
storage shed

Design for an Outdoor Play Area

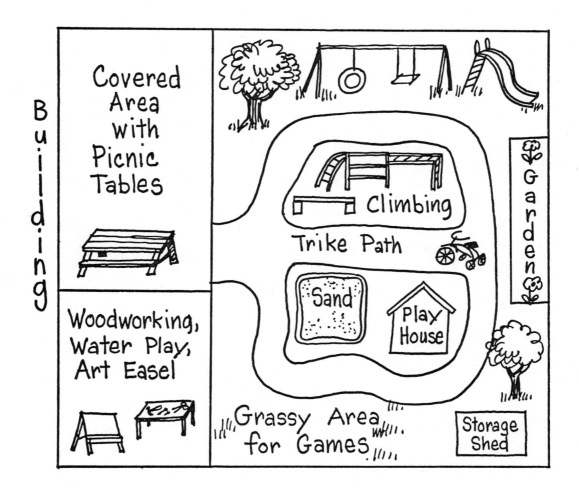

CURRICULUM

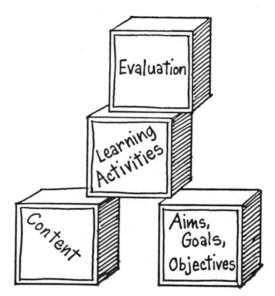

Curriculum is your plan for learning that should include a statement of your philosophy, as well as goals, objectives, content, learning activities, and evaluation. Planning takes a great deal of work, but the payoff will be worth it for you, as well as your students. The remainder of this book will provide you with the methods and materials for planning language, math, science, art, music, small motor, large motor, and nutrition experiences for children.

What Is Curriculum?

"Curriculum" means different things to different people. To some curriculum is a list of goals and behavioral objectives for different age levels. Others view curriculum as daily lesson plans and activities. Some consider only academics when they talk about curriculum, while others consider everything that happens in the school as part of the curriculum. Basically, curriculum is the plan for learning in your school. It is the foundation for teaching and gives meaning and direction to your program.

These are the key components in developing a curriculum:

Philosophy—The first step in writing a curriculum is to establish a statement of philosophy. It will reflect the purpose of your school and your values and beliefs about how children learn. Your philosophy will strongly influence the decisions you make.

Aims, Goals, and Objectives—Aims, goals, and objectives set the course for your program by stating what you want children to learn. Aims are broad generalizations about what your school hopes to accomplish. Based on aims, goals and specific behavioral objectives should be written for each age group. Objectives should be stated in observable terms so you can assess if your curriculum is accomplishing what you intend. Further, objectives should be based on what research suggests is normal for children at a particular age. Since children learn at different rates, every child in your room should not be expected to master every objective. You may need to modify the objectives for some, or you may need to expand the objectives for others.

Content—Content refers to the information, subject matter, or units that you select to accomplish your aims, goals, and objectives.

Learning Activities—These include all the experiences, activities, and materials you plan for your students. Learning activities should be related to the content and objectives and should match the children's needs and level.

Evaluation—Evaluation is the final component of curriculum and the one that is often overlooked. Evaluation is the process of assessing if you achieved your aims, goals, and objectives. Evaluation should be done formally with checklists, as well as informally with observations and anecdotal records. Evaluation will enable you to make adjustments in your teaching strategies and improvements in the curriculum.

What Principles Should Be Considered in Developing a Curriculum?

These principles should underlie curriculum planning and development:

1. *Child-Centered*—Curriculum should be written with a thorough understanding of child growth and development. It should reflect the interests, needs, abilities, and natural learning styles of children. The program should fit the children; the children should not be expected to fit the program!

2. *Balance*—Balance is a great principle in our universe and to nurturing well-adjusted children. There should be a commitment to meeting the needs of the total child with learning opportunities for social, emotional, physical, and intellectual development.

3. *Relevance*—The curriculum should contribute to the child's overall development and should be relevant to what they need today, as well as to what they will need in the future. Ask questions such as, "Do children need to learn this?" "Why?" "So what?"

4. *Sequence*—The curriculum should be organized so that acquisition of skills and concepts goes from simple to complex, and from the concrete to the abstract. By building on previously learned skills, children can be successful and can master one step at a time.

5. *Scope*—Scope refers to the breadth of the curriculum. Children need broad exposure and a wide range of activities to develop all their special talents and interests.

6. *Integration*—Learning in all areas should be integrated so as to give a wholeness to children. Skills must be reinforced with many hands-on experiences in different contexts.

7. *Continuity*—Learning and development are a continuous process from birth on. The curriculum needs to be ordered so that each child can learn and grow at his or her own pace regardless of chronological age.

8. *Interest*—When children are interested and challenged, they will learn and be excited about school.

Curriculum is not stagnant; it should be dynamic and meaningful. Curriculum must continually change and improve to meet children's needs and to include new information and materials that are emerging in the field of early childhood.

Do I Have to Write Lesson Plans?

Only if you want to be a good teacher! Planning is truly one of the most important jobs of a preschool teacher. Planning will help you feel prepared and in control of the direction in which your class is moving. In addition, planning will improve classroom management, can help you meet the needs of individual children, and can eliminate some of the stress in teaching.

What Is Long-Range Planning?

Long-range planning involves a yearly or monthly overview of the units you will teach and the skills you plan to focus on. Long-range planning allows you to capitalize on holidays, seasons, and special community events. In addition, with long-range planning you will have ample time to collect materials and plan learning centers and field trips.

What Is Short-Range Planning?

Short-range planning refers to weekly and daily lesson plans. Weekly planning enables you to provide a wide variety of learning opportunities and to integrate learning so children have the repetition and reinforcement they need. Weekly plans should include concepts, skill objectives, learning centers, and small and large group activities. The form on the following page is a useful one for weekly planning. By posting a copy of this on the bulletin board, parents will be aware of the many experiences their children are having each day and can follow through on learning at home.

Age Group _____

Date _____

Theme _____

Concepts _____

Objectives _____

	Monday	Tuesday	Wednesday	Thursday	Friday
Circle Time					
Language/ Reading Readiness					
Math					
Science					
Art					
Music & Movement					
Small Motor/ Manipulatives					
Blocks					
Dramatic Play					
Sand/Water					
Outdoor Play/ Large Motor					
Special Activities (Field trip, cooking, etc.)					

With your weekly plan and daily schedule, you are then ready to write more detailed lessons for each day. These are some things to consider when planning daily activities for children:

1. *Objectives*—What do you want the children to learn?
2. *Materials*—What visuals and concrete objects will you need? Remember, the more senses you involve, the more likely your children will learn.
3. *Introduction*—How will you get their attention? What can you do to get them interested?
4. *Procedure*—What will you do first, second, and so on? What are some key questions you can ask?
5. *Conclusion and Evaluation*—How will you summarize and end the lesson? How will you know if your objectives were achieved?
6. *Follow-Up*—What are some follow-up activities that you can use to reinforce and enrich your lesson? Art projects, music, stories, games, and centers are great ways to follow up a lesson.

How Do You Plan a Positive Circle Time?

Circle time, large group activity, class meeting, pow-wow, opening exercise, or whatever you choose to call it, is a special time in your school day when you sit down with your class. It is a time to introduce new information and activities, talk about the day, and have children share ideas. You may want to put tape on the floor in the shape of a circle for children to sit on, arrange chairs in a semi-circle, use carpet squares, or simply have them sit in a close group.

It is good to open your circle time with a short routine, such as:

opening song
pledge
attendance (Call roll; count the number of children.)
date (Have children repeat the day of the week, month, year. Ask questions about, "What was yesterday?" "What is tomorrow?")
weather report (Talk about the weather, appropriate clothing, etc.)
review letter of the week, color, shape, numeral, etc.
group lesson, sharing time, introduction of centers

Your lesson at circle time can be tied in with the teaching unit, skills or concepts you are working on, holidays, current events, or other appropriate topics. Use real objects that the children can see, touch, and will be interested in. Above all, don't talk too much or make the children sit too long!

Here are some bright ideas to capture children's attention at circle time:

- Get children's attention with a song, poem, or finger play.
- Tell a riddle or joke.
- Use a visual or prop.
- Hide something in your pocket.
- Read a story.
- Show a picture or poster.
- Put on a costume, hat, etc.
- Ask a question. Why? Who? How? What?
- Act out something or pantomime.
- Change your voice. Make it high, low, gruff, or silly.
- Hide an object in a "surprise box," pass it around, and let the children guess what it is.
- Use a puppet or stuffed animal.
- Ask children to bring things from home that relate to the lesson.
- Put something in a bag or sock and let the children feel it.
- Teach children a new word—a magic word!
- Encourage children to use their imagination and pretend.
- Use guided visual imagery. Take children on a plane, ship, or magic carpet and fly to a distant country.
- Invite a guest speaker.
- Share an object from nature.
- Bring in food that relates to the lesson.
- Use a map or globe.
- Bring in a newspaper article.
- Show a film, filmstrip, tape, or video.
- Brainstorm.

5

LANGUAGE DEVELOPMENT AND READING READINESS

The whole language approach to teaching, which focuses on using developmentally appropriate activities that integrate reading, writing, listening, and speaking, is explored in this section. Included are suggestions for developing oral language and listening skills, games and ideas for developing reading readiness and beginning writing, and strategies for creating a literate environment.

How Do You Foster Language Development?

Language is the key to intellectual development and the key to expressing thoughts and feelings. Language development begins at birth as the infant cries to express his or her needs. Soon the baby coos, then says one word, two words, short sentences, and before long is using extended sentences. During the first five years, language growth is dramatic and children will learn the basic patterns of speech they will use throughout their lives. How exciting for preschool teachers to be a part of this process!

Children naturally absorb language by listening and imitating others. Each child's speech is unique, and they will progress at their own rate. Since language development is influenced by children's social and cultural background, it is important to provide them with a wide variety of experiences and many opportunities for social interaction. They also need good models who encourage and accept them.

Teachers can foster language development by using appropriate language. Do not baby talk or use a high voice, but do try to speak slowly and clearly. If a child mispronounces a word or speaks incorrectly, do not criticize them, but do repeat the sentence properly. For example, if the child says, "Dookie gone," you could say, "Yes, your cookie is all gone." Also, try to expand children's language whenever you can by repeating what they say and adding another phrase. If the child says, "Pretty flower," you might say, "It's a pretty red flower and it smells good, too."

What Is the Whole Language Approach?

Speaking, listening, reading, and writing are all developmental and are all interrelated. Expressive language refers to speaking and writing; receptive language includes listening and reading. The whole language approach integrates these to make language meaningful and to give children a broad foundation. Through the whole language approach, children are able to make the connection between listening, speaking, reading, and writing.

> What I hear I can say—
> What I say I can write—
> What I write I can read!

The whole language approach recognizes that children learn when they are active and involved in multi-sensory experiences. Language is not taught in isolation, but is integrated across the curriculum and throughout the day. Children are encouraged to describe their block structures, express their feelings in dramatics, verbally share their artwork, label their science experiments, repeat finger plays, and listen for comprehension at storytime. A total language approach will also foster the total needs of children by helping them grow intellectually, socially, emotionally, and physically.

How Can You Promote Speaking Skills?

The best way to develop speaking skills is to get children to talk. But you must listen to them if you want them to talk. Look at them and really focus on what they are saying. Smile, nod your head, and ask them questions that will encourage them to expand. You must also accept a noisy classroom, for children need to verbalize and interact as they perform different activities in the room.

If there are shy children in your room, they may feel more comfortable talking to you individually or in small groups. You should never force children to speak in front of the group. Generally, as children gain confidence through successful experiences, they will be more willing to share with their classmates. When you suspect a child has a speech or language problem, seek help from a trained specialist.

Children need exciting experiences so they will have something to talk about. Here are some topics that will help you get on their level and find out about their interests and feelings:

family	pets
toys	television
friends	movies
neighbors	books
likes	their room
dislikes	games and sports
food	wishes
birthdays	fears
holidays	vacations
going to the doctor	ask parents about interests

In addition to informal play, these planned activities will foster oral language development:

- Decorate an old box and fill it with interesting props, such as glasses, hats, costumes, and masks. Encourage children to select an item and make up a story with it.
- Let children make puppets or use classroom puppets or stuffed animals. Have them pretend they are the puppet character and talk.
- Ask children to bring in photographs of their families from home and tell the class about them.
- Use routine opening exercises each day to involve the children in speaking. They might say the date together, count the children present, repeat the pledge, or sing.
- Finger plays, chants, songs, poems, and nursery rhymes all encourage children's speech.
- Ask children to repeat animal sounds or to make the sound effects when you read stories.
- Let children retell stories using the flannel board.
- Say part of a sentence, then ask the children to complete it.
- Read or tell a story, stopping before the end. Encourage children to make up their own ending.
- Have children speak into a tape recorder, then play it back for them.
- Video children playing, singing, and working, then let them watch their very own movie.
- Teach children mannerly phrases, such as "Good morning (teacher's name)," "Yes, please," "No thank you," "Excuse me," etc. Be consistent with this and praise them when they remember these courtesies.

- Encourage children to speak in complete sentences. If the child says, "Apple juice," say "I would like some apple juice, please," and have them repeat it.
- Show and tell can be fun and effective if you are careful not to allow children to ramble. You might want to assign each child a different day to bring something from home, or you might have a different theme for show-and-tell each week. For example, you might ask them to bring in something from nature, something they've made, a favorite book, a baby picture, or something that begins with "t."
- Have class discussions when there is a problem in the room. "People are forgetting the rule about walking in the hall. What can we do about it?"

- Hide a mystery object in a bag. It might be bubbles, peanuts for snack, or a new puzzle. Let children take turns asking questions and guessing what it might be.
- Have children look at books in pairs. Encourage them to take turns talking about the pictures or making up stories.
- Make a story wheel from a pizza board or large cardboard circle. Divide the circle into eighths and put a picture of an object, person, or animal in each section. Attach a spinner to the center. Have children take turns spinning and making up a story about the picture they land on.

- Bring in a box full of unusual items from home or nature. You might include a hair curler, egg beater, or seed pod. Let children take turns selecting an item and describing it and telling how it is used.
- Have children tell riddles and jokes to each other.
- Give children a play telephone to practice having conversations. They will also enjoy a play telephone booth. Take a large appliance box and cut out windows. Put in a chair to sit on and make a telephone from two paper cups and a toilet paper roll. (Their conversations will have you roaring!)
- Cut out pictures representing different emotions, such as happiness, fear, anger, surprise, sorrow, etc. Ask children to describe how the characters in the pictures feel and to make up stories about them.
- Involve the class in a group story. The leader starts the story off, then each person adds to the story as you go around the circle. It is helpful to pass a prop from one to another as the speaker changes. You could pass a stuffed animal, paper wand, or "magic" marble. Story starters might include finding a secret fairy who grants wishes, riding a rocket to outer space, taking a pill that makes you shrink, finding a treasure chest, etc.

- Ask children to dictate sentences and stories about their drawings and paintings.
- Let children dramatize stories, nursery rhymes, and poems.
- Have children role-play different life situations, such as getting a new puppy, going to the circus, being frightened by a storm, or moving to a new school.
- Get children to think creatively with questions like, "What kind of animal would you like to be? Why?" "How old would you like to be?" "If I gave you three magic wishes, what would you wish for?" "What would you do with $100?"
- Bring in a simple object, such as string, a rubber band, or a box of raisins. Let children brainstorm all the things they could do with the object.
- Give children a common ground for discussions with walks, field trips, holidays, parties, dress-up days, family programs, etc.
- At the end of each day, encourage children to talk about all the things they have seen or done.

How Do You Develop Listening Skills?

Listening is important for school success, as well as life success. However, children do not naturally come to school with good listening skills. They must be practiced and developed like other skills. Maturity, vocabulary, attention span, and background will all influence a child's ability to listen.

Children are bombarded by sounds from the telephone, radio, machines, and people. It is not surprising that they are able to "turn the teacher off" and not hear anything you say! We must teach children how to listen actively, attentively, and selectively. Give children a reason for listening and make it a habit to give directions just *one* time. Vary your tone, pitch, and volume to keep children interested, and model good listening skills. If a child continually has difficulty hearing and following directions, refer him or her to a specialist for screening.

These activities will be helpful in developing good listening skills:

- Give directions one time, then ask a child to repeat what you have said to the rest of the class.
- Provide children with records, tapes, stories, songs, and poems that they will want to listen attentively to.
- Set up a listening center in your classroom with headsets so children can listen to story records or tapes undisturbed.
- Describe an object or child in the room. Ask children to listen, play "detective," and guess what or who it is.
- Set three objects in front of the children, such as a glass, can, and box. Strike each one with a spoon. Have the children close their eyes while you strike one and try to identify which one you hit.
- Play Simon Says and other games that require children to listen and follow directions.
- Ask children riddles and simple trivia questions.
- Play echo games where you make a sound or say a word or phrase. The children listen and then repeat it as a group or individually.

- Say a rhyme or finger play and leave out a word. Ask children to identify the missing word.
- Have children close their eyes. Tell them to raise their hand when they hear a sound and to lower their hand when it stops. Use a xylophone or other musical instrument to make the sound.
- Give each child a small toy or paper cutout. Ask them to put it on their head, behind their back, above them, in front of them, between their elbow and knee, etc.
- Take children on a listening walk in the building or outside. When you return, ask them to identify all the different sounds they heard.
- Tell the children when you say "rag doll" they should flop over, but when you say "soldier" they should stand up straight and tall. Alternate softly saying "rag doll" and "soldier" as the children move accordingly.
- Set a stuffed animal, such as a bear, in the front of the class. One at a time, ask children to touch something on the bear. You might ask one to touch his nose, another to wiggle his ear, shake his paw, etc.
- Place several objects on a table on one side of the room, while you and the children sit on the opposite side of the room. Give one child at a time a basket or bag and ask them to bring you one of the items from the table.
- Arrange three picture cards or real objects in front of the children. Describe one and ask children to identify it. For example, you might use a pencil, baby bottle, and hammer.

 Which one would you use if you wanted to build something with nails and wood?

- In addition to asking children comprehension questions after a story, have them color a picture about the story.
- Ask children to listen carefully while you give them directions for drawing a picture. You might say, "Make a circle in the middle of your paper with your red crayon." "Next, make a flower out of the circle." "Take your green crayon and draw a stem on the flower." "Now put some grass at the bottom of the page," and so on.
- After "show and tell" ask children comprehension questions about what different class members shared.
- Read a story with a whisper voice.
- Whisper a special message in each child's ear. "I love you." "Thank you for sharing your snack with Maria." "I like the way you cleaned up the blocks."

What Different Methods Can Be Used to Teach Reading?

Nothing receives more emphasis in our education system than reading. And no wonder why—for reading is the tool through which other information is learned. For years educators have sought a miracle method that will successfully teach all children to read. Unfortunately, after years of research, studies have shown that there is no one reading approach that is best for all children. Regardless of the sales pitch or the pretty packaged materials, the single most important ingredient in teaching children to read remains an enthusiastic and well-trained teacher.

These are some of the major approaches to reading instruction:

Whole-Word Approach—This approach emphasizes visual memory skills, for children learn to recognize words by memorizing them. The "Dick and Jane" series was based on this "look and say" approach. An advantage of this approach is that children can quickly experience success and feel like they are reading. One disadvantage of this approach is that children cannot "decode" or read words on their own.

Phonetic Approach—Using this method, children are taught the individual letters and the sounds they represent. When these sounds are blended, they form words. This approach enables children to decode words they don't know on their own. The phonetic approach also supports early writing, for children have the skills to spell their own words.

Language Experience—This approach capitalizes on children's natural speaking vocabulary and their personal experiences. Children dictate sentences and stories to the teacher, then attempt to read them back. The idea is whatever the child says can be written down, and what is written can then be read.

These are other skills that will help children read:

Picture Clues—The picture on the page represents what is written in print.

Configuration Clues—The outline of the word can help children remember it.

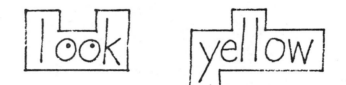

Context Clues—The content of the sentence gives the child a hint as to what the word is.

    I w_____ an ice cream cone.

    There is no one best way to teach children to read; therefore, a combination of these approaches will give children more skills and will appeal to their different learning strengths and styles.

What Guidelines Should Be Followed in Teaching Young Children to Read?

A highly debated issue is, "Should you teach preschoolers to read?" If you use drill, pressure, and ditto sheets, the answer is NO! If you use developmentally appropriate activities and follow the guidelines below, the answer is YES!

    1. Teach reading so that each child can experience success and feel confident.

2. Offer children broad experiences that include active learning through the senses. Give them activities where they can taste, smell, hear, see, and touch.
3. Do not teach reading in isolation, but integrate it with writing, listening, and speaking activities across the curriculum.
4. Relate to the child's background of experiences and build on what they already know. Assess them continually and allow them to learn at their own pace.
5. The age at which children will read varies. Never group or label preschool children so that they feel inadequate or inferior.
6. Recognize children's individual learning styles. Be flexible and offer a variety of approaches and skills.
7. Provide children with a rich environment where they are exposed to books, print, and writing materials.
8. Be enthusiastic about reading. Help children understand that reading is useful, as well as enjoyable.
9. Have realistic expectations for your students. It takes a long time to develop readiness skills and to teach children to read.
10. Communicate with parents so they understand reading readiness and active learning. Suggest ways they can help their children at home by reading to them, writing down their stories, playing visual and auditory games, etc.

What Is Reading Readiness?

Although formal instruction in reading may not begin until elementary years, reading readiness should begin when children are very young. Reading readiness will provide children with the foundation, skills, and attitude they need to be successful readers in future years. Readiness cannot be taught or hurried, but must be developed gradually through firsthand experiences. Consider these skill areas in planning your curriculum:

Visual Discrimination (Visual Perception)—This is the ability to recognize similarities and differences in objects, pictures, shapes, letters, and words.
Visual Memory—Children need to remember letter forms and words.
Perceptual Motor Skills—Children need the eye-hand coordination to track words and a line of print with their eyes. They also need the motor skills to write letters and words.
Orientation—The eyes must be trained to go from left to right, and from the top to the bottom.
Auditory Discrimination (Auditory Perception)—Children must be able to discriminate between various sounds and to hear different sounds before they can associate a particular sound with a letter.
Auditory Memory—This refers to the ability to remember the sounds letters make so they can be reproduced and blended together to make words.
Concept Development—Children need firsthand experiences they can relate language and reading to in order to bring meaning to the printed page.

Readiness for Books—Children should know how to open books, turn the pages, and care for books.

Oral Language—This is the ability to put words together to make sentences, and to use sentences to convey thoughts and information.

Attitude—Learning to read involves not only the development of skills, but also a love of reading and books.

Letters—There are 26 upper case letters (capital) and 26 lower case letters in the alphabet. These letters make sounds, and when you put them together they make words.

Consonants are letters that make a constant sound.

b c d f g h j k l m n
p q r s t v w x y z

Diagraphs are two consonants whose sounds change when they are together.

ch   sh   th   qu

Vowels are letters whose sounds change. The vowels are a, e, i, o, u, and sometimes y and w.

	A	E	I	O	U
long sound	āte	ēat	īce	ōat	ūse
short sound	ăt	ĕnd	ĭt	ŏn	ŭp
"r" controlled	art	her	girl	or	fir

What Materials and Activities Can Be Used to Develop Readiness Skills?

There are many activities, games, experiences, and materials that can be used to develop readiness skills. You will be the best judge in determining which ones are the most appropriate for the age, interests, and abilities of the children you teach. These questions will guide you in making your decision:

- What are my aims, goals, and objectives?
- Will the activity help achieve a skill or objective that I am working on?
- Does the activity relate to my students' experiences?
- Is it suited to their level? Will they be successful?
- How can the activity be modified for individual children? Can I make it easier? More difficult?
- Is it interesting? Will the children enjoy it?
- Will the children be actively involved? How many senses will they use?
- Does it require children to integrate a variety of skills?
- How can I adapt it for a theme or unit I am teaching?

Visual Discrimination

Children need to begin visual discrimination by recognizing likenesses and differences in colors, pictures, and shapes. As they master these, move to increasingly difficult symbols, such as letters, numerals, and words.

- Focus on one color each week. If it is "red" week, then fingerpaint with red, make red birds for art, ask the children to bring in something red for show-and-tell, eat red apples or red strawberries for a snack, and ask all the children to wear red to school on Friday.
- Collect a basket of objects that are red, yellow, blue, and green. Ask children to sort the ones that are alike, or hold up one object and let them find all the others that are that same color.
- Sing color songs.
- Ask children to line up by the color that they are wearing. For example, "If you have on blue, you may line up for play time."
- Cut out felt objects of the basic colors. Put one on the flannel board, then ask children to find another one that matches it. Later, have children group cutouts that are the same color on the flannel board.

- Use construction paper or poster board to make 8″×10″ color cards. When you hold up a particular color, have children tiptoe around the room and touch another object of that color.
- Take a foam cube and glue a different color to each side. When the cube is rolled, the children wearing that color must stand up and do an exercise, such as jumping jacks, toe touches, etc.
- Make games where children must match objects of like colors.

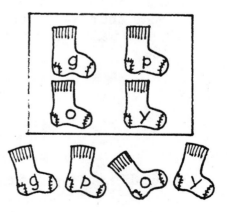

- Make a lotto game where children must match color cards to like colors on their game board.

- Take a paper plate or pizza wheel and divide it into eight sections. Color each section a different color. Take eight clothespins and color them a matching color. Have the children match the appropriate clothespin to the color on the wheel.

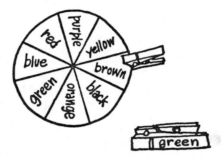

- Get two samples each of paint chips. Cut them apart, then let the children match like colors.
- Use Old Maid cards or other old cards to make a picture discrimination game. Cut 6″×8″ pieces of cardboard. Glue cards that are alike on half of the cardboard, and cards that are different on the other half. If the pictures are alike, the children put them in one pile; if the pictures are different, they go in another pile.

- Cut different types of clothing from construction paper. Let children use clothespins to hang up those that are alike together.

- Collect large and small pictures of similar objects, and ask children to match those that are alike.

- Make visual matching games from old workbooks, stickers, or newspaper advertisements.

- Cut wallpaper, fabric scraps, or wrapping paper into 3″ squares. Ask children to match up those that are alike.

- Make two cards of each of the expressions below. Have children match up the two that are alike. Encourage them to describe how that person feels and why.

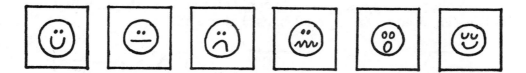

- Take three objects and place them in front of the children. Two should be the same and one should be different. You can use common objects found around the classroom such as blocks, crayons, beads, or small toys. Ask the children which two are alike, then ask them to remove the one that is different. (A similar game can be played with cutouts on the flannel board.)
- Make games where children must identify which ones are the same.

Circle the ones that are the same							
☆	☆	△	☆	☆	∧	☆	∨
⬦	◇	□	⬦	△	⬦	⬦	▽
⊤	⊤	⌐	⊥	⊤	✗	⌐	⊤
go	og	ga	go	po	go	qo	go

- Construct games where children must mark which one is **different**.

Which one is different?							
○	○	○	⬭	○	○	○	○
B	B	B	B	P	B	B	B
☺	☺	☺	☺	☺	☺	☺	☹
□	◇	□	□	□	□	□	□

- Cut 3″×5″ cards from construction paper or poster board. Print the letters you are learning on the cards. (You should make three or four of each letter.) **Have children match the letters that are alike.**

- Give children a newspaper and ask them to circle all of a certain letter. For example, you might ask them to circle all the "m's" they can find.
- Have children match up road signs that are alike.

- Make a mail game where children can match up letters (envelopes) with **the** correct person's house. (This is fun to play with cubbies, too.)

- Have children match objects that go together, such as a shoe and sock, spoon and fork, ball and bat, soap and towel, etc.

Visual Memory

Visual skills are important in reading, as well as math and other areas. Children will develop visual memory as they play these games and have fun.

- Arrange three or four objects on the floor or table. Cover the objects with a "magic" blanket, then ask the children to name the objects. As children improve, add more objects for them to remember.
- Place three or four objects in front of the children. Have them close their eyes while you hide one object behind your back. When the children open their eyes, see who can tell you which one is missing. (You can play a similar game by placing felt cutouts on the flannel board, then removing one or two.)
- Dress a bear or doll in clothes and tell the children to look carefully. Have them close their eyes while you change or remove one item. You might take off a shoe, move an arm, etc. When the children open their eyes, they can stand up when they figure out what is different.
- Go on a memory walk around the school. Tell children to "take picutres" of all the things they see with their eyes. When you return to the classroom, make a list of all the things they can remember seeing.
- Have children sit in a circle. One child is "it" and must leave the room or close his or her eyes. Another child is picked to hide in a corner. "It" returns to the room and tries to identify who is missing.
- Show children an interesting picture from a book for 10–15 seconds. Put the book down, then ask children to tell you something they saw.

- Take 5 to 10 common classroom items and lay them down on poster board or a file folder. Trace around them with a marker, then let the children take turns identifying the outlines and matching the appropriate objects to them.

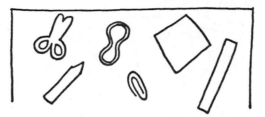

- Give each child 5 to 10 blocks. Make an arrangement in front of the children with your blocks, then cover it up with a box or blanket. Challenge the children to copy you and build the same thing with their blocks.
- Cut a 3″ circle from the front of a file folder. Cut 8″×10″ pictures from magazines, advertisements, or food cartons. Place one picture at a time inside the folder. The children are to look through the peek hole and try to identify the picture.

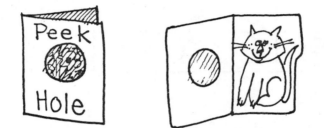

- Take a magazine picture and fold it back and forth from the top to the bottom in 1″ strips. Reveal the picture 1″ at a time until the children identify what it is.

- Make several shapes, designs, or letters on poster cards. Give each child a piece of paper and crayon or pencil. Hold up one card at a time for 10 seconds while the children study it. Put the card down and ask the children to reproduce what they remember on their paper.

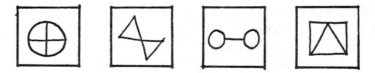

- Make concentration games with shapes, stickers, or letters. Start with five pairs and increase the number of pairs as the children improve. Place all the cards face down on the floor or table. One player at a time turns over two cards. If the cards match, the player gets to keep them and gets another turn. If the cards don't match, the cards are turned over and the next player gets a chance to match up like cards. The one with the most cards wins.

- After reading a story, ask children questions about the illustrations in the book. For example, "What color was Sally's hair?" "How many windows did Jack's house have?"
- Follow-up nature outings, bus rides, and field trips with questions where children must recall things they have seen.

Perceptual Motor and Orientation

The chapter on small motor skills will provide you with many ideas for developing perceptual motor skills.

These activities will improve children's orientation skills:

- Sweep your hand in a left-to-right direction under words, sentences, and pictures whenever possible.

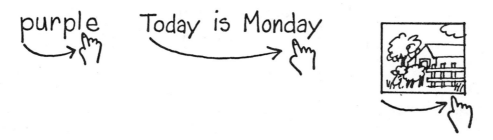

- Demonstrate how to open books and turn the pages. Provide children with many opportunities to look at books and turn the pages.
- When reading a book, point to pictures on the left-hand side, then to the right-hand side.
- Give children tracing games where they must move an object, pencil, or crayon from left to right.

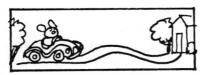 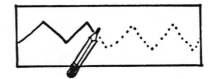

- Have children follow a piece of tape or a chalk line from left to right.
- Ask children to walk, hop, crawl, fly, tiptoe, skip, etc. in a left-to-right direction.
- When singing songs or doing finger plays, do the movements from left to right. (Remember, if you are facing the children you will need to go from your right to your left.)
- As children do art projects, encourage them to go in a left-to-right direction. They might do printing, weaving, painting, pasting, or other projects by starting on the left.

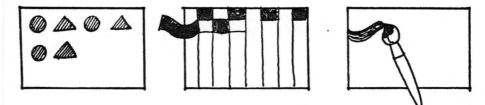

- When using the flannel board or other objects, always arrange them from left to right.
- Teach children their left and right hands. Print the letter "l" on their left hand and "r" on their right hand.
- Have children trace around their left and right hand and foot and label them.

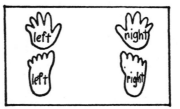

- Make a yarn bracelet for each child from *r*ed yarn for "*r*ight day." Throughout the day say, "Show me your right hand." "Shake your right leg." "Touch your right ear." (On "left day" give the child a *l*emon yellow yarn bracelet.)
- Play games, such as the Hokey Pokey and Simon Says, that require children to practice using their right and left.

Auditory Discrimination

These activities will encourage children to discriminate between various sounds and will prepare them for learning different letter sounds:

- Sing songs where children must reproduce different animal sounds.
- Take turns making animal sounds and guessing which animals you are.
- Ask silly questions that require children to listen carefully. For example, "Does a horse have a tail or a mail?" "Do you cook in a pat or a pot?"
- Let individual children say a rhyme or sentence in a tape recorder. Play it back for the class while they try to identify different voices.
- Rhyming words are words that sound alike at the end. Say nursery rhymes or read rhyming books. Ask children to identify the words that rhyme.
- Use each child's name to make up silly nonsense words that rhyme. For example: Beth – Meth – Teth – Reth – Leth, etc.
- Say three words, two of which rhyme. Children listen and pick out the rhyming pair. For example: bell, frog, tell; book, take, make.
- Play rhyme time ball. (Roll the ball when you are inside, and throw it when you are outside.) Say a word, then roll the ball to one child. The child must say a rhyming word as they catch it.

- Make games where children must match up pictures that rhyme.

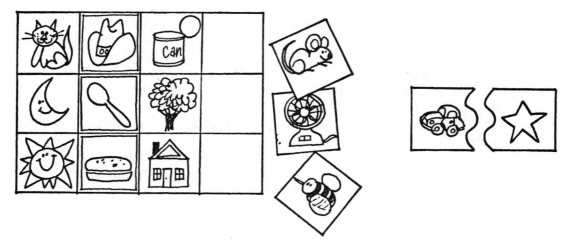

- Say two words. If they are the same, children stand up. If they are different, children sit down. For example: pail, pail (children stand up); man, men (sit down).

- Use musical instruments and songs to improve auditory discrimination by having children identify high and low, loud and soft.

Auditory Memory

Auditory memory can be developed through songs, finger plays, chants, rhymes, or activities similar to the ones below:

- Listen up! Give children a series of directions to follow. Start with two commands, then make them increasingly longer. For example: Put your hand on your head, then clap once. Put your hand on your head, clap once, touch your toes. (This is also fun to play outside.)
- Collect a box of toys and classroom objects, such as blocks, little dolls, cars, crayons, or eating utensils. Name three things. See who can remember what you said and take those items out of the box. Increase the number of items as the children improve.
- Arrange three or four felt pieces on the flannel board. Say them in a specific order, then ask one child to rearrange them in that order.
- Clap, slap, or snap a pattern. Have the children listen, then try to repeat the same pattern. For example: snap, snap, clap.
- As you sing a familiar song or say a nursery rhyme, change one or two words. Ask the children to tell you what was wrong.
  Example: Jack and Jean went up the hill
                    to fetch a pail of water.
                    Jack fell down and broke his crown,
                    and Jean came tumbling after.
- Play games similar to "Going on a Picnic," where children must remember what is said. The first person says, "I'm going on a picnic and I'm taking (*names an item*)." The second person says, "I'm going on a picnic and I'm taking (*first item*), (*second item*)." The game continues with each person adding an item to the list. When a person forgets, the game starts all over again.
- Let children take turns retelling familiar stories to a friend or small group.
- Cut up old fairy tale books and have the children arrange the pictures in sequential order.
- After story time, ask children to recall characters, events, and other details in the story.
- Take a word and break it down into the individual sounds of letters. The children listen, then try to blend the sounds together to make a word. For example: $b - 1 - \breve{a} - k$ = black; $s - n - \bar{o}$ = snow; $p - 1 - \bar{a}$ = play.

Letters

There are a variety of ways to introduce letters to children. Remember that letters and sounds are abstract for little ones, so you must make them real with objects they can associate with, art projects, manipulatives, and games. Generally, it is best to introduce one letter at a time, teaching the sound along with the letter name. You can go straight through the alphabet from A to Z, introduce all the consonants and then the vowels, or skip around.

Many teachers choose a "letter of the week" and integrate a broad variety of learning experiences similar to the ones below:

Letter Friend—Make a different puppet from a paper sack, sock, or other materials for each letter. Name the puppet after the letter and write the letter on the puppet. You can also take a stuffed animal and simply change its name each week as you study a different letter. Hide the letter friend in a box each Monday and make it a special occasion when the letter friend is introduced.

Here are some names for "letter friends":

A – Andy or Abby Alligator
B – Barney or Becky Bear
C – Carl or Cathie Cat
D – Denny or Dotty Dog
E – Ed or Edna Elephant
F – Fred or Fran Fish
G – Gary or Gail Goat
H – Harry or Holly Horse
I – Ike or Irene Iguana
J – Jack or Jill Jaguar
K – Kirk or Karen Kangaroo
L – Larry or Lucy Lion
M – Mikey or Mandy Mouse
N – Nick or Nancy Nightingale
O – Ollie or Olive Owl
P – Patrick or Patty Pig
Q – Quintella Queen
R – Ricky or Robin Rabbit
S – Sammy or Sallie Snake
T – Teddy or Tammy Turtle

U – Ugene Unicorn
V – Vern or Veronica Vulture
W – Will or Wanda Walrus
X – X-Man
Y – Yodi or Yolanda Yak
Z – Zeke or Zana Zebra

Letter Can—Cover a large can or oatmeal box with construction paper, wallpaper, or contact paper. Each week write the letter you are studying on a piece of paper and tape it to the bottom of the can. Let one child at a time take the can home and collect objects around the house that begin with that sound. When they return the can to school the next day, let the child share the objects they have found at circle time.

Letter Table—Write the letter you are studying on a piece of cardboard and stand it up in the middle of a small table or on a shelf. All week long, the children can bring objects from home that start with the sound and place them on the table or shelf.

Letter Book—Give each child a sheet of paper. Ask them to write the letter you are studying on the paper and draw pictures of the things that begin with that sound. You could also let them cut out magazine pictures of objects beginning with that sound. Label the objects on each child's page, then staple them together to make a book.

Dramatizations—Act out different things that begin with the sound you are studying. For example, if "L" is the letter of the week, you could "lick a lollipop," "love," "leap," "look," "laugh," etc.

Art—Plan art projects around sounds you are learning. Bubble painting would be good for B, puppets would tie in with P, and paper snakes would be fun for S.

Cooking—Cook a snack or eat a food that begins with the letter of the week. You could make applesauce for A, banana boats for B, carrot salad for C, and so on.

Hands Up—Take a washable marker and print the letter you are studying on each child's hand. Talk about the letter and the sound it makes. Instruct the children to raise their hand every time they hear you say a word that begins with that sound, then say a list of words for them to respond to.

Mobiles and Posters—Cut out a giant-size letter from poster board. Let the children draw objects beginning with that sound on the letter, then hang it in the room. You could also let the children cut out magazine pictures beginning with a particular sound and glue them on a poster.

Floor Letters—Take masking tape or cloth tape and make a giant letter on the floor. The children can walk on it, drive cars and trucks around it, etc.

Writing Letters—Children can follow the dots to make letters, trace around letter stencils, write letters in the air, draw letters in sand, cut letters out of paper, make letters out of clay or pipe cleaners, write letters on the chalkboard, make letters with glue and sprinkle them with Jello or colored sand, or practice writing letters with markers, crayons, colored pencils, or paints.

Language Experience—Print the letter of the week on chart paper or poster board. Let the children think of as many words as they can that begin with that sound. Write down the words as the children say them, then read over the list when you are finished.

```
┌─────────────────┐
│       Rr        │
│ Randy    red    │
│ run      rabbit │
│ rain     ride   │
└─────────────────┘
```

These are other activities that will stimulate children's interest in letters and sounds:

- Give children textured letters to explore and manipulate. You can purchase three-dimensional plastic, wood, and magnetic letters, or make your own from felt, sandpaper, yarn, glitter, etc.
- Let children make letter shapes from play dough or clay. (It's also fun to make letters from frozen bread dough or canned biscuits, then bake and eat them.)
- Challenge children to make different letters with their bodies.
- Make lacing cards of different letters for children to sew around.
- Sing alphabet songs.
- Trace letters on children's hands or backs while they try to identify them.
- Display the alphabet in a prominent place in your classroom. As you sing songs or talk about different letters, point to them.
- Dismiss children by pointing to a letter and telling them they can leave if their name starts with that letter; ask them to make that letter sound; or have them think of a word beginning with that letter.
- Make alphabet poster cards that you can use for many activities. Cut 26 sheets of 8″×11″ cardboard. On each sheet write a different letter (upper and lower case) and draw a picture of an object that begins with that sound. Laminate these or cover them with clear contact paper. Pass these out and ask children to stand up when their letter is called or when you say a word that begins with their letter.

- Have the children stand in a circle, then put the letter cards inside the circle on the floor. Choose two children at a time to play letter pick-up. The teacher calls out a letter, and the first child to find it and pick it up wins.
- Spread 10 letters on the floor. Take a small circle and draw a silly face on it. Have the children turn around and hide their eyes while you hide the silly face under one letter. The children turn around and take turns guessing where silly face is and looking under that letter. Whoever finds it may be the next one to hide it.
- Hide the letters around the room in plain sight. Let the children hunt for the letters, or assign each child a particular letter to find.

- Take inexpensive paper plates and write a letter on each plate. Spread these out in a circle on the floor, then have the children march around the letters while a record is played. When the music stops, each child should find a letter and stand on it. As you point to children, they must identify the letter they are standing on.
- Cut letters out of cardboard or construction paper and put them in a sack. One child at a time takes a turn reaching in the bag, drawing a letter, and naming something that starts with that sound.
- Play the alphabet game on field trips or bus trips. The object of the game is to find the letters in alphabetical order on signs, license plates, billboards, etc. Next, try to identify an object out the window that begins with each letter. For example, a–asphalt, b–building, c–car, etc.
- Take an alphabet walk around the school and try to identify something that begins with each letter. You might find an apple for A, ball for B, crayon for C, and so on. (This is fun to play outside, too.)
- Make a fishing game where children must identify different letters of the alphabet. Cut out paper fish and write a letter on each. Attach a paper clip and use a magnet tied to a stick for your pole. The children must identify the letter on the fish they catch and say a word that starts with that letter.
- Take a potato chip can or other tall can and cover it with colorful paper. Cut 60 strips of construction paper that measure $2'' \times 12''$. On the bottom of each strip write an alphabet letter, but on eight of them draw a bee. Put the strips in the can with the letters toward the bottom. Let the children take turns drawing a letter and identifying it. If they draw the bee they are out of the game. The game continues until one person is left.
- Let children identify and eat cereal in the shape of alphabet letters. They will also enjoy doing art projects with cereal and pasta in the shape of letters.
- Give children stencils of alphabet letters. Let them trace around their initials, the letter of the week, or any letters they like. Next have them cut their letters out, punch a hole in them, and string them on yarn to make a letter necklace.
- Make BINGO cards with alphabet letters. As you call out a letter or word, children can cover up that letter with a paper square, bean, cereal, or popcorn. The first one to fill up four corners or a row wins.
- Make puzzles where children can match upper and lower case letters.

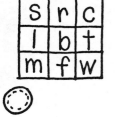

- Do the "alphabet stretch" and get rid of wiggles while reinforcing letters and sounds. Extend your arms in the air and say "A". Put your hands on your shoulders and make the sound "ă." Touch your toes and say a word that begins with "a" like "apples." Put your hands in the air and say "B," touch your shoulders and say the b sound "b," then touch your toes and say a "b" word like "ball." Continue for each letter of the alphabet.
- Take a piece of poster board and mark it off into nine sections. Write letters in the different sections. Give one child at a time a bean bag and let them throw it on a letter. They must identify that letter and think of a word that begins with that sound.
- Make games where children can put the letters in alphabetical order.

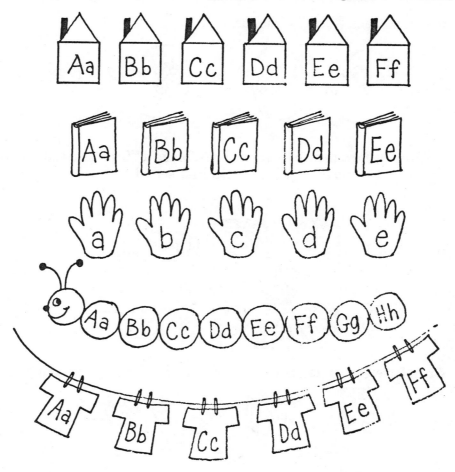

- Make games where children must match letters with beginning sounds.
  IT'S IN THE BAG! Put pictures of objects in the correct bag.

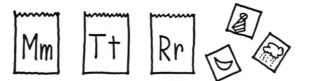

Put pictures in the correct pocket.

Match mittens with like sounds.

Cut a circle for a mouth in a cereal box. Make a "Letter Friend" out of the box and feed it pictures beginning with that sound.

Write letters on boxes. Sort small toys and objects by beginning sounds.

Sightwords

These activities can be used to expose children to sightwords or to help them learn to read simple words in a fun, natural way.

- Label centers and objects in the room. It is helpful to draw a simple illustration by the word so the children will learn to associate that word with the particular object.

- Write children's names on their cubbies, papers, and other belongings. Have a check-in system where they can identify their names every morning, or make a list of names and have them find their name and circle it when they arrive at school.

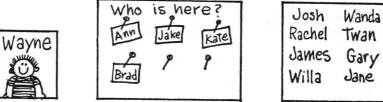

- Take food labels, cut out the product names, then have children match up like words. Store, restaurant, and product names from newspaper advertisements can also be made into matching games.

- Make textured words with sandpaper, felt, glitter, Jello, beans, etc.

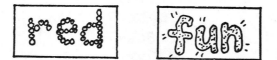

- Label pictures children draw, as well as their block sculptures and sand creations. Make labels for different themes in the dramatic play area.

- Let children copy words with magnetic letters, or let them type words on a typewriter.

- Make a list of class rules on chart paper and read over them every morning. Point to each word as it is said.

- Write out the words to songs, finger plays, nursery rhymes, or recipes on chart paper and follow along with the words as you read or sing together.

- Make love notes for the children that they will want to read. Also, write the daily schedule, homework assignments, and special events on the board and read over these together.

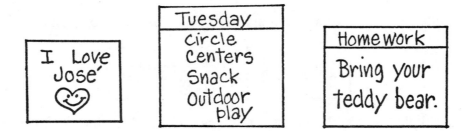

- Go on a word scavenger hunt around the school. Find words like "girls," "boys," "office," "fire extinguisher," "exit," and so on.
- Make puzzles from words. For example, write a color word on a sentence strip, then cut between the letters. Put the puzzle pieces in an envelope and write

the color name on the front of the envelope so children have something to look at as they work the puzzle.

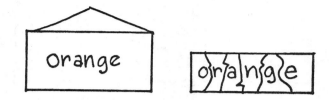

- Write a simple sentence on a sentence strip. Make two copies of it. Cut between the words of one, then have the children match up like words and read the sentence.

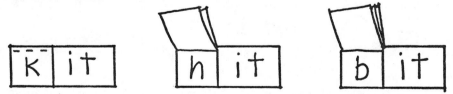

- Have children find and circle sightwords in the newspaper, or ask them to cut out words they can read.
- Make configuration games where the shape of the word will help children identify what the word is.

- Teach children word families. If they can learn a word such as "can," then they can change the beginning sound and read many different words like "man, fan, tan, Dan, ran, van, and pan."
- Take a 3″×5″ card and write a word ending on it, such as "an, "in, "at, "it, "ot, "ake, "ike, "ay," "all, "ill" and "ed." Cut five 3″×2″ strips of paper and staple them on top. Write a different consonant on each strip, then flip them over to make new words.

- Make games where consonants can be changed on word endings to make new words.

- Make a large set of alphabet letters on 8″×11″ paper. Let each child hold a letter. As you call out different letters, have children stand up next to each other to make words. In this way children can clearly see how letters can be moved and changed to build words.

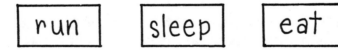

- Provide children with picture dictionaries to look at and copy words from.
- Write action words and verbs on poster cards, such as "run," "sleep," "eat," "play," etc. When the word is shown, have the children stand up and act out the movement.

- Make puzzles and games where children can associate words with pictures.

- Help each child collect words that they want to learn or that have personal significance for them. You might ask children to bring in a shoe box and to decorate it to be a "word bank." Write down words the children ask to learn on 3″×5″ cards, then have them read them and "save" them in their word banks.

They could also store their words in an index card file box, or they could punch holes in the cards and attach them to a metal ring. Children are then able to use these words for writing stories and for other activities.

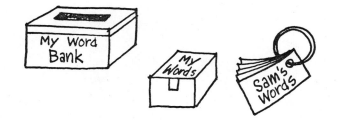

How Do You Encourage Beginning Writing?

Many exciting programs have been developed in recent years that promote early writing by young children. These programs emphasize the whole language approach and contend that reading and writing develop together and support each other. It is important to encourage all attempts at writing and to praise children enthusiastically. Whether children scribble, draw, or write, they are trying to use symbols to communicate. Correct letter formation and spelling will come as the children grow and learn.

The following activities will provide children with opportunities for integrating reading and writing skills:

Daily Journals—Ask each child to bring in a spiral ring notebook, or make a blank book for each child by stapling paper between construction paper. Set aside a special time each day when children can "write" in their journals. It can be the first thing in the morning, before lunch, or after rest, but you should be consistent and make it a routine part of your day. At first, ask the children to draw pictures about themselves or things that happen to them. Go to children individually and write down exactly what they dictate to you by their picture. Give children the opportunity to show their journals and talk about their pictures with their classmates.

Write down what the child dictates.

As reading and writing skills develop, children will begin to scribble on the page with their pictures or write isolated letters.

Gradually, children will start to copy words in the room and will write high interest words, such as love, mom, dad, cat, etc.

In the next stage, children will begin to use "invented" spelling and write down words according to how they sound.

Do not spell words for children or correct their writing. Be supportive and tell them just to write down the sounds they hear. With invented spelling children are able to write sentences and stories at a young age. The real advantage of journals is that each child can progress at his or her own rate and that writing and reading are integrated and meaningful for them.

Chart Stories—Let children dictate stories as a group while you write them on chart paper. This is a good follow-up activity after a walk, field trip, science experiment, or cooking lesson.

The Farm
We went to the farm.
We saw cows.
We fed ducks.
Jim got wet.

Home Story—Take a spiral ring notebook and begin writing a story in it. Let one child at a time have a turn taking the notebook home and adding to the story with their parents. Read what they have written to the class the following day, then send the story home to be added to by another family.

Cards—Let children make homemade cards for friends and family members for birthdays and other holidays. Write down the words they dictate to you, or encourage them to write their own greeting. (It's also good to have children make thank you notes for speakers, field trip guides, school helpers, and others.)

Take Home Teddy Story—Choose a stuffed bear or other animal to be your class mascot. Each weekend let one child take home the animal along with a spiral ring notebook. The parent writes a story about the adventures "Teddy" has with his or her child, such as where they went, what they played, what they had to eat, what they watched on television, etc. The story is read to the class on Monday morning when it is returned along with "Teddy." The parents enjoy participating, and you end up with a wonderful tale of Teddy's adventures.

Autograph Books—Staple blank sheets of paper together and let children decorate the cover for an autograph book. They can get their friends to sign their names, draw pictures, or write messages in their books. (This is a great activity for the end of the year.)

Mailboxes—Have children make their own mailboxes from a shoe box, cereal box, or paper sack. Give them scrap paper, envelopes, pens, and pencils and let them write and deliver letters to their friends.

Birthday Books—These are a special treasure that children will want to save. Each child is given a sheet of paper on which to draw a picture or write a message for the birthday child. The birthday child gets to decorate the cover from construction paper. Collect the pictures and staple them in the cover for a unique book.

Class Book—Make books for different letters, colors, and themes you are studying. Titles might include "If I Had a Magic Wand," "If I Were President," "When I Grow Up," and "Happiness Is." Give each child a sheet of paper and ask them to cut out magazine pictures or draw their own picture related to the theme of the class book. Have each child dictate a sentence to you describing their paper, then staple them together to make a book. Put the book in the classroom library and let children have turns taking the book home.

Friend Book—At the beginning of the year ask each child to bring in a photograph, or take a picture of each child. Glue their picture to a piece of paper and ask them to tell you a story about themselves. Put all the pictures together to make a book about "My New Friends." Each night a different child can take the book home and introduce his or her family to new school friends.

Blank Books—Keep a large supply of blank books for children to write and draw in. It works well to take two sheets of 8½″×11″ paper, fold them in half, then staple them together. For a change, make children "itty-bitty books" from paper cut in 2″ squares, or make "great big books" from large sheets of newsprint.

Homemade Books—These are a great motivation for beginning writers. It's fun to make them in a shape to go with a theme you are studying.

Baggie Books—Books from plastic bags are easy to make and are durable for little ones. Cut construction paper to fit into sandwich size zip lock bags. Let the children draw pictures, cut out magazine pictures, or glue photographs on the paper. After dictating a sentence or writing their own sentence, insert the paper in the bag and zip it up. Punch holes and attach the bags together with a pipe cleaner or yarn.

Cloth Books—For a real treat, make cloth books for children. Start with a 12″×15″ piece of fabric and two pieces of 9″×6″ cardboard. Glue the cardboard in the middle of the fabric, leaving ½″ between them. Trim the fabric at the corners, then glue the fabric to the cardboard. Take 5–10 sheets of paper, fold them in half, then sew them to the middle by hand or on a machine. If you wish, glue another 9″×6″ piece of cardboard over the inside covers.

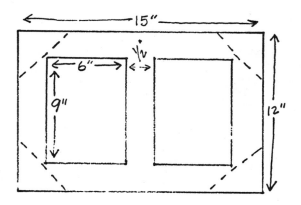

6

MATHEMATICS

Throughout the day, you can make math interesting and meaningful for children with the materials, games, and activities presented in this section. Major concepts introduced are one-to-one correspondence, patterns, sorting and sets, counting, number recognition, shapes, comparisons, measurement, time, money, addition, and subtraction. The use of computers in the classroom is also discussed.

What Is "New Math"?

"1–2–3–4–5–6–7–8–9–10." Okay, Suzie can count. That's all there is to preschool math, isn't there?

The difference between "new math" and math taught in the past is that new math focuses on understanding and hands-on experiences, rather than rote memory. New math takes into account the cognitive development of young children and provides the groundwork and foundation for future mathematical processes. Further, when math is interesting, concrete, useful, and fun, children will have successful experiences and develop a positive attitude about math.

How Do Children Learn Mathematics?

Most of what children learn about math is not from dittos and workbooks, but from play and daily activities. For example, when children set the table for a snack, they are matching one-to-one; when they play with the blocks, they are experimenting with different shapes; when they remind you that the big hand is on the 12 and it's time to go outside, they are telling time; when they sing about "Five Little Monkeys," they are counting. Throughout the day children use math and learn in ways that are natural to them.

In addition to play activities, teachers need to offer children carefully sequenced learning experiences in mathematics. Observe children to assess what they already know, then plan activities that will be challenging, yet provide for the varying abilities of the children in the class. Math is a continuous process, and children need to move from concrete experiences to visual, symbol, and abstract activities.

> 1st —*Concrete*—Give children real materials to manipulate and work with. They need to see and touch objects and verbalize their thoughts.

example:    (4 actual cookies)

2nd—*Visual*—Expose children to illustrations or pictures representing concepts.

example: (card illustrating a set of 4)

> 3rd —*Symbol*—Introduce the symbols that represent the concept.

example: 4

4th —*Abstract*—Children are mentally able to understand the concept of "4."

Whenever you plan math activities, you will want to follow the above sequence. Remember, children will need a variety of real experiences with concrete objects before moving to the visual and abstract. Even then, some children will never move beyond the concrete stage. You cannot force or pressure children to learn mathematical concepts, but you can encourage them with stimulating activities, time to explore, materials to manipulate, and praise and reinforcement.

What Vocabulary Should Children Be Exposed To?

The ability to use mathematical words is important for children's understanding. When the vocabulary is used in connection with experiences, then it will make sense to children. The words below are ones you should use frequently as you explain activities, identify objects, talk to children, sing songs, tell stories, and ask questions.

Time	Measurement	Size	Position	Amount	Operations
date	cup	big	up	set	add to
clock	pint	little	down	group	take away
calendar	quart	fat	here	one, two,	multiply
second	gallon	thin	there	three, etc.	divide
minute	ruler	tall	top	pair	equal
hour	inch	short	bottom	dozen	separate
day	foot	long	far	cent	count
week	yard	heavy	close	nickel	compare
month	mile	light	right	dime	measure
year	scale	more	left	quarter	
season	pound	less	inside	dollar	
after	ounce	greater	outside	how many	
before	thermometer	full	first	how much	
today	degree	empty	last	whole	
yesterday	meter	all	middle	half	
tomorrow		some		part	

Signs—Mathematical symbols and signs are like road signs that tell you what to do. Many common mathematical errors are made in older years *because children do not pay attention to the signs.* Therefore, begin exposing preschoolers to these symbols and terms:

+ plus sign; put together, add
− minus sign; take away or separate
= equals; numbers on either side must balance
> greater than
< less than

What Manipulative Materials Can Be Used for Teaching Math?

Manipulative materials are at the heart of preschool math, since they provide children with the concrete experiences they need to learn. Choose familiar objects that are safe and durable, and change them frequently to keep children interested. Also, try to choose equipment that is versatile and leads to exploration and self-discovery. Most of the objects below are free, inexpensive, or are easy to make.

For Counting	Shapes	Measurement	Time and Money	What Else?
seashells	unit blocks	ruler	3 min. timer	play phone
seeds	color cubes	yardstick	stop watch	cuisenaire

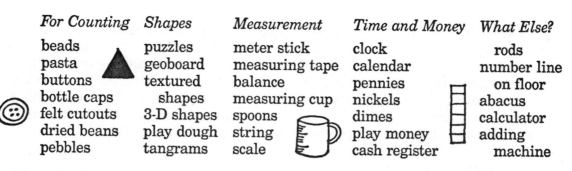

For Counting	*Shapes*	*Measurement*	*Time and Money*	*What Else?*
beads	puzzles	meter stick	clock	rods
pasta	geoboard	measuring tape	calendar	number line
buttons	textured	balance	pennies	on floor
bottle caps	shapes	measuring cup	nickels	abacus
felt cutouts	3-D shapes	spoons	dimes	calculator
dried beans	play dough	string	play money	adding
pebbles	tangrams	scale	cash register	machine

You can also use small toys, golf tees, plastic cups and plates, silverware, pencils, balloons, clothespins, food, stickers, popsicle sticks, toothpicks, styrofoam packing, egg cartons, and anything else that is plentiful and fun.

What Mathematical Concepts Should Be Introduced to Children?

In preschool years, the emphasis is on exposure, not mastery. The following concepts are ones that young children should be introduced to through readiness activities:

One-to-one Correspondence—In order for children to count with meaning, they must know how to pair objects or match them one-to-one. For example, one book for each child, or one hat for every clown.

Patterns—Patterning is the ability to reproduce an arrangement of objects. Math itself is a pattern that repeats over and over.

Sorting and Sets—Children need to learn how to classify objects and put them into sets and groups according to some attribute or characteristic, such as color, shape, etc.

Counting—Rote counting is the ability to recite numerals. Rationale counting involves understanding the meaning of numbers.

Number Meaning and Recognition—Each number represents an amount or quantity which is represented by a symbol or numeral. Number is the abstract— "three balls"; numeral is the symbol—"3."

Shapes—Children should be able to recognize similarities and differences in shapes, and to name shapes.

Comparisons—Children can learn to determine if objects and sets are alike or different through comparisons.

Measurement—Measuring is a formal way to compare objects. Children need experiences with linear, weight, and volume measurement.

Time and Money—Time and money are a daily part of everyone's lives and are useful concepts for children.

Addition and Subtraction—Simple operations in addition (joining sets) and subtraction (separating sets) can be introduced to preschoolers with manipulatives and firsthand experiences.

What Activities Can Be Used to Teach Children Mathematics?

Children at all ages can be involved in learning the previous concepts, but you must choose activities that are appropriate to the abilities and interests of your particular class. Some of the activities listed in this chapter can be used with large groups, some are more appropriate for small groups, still others are best for individual exploration at the math center. Many of these concepts can be reinforced in art, science, music, and other play activities. As with other areas of the curriculum, go from simple to more complex tasks and sequence activities so that children can experience success. For example, teach children to count to 5, then to 10, 15, and so on. Focus on learning one shape at a time, rather than overwhelming children with four shapes all at once. Also, encourage children to repeat activities to build their confidence.

One-to-One Correspondence

- Give children three plates and three cups and ask them to set the table. Increase the number of items as the children improve.
- Let children pass out books, crayons, and snacks to their classmates. Ask questions such as, "Do you have enough for everybody to have one? How many more do you need?"
- Have children match up blocks to squares on pattern cards.

- Ask children to match up pegs to holes on a pegboard, or to match up puzzle pieces to their appropriate space.
- Play group games, such as Duck-Duck-Goose, where children tap one person at a time.
- Make folder games where children must match up objects one-to-one. For example, put a flower in each pot, give each elephant a peanut, or put a hot dog in every bun.

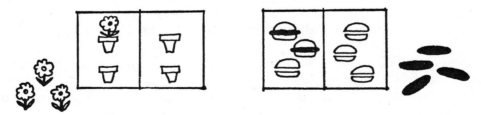

- Tell flannel board stories, such as The Three Bears and Three Little Pigs, then let children retell them, matching objects one-to-one. (One bowl for every bear, one house for every pig, etc.)

Patterns

- Clap out a pattern, then ask children to repeat it.
  For example: clap-clap, clap-clap.
- Ask children to copy body movement patterns.

For example: touch your toes, your head, then jump.
(Make these increasingly longer and more complex.)

- Let children reproduce patterns with beads, parquetry blocks, and pegboards.
- Have children copy patterns using popsicle sticks, blocks, and other small toys.

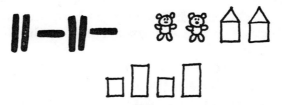

- Ask children to reproduce a pattern of fruit on a toothpick for a snack.

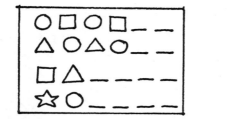

(banana, grape—banana, grape)

- Children can make patterns in art with sponge prints, vegetable prints, and other media.

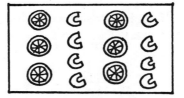

- Make folder games that require children to complete a pattern.

- Have children copy patterns on paper for a pre-writing experience.

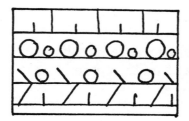

Sorting and Sets

- Let children sort spoons, forks, and knives into a silverware tray.
- Give children a box with two or three of several different things to sort. You might use balloons, pencils, bandaids, toy cars, etc.
- Group children in the room according to the type of shoes they are wearing, the color of their clothing, or some other characteristic.
- When children clean-up, encourage them to group the blocks that are alike and to sort toys that are alike.
- Cut out three, four, and five of several different objects from felt, then ask children to group them on the flannel board.
- Use a muffin tin, egg carton, or partitioned box to have children sort various objects, such as mixed beans, buttons, colored golf tees, coins, etc.

- Ask children to sort playing cards by suit.
- Make a sorting box from a shoe box. Put a cardboard divider down the middle, then let children sort picture cards of living and non-living things, animals and people, big and little objects, different-colored objects, etc. Coordinate this activity with skills you are working on in other areas of the curriculum.

- Make lollipops by gluing 3″ circles of construction paper to popsicle sticks. (Make several of each color.) Let children sort these by color into juice cans covered in the same color.

- Make a folder game with three or four different types of fruit trees. Let children put cutouts of the fruits on the appropriate tree.

Other similar games can be made where children sort furniture into the appropriate room, clothing to the corresponding season, foods into the four food groups, etc.

- Introduce sets to the children with the "Set Dinosaur." He's an imaginary character that loves to eat sets of things. Ask the children to find all the sets in the classroom that he could eat, such as a set of books, a set of chairs, a set of blocks, etc.
- Go outside for a walk and look for sets on the playground and in nature.
- Give children a box with one of the first item, two of the second item, three of the third item, etc. Ask children to make sets and count the objects in each set.
- Tell children that a set that has nothing in it is the empty set, represented by "0". There are "0" ghosts in the room; "0" horns on your head. What else can you think of?

Counting

- Songs, rhymes, finger plays, and stories are a wonderful way to introduce counting to children. The chapter on "Music and Movement" will give you some good ideas.
- Count as you do various exercises, such as jumping jacks, toe touches, waist bends, etc.
- Count as you bounce a ball, swing, or jump rope.
- Count how many apples you need for a snack, how many cotton balls they can use for an art project, how many blocks you can stack in a tower, how many steps to the playground—count everything!
- Use counting as a transition technique. "Let's see if you can line-up by the time I count to 10." "Let's count to 15 and see if everyone can be ready for a story by then."
- Count while you're waiting for lunch, riding on the bus, or between activities.
- Make a counting chart for your room with numerals 0–100. Point to each numeral as the children count together orally.
- Count to 100, count by 2's, 5's, and 10's.
- Practice counting backwards. Stoop down, count backwards from 10, then jump up like a rocket blasting off.
- Ask a different child each day to count all the boys and girls in the room. You will have to help them learn how to touch one person as they say each number.

- Post a calendar in your room and orally count the days as you point to the numerals.
- Give children lots of interesting things to count in the math center, like feathers, rubber fishing worms, shells, and trinkets.
- Hide sets in plastic eggs, small boxes, or paper sacks. Let children take the objects out and count them.
- Make a number line on the floor with tape. Let children name numerals as they walk on the number line. (Make a number line on the playground sidewalk with chalk or paint.)

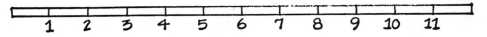

- Make small posters of the numerals 1–10. Give each child a numeral and let them get in proper order.

- Slowly sing "Ten Little Indians" and have children hold up their numeral as it is sung.
- Let children hang up numeral cards with clothespins on a clothesline in your room.

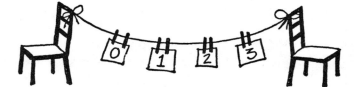

- Ask children to put magnetic numerals in order on a metal surface.
- Make a paper train with an engine and 10 separate cars. Write "0" on the engine and the numerals 1–10 on the cars. Have children line the cars up in order from left to right.

- Make a Numbo worm puzzle where children can arrange the parts of the worm's body in order.

- Make folder games where children must put objects in numerical order.

- Make an obstacle course on the playground with numbers to follow.

- Make board games where the children must count and move the appropriate number of spaces.

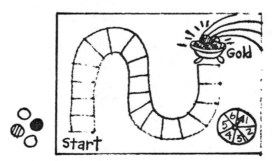

Use dice, a spinner, or cards on which numerals are written.

- Let children complete dot-to-dot pictures by counting and following the numerals.

- Play number detective where children must tell you what number comes before, after, or between what you say. For example, "What number comes before 6?", "What number comes after 9?", or "What number comes between 2 and 4?"
- Teach ordinal numbers with everyday questions like, "Who is the first person in line? The second? The third?"
- Introduce children to estimating by asking them to guess how many objects there are in different sets. For example, ask them how many balloons there are in a bag, grapes on their stem at snacktime, or books in the classroom library. Encourage them to count to verify their estimate.
- Fill a jar or other container with marbles, popcorn, jelly beans, etc. and let the children estimate the quantity. The child who guesses the closest amount gets to keep the jar and contents, or they may share it with their friends. (This is a fun game to play at parties, too.)

- Children can use poker chips, pennies, or any other plentiful objects for "loot" in this game called "Lucky Loot." Give each child a plastic container to store their winnings in. Children take a die one at a time and throw it. Whatever number shows up, they may count out that number of the "loot" and put it into their container. At the end of the game, estimate who has the most "loot," then count to see if they predicted right.

Number Meaning and Recognition

- Give children real objects to make sets with. For example, staple paper flowers to straws, then put them in numbered cans. Give children shelled peanuts and ask them to put the correct amount in numbered bags.

- Take an egg carton and write the numerals 1–12 on the sections. Ask children to make appropriate sets in each section with beans, seeds, or buttons.
- In the bottom of cupcake liners or on small paper plates, write the numerals that you are working on. Give children cereal, peanuts, popcorn, raisins, or other small pieces of food with which to make sets. (The best part is eating the sets when you're finished!)

- Ask children to clip the appropriate number of paper clips to index cards on which numerals are written.

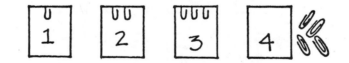

A similar game can be made by having children attach clothespins to a paper plate or card on which numerals are written.

- Take index cards or 3″×5″ pieces of paper and write numerals on them. Give children a hole punch and have them punch out the corresponding number of holes for each set.

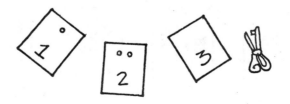

- Make folder games that require children to make sets for specific numerals. You can put chocolate chips on cookies, petals on flowers, seeds in a pumpkin, eggs in a nest, fish in a bowl, and many other combinations that will delight children. Seasonal games of this nature are also a big hit. (Use the patterns in the Appendix or create your own.)

- Make puzzle games where the pieces will fit when the correct numeral and set are matched.

- Have children match up equal sets of different objects.

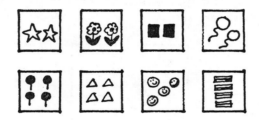

- Let each child make a set book. Take 5–10 sheets of paper and write a numeral on each page. Have children draw sets or use stickers or stamps to make sets to match the numerals on each page. They can also cut sets from magazines or newspapers.

- Go on a set scavenger hunt outside. Ask children to find 1 flower, 2 seeds, 3 rocks, 4 leaves, etc.

- Write the numerals 0–15 (or however many children you have) on paper and arrange them in a circle on the floor. Play some music and have children march around the numerals until the music stops. Call out one numeral. Whoever is on that numeral must clap or do jumping jacks that number of times.
- Make each child a set of cards with numerals 0–10 written on them. The children lay out the cards in front of them. The teacher draws a set on the chalkboard or claps a certain number of times. Each child then holds up the correct numeral. (This is a good way to check addition and subtraction facts, too.)
- Give children sandpaper numerals to trace and touch.
- Have children form different numerals out of clay or play dough.

- Let children make numeral collages from different materials, such as yarn, cotton, beans, and toothpicks.

- Make a Numbo game similar to BINGO. Draw off 9–16 spaces on cards and write different numerals in each space. (Make each card different.) As you call out a number, each child tries to find it on their card. They may cover it up with a piece of paper, beans, cereal, etc. The first child to fill up four corners, a row across, or other combination wins. (You can also use these cards for addition and subtraction games.)

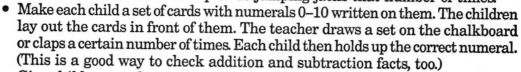

- Make set dominoes by gluing stickers or drawing sets on cards. Let the children take turns drawing cards and matching up like sets.

- Make a concentration game with sets and numerals. Write numerals on half of the cards, and draw sets on the other half. Turn the cards face down and let the children take turns matching them up.

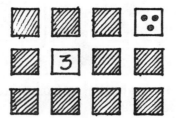

- Play Go Fishing. Make 6″ fish from construction paper. Write different numerals on the fish and attach a paper clip to each. Tie a magnet to a 3′ string which has been tied to a stick. Spread out the fish on the floor, then let the children take turns fishing and identifying their numeral.

- Measure off a sheet of poster paper into nine sections. Write a different numeral in each section. Let each child take a turn throwing a bean bag and identifying the numeral it lands on. Add to this game by asking them to jump, hop, clap, etc. the appropriate number of times.

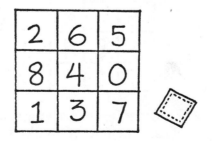

- Make numeral set cards. On 8″×11″ heavy paper write the numerals 0–10. Draw a corresponding set on each card. When you hold up each card, ask the children to clap, snap, stomp their feet, or do other movements that number of times.

- Use a play telephone to help children learn to recognize numerals and how to dial their phone number and other emergency numbers.
- Teach children to recognize their address, phone number, and birthday by using matching games and flash cards.

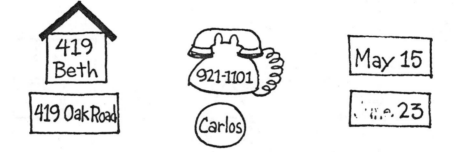

- The section on small motor skills has many good ideas and rhymes that will help children learn to write numerals.

Shapes

- Make shapes out of different textures, such as fabric, sandpaper, glitter, foil, cotton, cardboard, styrofoam, felt, etc. Encourage children to manipulate these.
- Challenge children to make shapes with their individual bodies. Then divide them up into groups of four and ask them to make a circle, square, rectangle, and triangle with their bodies.
- Put cardboard shapes or three-dimensional shapes in a paper bag. Let children take turns reaching in and identifying the shapes by touch.

- Plan shape snacks, such as round crackers, triangle sandwiches, square cheese, and rectangle cookies.
- Use shapes in various art projects. Cut sponges into shapes for printing, cut construction paper into various shapes for collages, create people and animals from shapes, do crayon relief pictures of shapes, construct a mobile from shapes, or make shapes with clay and play dough.

- Make shape puzzles from heavy poster board.

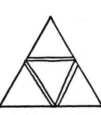

- Ask children to make shapes with a geoboard.

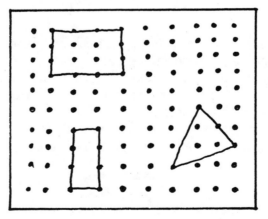

Take a 12″ square of wood that is ¾″ thick. Using 2″ nails, hammer in ten rows and columns. Give children rubber bands to stretch over the nails to make shapes.

- Ask children to make various shapes with pegs on a pegboard.

- Give children blocks of various shapes to experiment with and build with.
- Cut out shapes from felt of various sizes and colors. Let children group them and arrange them to make objects.
- Make shapes on the classroom floor with cloth tape. Encourage children to walk around them and play in them.
- Draw or paint shapes on the sidewalk.
- Draw pictures of circles, triangles, squares, and rectangles on cardboard. Make several different sizes and colors of each shape, then let children categorize them into groups that are alike.
- Make a shape lotto game where children draw cards and match them up to shapes on their game board.

- Make a game of shapes and colors similar to Bingo. Children can cover up the shape of the appropriate color when you call it out.
- Make a concentration game out of different shapes. Make two of each of the shapes below for the children to remember and match.

- Encourage children to verbalize and describe the different shapes. For example, "A circle is round like a ball." "A square has four sides that are all the same, and it looks like a picture frame."
- Have children trace, draw, and cut out various shapes.

- Take a shoe box and put one cup of sand or salt in the bottom. Have children practice tracing shapes in the sand or salt.
- Make books of shapes as you study them. Children can practice drawing the shape on one page, cut out magazine pictures of the shape to paste on another page, cut out the shape and glue it on a page, and make animals or objects from the shape.

- Play the game "I Spy" with shapes. One child says, "I spy a _____," then the rest of the class tries to guess what it is.   shape
- Take a shape walk and look for different shapes around the school and playground.
- Introduce children to fractions by having them cut pieces of paper in half, food in half, etc. Cut cereal boxes, an old T-shirt, napkin, paper plate, and other real objects in half, then let children match halves to make wholes.

Comparing

- Compare children's hands, feet, length of hair, family size, etc.
- Compare objects in the environment using vocabulary such as heavy and light, large and small, tall and short, light and dark, wide and narrow, etc.
- Match flannel board objects from Goldilocks and the Three Bears by size. Baby Bear gets the small bowl, small chair, small bed, and so on. (You will find patterns in the "Story Time" chapter.)
- Take cardboard rollers from paper towels and make tubes for children to seriate by size. Cut one 7", 6", 5", 4", 3", 2", and 1". You can also make a seriating game with egg cartons. Cut 1 section, 2, 3, 4, 5, and 6 section lengths. Encourage children to arrange these in both ascending and descending order.

- Get paint chips from a paint store and cut the colors apart. Have children arrange the chips in order from dark to light.
- Ask children to seriate set cards.

- To show comparisons visually, make bar graphs for your class. You could graph the number of people in each child's family, their favorite animals, how many children have a birthday in each month, or how many teeth each child has lost.

How many in your family?						
Name	1	2	3	4	5	6
Maria		▨				
Will	▨	▨	▨	▨		
Wang	▨	▨	▨			
Shawn	▨	▨				

- Introduce children to the inequality signs with Alfred the Alligator. Alfred is always hungry so his mouth will always be trying to eat the larger set.

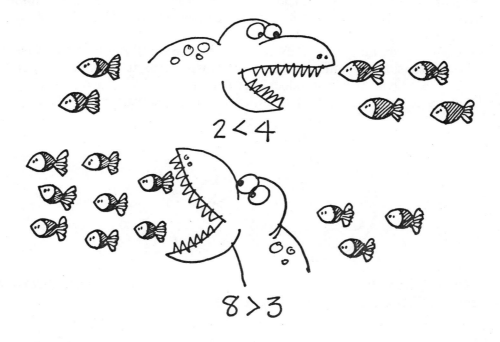

2 < 4

8 > 3

Measuring

- Have children measure tables, chairs, books, and other objects in the room with their hands, a crayon, a block, or shoe. They can report how long it is to the class; for example, "5 hands long," or "10 crayons long," and so on.
- Have children jump or hop a distance, and then measure that distance with a pencil or block.
- Make a 12″ ruler for each child in the class out of cardboard. Show them how to measure the length of objects, then let them experiment measuring things in the classroom and outdoors.
- Give children their rulers and challenge them to find something 1″ long. After everyone has found something, ask them to find something 2″ long, and so on.
- Measure children with a piece of yarn. Have them draw a picture of their head on a paper plate and attach it to the yarn.
- Bring in a bathroom scale and weigh each child.
- Give children cup, pint, and quart containers to experiment with in sand or water. Ask them how many cups it takes to make a pint, or how many pints it takes to make a quart.
- Provide children with opportunities to measure liquids and solids with cooking experiences.

Time

- Place a digital clock alongside your classroom clock. Children will begin to associate the numerals on the digital clock with those on the manual clock.
- Let each child make a clock from a paper plate. You will have to write the numerals in pencil and let them trace them in crayon. Cut a long hand and a short hand from construction paper and attach them to the center of the plate with a brad.
- Teach children how to identify the hour by the small hand on the clock. Call their attention to your classroom clock whenever it reaches the hour. For example, "Look! It is ten o'clock and time to get ready for a snack."
- Make a clock puzzle and have children fill in the numerals.

- Have children sequence pictures of different things that happen to them during the day. Write the hour on each picture.

- Talk about why it is important to learn how to tell time.
- Teach children the days of the week and go over the calendar every morning. Ask questions like, "What was yesterday?" "What is today?" "What is tomorrow?"

Money

- Give children a container full of coins and ask them to group the ones that are alike together.
- Give children a container with two of each coin. Have them match the coins that are alike.
- Put different amounts of pennies in small cups. Ask children to count and tell you how many cents are in each cup.
- Make a "Penny Store" in your room where all items cost one cent. You might have cereal, pretzels, raisins, or peanuts. Give each child 10 pennies and let them purchase the amount of each they would like. (Let the children take turns being the clerk in the store, too.)
- Make a game with paper piggy banks. Write a different numeral on each bank and have children count out the appropriate number of pennies for each bank.

- Make a restaurant or grocery store in the dramatics area. Put price tags on items and let children take turns "buying" and "selling" items.
- Take grocery coupons and have children match up those that are worth the same amount.

Addition

- Make sets of different children in your room. Put the sets together and encourage children to count and tell you how many in all.
- Make sets of different objects in your classroom, then put them together. You can use books, crayons, blocks, chairs, and other common objects.
- Let children make sets and join them with food they have for a snack.
- Show children how to add using the number line. Put a large number line on the floor. Let one child at a time put on some paper bunny ears and hop out addition problems.

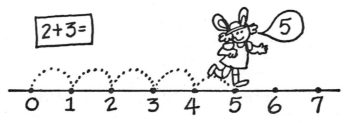

- Give children fun objects to make sets and add with in the math center, such as balloons, toy figures, birthday candles, etc.
- Give children felt cutouts and have them make sets and join them on the flannel board.
- After children have had many concrete experiences, introduce them to the addition equation. Make small cards of the addition facts (0–10) and make games where they can manipulate objects to work out the problems.

Make sets of candles on the birthday cake.

Put scoops on the ice cream cone.

Put buttons on the clown.

- Have children illustrate joining sets by drawing them on a sheet of paper, or let them stamp out addition problems with rubber stamps.

- Let children roll dice and add up the numerals on them.

- Each morning count the number of girls in the room. Then count the number of boys in the room. Ask who can tell you how many in all.

- Give children word problems or number stories to solve. Use their names to make it more exciting. For example, "Nick had two cards. His grandmother gave him one for his birthday. How many does he have in all?"
- Show children how to do addition with a pocket calculator.

Subtraction

- Subtraction is the opposite of addition. Make sets of children, then ask a subset to sit down. How many are left?
- Demonstrate subtraction problems with objects in the classroom.
- Let children work out subtraction problems with pegs on the pegboard or stringing beads.
- Have children hop backwards on the number line to illustrate subtraction.
- Let children play "Yum-yum eat 'em up" at snack. Give them popcorn, sunflower seeds, or other small pieces of food. Ask them to make a set. Tell them to eat a certain amount, then ask how many are left.
- Introduce children to the subtraction equation. Give them real objects to use to work out problems. Toy cars, pennies, plastic bracelets, and seashells are all fun.

- Make games where children can manipulate objects and work subtraction problems.

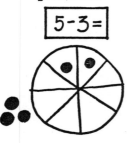

Take away pepperoni on the pizza.

Take away lollipops from the can.

Take away leaves from the tree.

Why Should You Use Computers with Children?

We live in a world of computers, and children, too, can learn how to use them and feel comfortable with them. Most preschools and day care centers already have computers or have plans to purchase them soon. Computers are neither a miracle machine that will replace teachers, nor a monster that will destroy children. However, they can be a valuable teaching tool and can supplement, enrich, and reinforce classroom learning.

Computers should be available to children in centers, similar to blocks, manipulatives, and other interest areas. You do need to monitor children to balance computer time with hands-on learning in other centers. Initially, children will need adult support to learn how to use the computer, then you will need to be available to answer questions or help with problems. Children can work independently at computers, or they can work with a friend and learn from each other. An advantage of computers is that they provide for individualized learning. Children can start where they are and progress as far as they can. In addition, children can see their success, can repeat difficult material, and are not penalized for making mistakes.

How Do You Choose Appropriate Software?

The value of computers rests primarily on the software you put into it. You should try out software whenever possible to see if it will achieve your goals and if it appeals to your students. These are other questions to consider when selecting software:

Is it appropriate for the age and abilities of the children you teach?
What concepts and skills does it teach?
Are children actively involved in the game or program?
Are the directions clear?
Can children work this program independently?
Does it provide for increased complexity?
Is there positive reinforcement?
What happens if the child makes a mistake?
Is it fun enough to keep children interested?

Are the graphics colorful and appealing?

Are there endorsements by professional education organizations?

What Can Children Learn from Computers?

These are a few of the skills and attitudes children can develop as they work and play with computers:

- thinking skills
- problem-solving
- comprehension
- eye-hand coordination
- visual memory
- decision-making
- number and letter skills
- how to follow directions
- increased attention span
- positive attitude toward computers
- independence and confidence

Above all, computers make children feel like they are a part of the world of grown-ups, and, they are fun!

7

SCIENCE

Science taps into the natural curiosity children have about the world around them. Through science, children learn to observe, question, explore, experiment, predict, and solve problems—skills they will continue to use throughout their lives. This section presents activities for motivating children and giving them first-hand experiences with the human machine, plants, animals, weather, the earth, space, ecology, and physics. Suggestions for field trips and guest speakers are also provided.

What Is Science?

Many teachers are afraid of science because they think it is complicated experiments, test tubes, and abstract facts. This couldn't be farther from what preschool science is all about. Science is not isolated information that you teach children. Rather, science is the real world and everyday experiences: science is the wind blowing and the windows fogging; science is leaves falling and Julie's new kittens; science is baby teeth coming out and magnetic sticks. Science is not only knowledge about all the living and non-living things in our environment; science is also a process—a way of finding out about the world, asking questions, and learning how to solve problems. Above all, science is a sense of wonder and excitement for children.

How Do Children Learn Science?

Children do not think abstractly. They must have concrete, hands-on experiences or they will not understand. Children learn through their senses: they must *see* science, *hear* science, *touch* science, *taste* science, and *smell* science. Teachers should also emphasize the following scientific processes, for these are lifelong skills that will enable children to continue to learn independently:

Observing—Call children's attention to various objects and changes in their environment.

Classifying—Encourage children to group and organize objects according to certain criteria.

Experimenting—What will happen if _____ ? Use trial and error to find out. (P.S.: It's okay to make mistakes.)

Predicting—Try and guess what the outcome will be.

Questioning—Ask open-ended questions. Why do you think that _____ ? How did it happen _____ ?

Researching—Show children how to find information in books or how to ask experts for help.

Communicating—Ask children to describe their experiences and report results to you and their classmates.

What Is the Teacher's Role?

The role of the preschool teacher is to be a facilitator and to help children "teach themselves science." Here are a few suggestions for encouraging self-discovery and a positive attitude toward science:

1. Motivate children by providing them with a rich environment full of materials they can discover on their own.
2. Find out what children know and what they want to know, then select appropriate topics and activities.
3. Involve all children by choosing activities that they can do alone or in a small group.

4. Give children the time and freedom they need to explore.
5. Respect individual differences. The way a child approaches a problem might be different from the way adults would do it. Realize that since children learn at different rates, all children may not fully understand every concept presented.
6. Ask many open-ended questions and accept divergent answers. Science is not "right" or "wrong."
7. Give children frequent feedback and reinforcement during the learning process. Clarify ideas, introduce vocabulary, and provide additional information. If you don't know the answer, admit it and then look it up in a book or ask someone for help.
8. Interrelate science to other content areas, such as language, math, art, music, and outdoor play.
9. Expand studies with field trips, stories, films, and guest speakers.
10. Model a positive attitude about science and share in children's enthusiasm and fascination for the world around them.

What Science Materials and Equipment Should Be Available in Preschool Classrooms?

Science takes place at the art center, while cooking, on the playground, in the block center, and in every area of your classroom. The science area, or discovery center, should be a special place full of interesting materials, books, tools, and objects that children can touch, hear, see, smell, and taste. Curiosity leads to learning, so it is important to rotate materials frequently to keep children interested. Children will also enjoy bringing their own treasures, discoveries, and collections for the science center. Look around your home, classroom, yard, and playground for items that will capture children's attention.

magnifying glass	magnets
large stool magnifier	prism
balance scale	thermometer
flashlight	kaleidoscope
color paddles	stethoscope
posters and pictures of nature	science magazines for children
books and encyclopedia	(*Ranger Rick, World*)
balloons	shells
rocks	bird nest
mirrors	feathers
plants	classroom pets
seeds	feely sock
leaves	simple machines
ant farm	collections
aquarium	terrarium

What Science Topics and Activities Are Appropriate for Young Children?

It is important to plan a balanced, orderly science program, as well as to take advantage of the "teachable moment." A "teachable moment" would be when a child finds a caterpillar or when someone sees a rainbow on the playground. A good way to organize science in the classroom is around major concepts or ideas. By providing children with various materials and experiences around a broad topic, concepts will be reinforced and learning more permanent. Many times children will need to repeat activities and experiments for verification and in order to understand cause and effect.

This section offers a wide range of lessons and topics for study in your classroom from the human machine to physics. Consider your students' developmental level, their interests, and environmental changes in selecting topics and activities from this resource list.

Sense of Sight—Examine children's eyes using an eye chart.

- Take a "blind walk" where children close their eyes or wear a blindfold to experience what it would be like without their eyes.
- Show children an example of Braille and discuss how blind people use seeing eye dogs and canes.
- Talk about how to care for your eyes and keep objects away from them.
- Have children draw a picture of things they like to see.
- Take a sheet of paper and poke a small hole in it. Look through the peep hole and what do you see?
- Lay on the ground and get a "bug's eye view." Climb to the top of the slide or playground equipment to get a "bird's eye view."

Sense of Hearing—Make sound cans from empty film containers. Fill two cans with paper clips, two with rice, two with pennies, two with cotton balls, and two with sand. Let children match up the cans that make the same sound.

- Make a tape of different environmental sounds for the children to recognize.
- Hide a portable radio or music box that is playing in the room while the

children hide their eyes. The children then go on a sound hunt and **try to** locate it.

- People who can't hear are called "deaf." They can use hearing aids or learn sign language. Invite a guest speaker in to teach the class some sign language.
- Ask children to bring in something from home that makes a sound they like.
- Discuss noise pollution and sounds they do not like to hear.
- Let children take turns making different sounds in the classroom while others try and guess the source. They might turn on the water, open the door, push a chair, etc.
- Have one child sit in a chair with their back to the class. Let other children come up one at a time and say something while "it" tries to identify them by their voice.
- Make paper cup telephones. Take two paper cups and make a small hole in the bottom of each. Take a piece of string 4' long and insert the ends in the holes of the cups and tie a knot. Two children take the cups and take turns talking and listening.

Sense of Taste—Have a tasting party where each child brings in a different food for the class to sample.

- Categorize foods that are sweet or salty; categorize foods that are good for you or are junk foods.
- Discuss the four food groups, then let children cut pictures out of magazines and classify them under the appropriate group.
- Make a bar graph of favorite foods the children like to taste.
- Sample foods that are similar in looks, such as sugar and salt, flour and powdered sugar, apples and pears, etc.
- Give each child a paper plate and let them draw their favorite foods.

Sense of Smell—Take film cans or baby food jars which you have spray painted. Put items with a unique fragrance in the bottom of each and cover with cotton balls. You might use coffee, bubble gum, vinegar, peppermint, lemon, or peanut butter. Let children take turns smelling the jars and identifying the items, or have them match up pictures of the items with the fragrances.

- Taste and smell work together. Have children hold their nose and see if they can taste various foods.
- Go on a "smell walk" where children close their eyes at different intervals and identify smells in nature.
- Discuss how different animals use their sense of smell.

Sense of Touch—Place objects with various textures in a paper bag. Let children take turns reaching in the bag and identifying the objects.

- Take old socks and put an object in the bottom of each. Let children identify the objects, then match up pictures of the objects with the appropriate sock.
- Classify objects by texture, such as hard, soft, rough, smooth, etc.

- Give each child a paper bag and let them find one object out on the playground and put it in the bag. Let children take turns reaching in each other's bags and identifying objects.

Sense Books—Make a book about the five senses with "things I like to feel," "things I like to hear," etc.

- Talk about combining senses. What senses do you use when you eat a banana; ride a bike; listen to a story?

Body Parts—Ask children to point to body parts as they are named.

- Play "Simon Says" and sing songs about body parts like "The Hokey Pokey."
- Identify pictures of body parts cut from magazines.
- Have children point to body parts on a stuffed animal or doll.
- Ask children to describe the function of different body parts. For example, "How do you use your neck?", or "What does your mouth do?"

Skeleton—Explain how bones protect parts of the body and help you stand up. Have children feel their skull and tell you what it protects. Have them feel their ribs and tell you what they protect.

- Obtain old x-rays from a hospital or physician for the children to examine.
- Bring in bones from chicken, fish, and other meats for the children to compare.
- For an art project, make a skeleton by gluing drinking straws which have been cut in various lengths on paper.
- Let children draw their face on a paper plate, then construct their skeleton in the block area by using unit blocks.

Muscles—Stretch rubber bands to show how muscles stretch.

- Ask children to show you how many parts of their bodies they can bend and stretch.

Organs—Talk about what a pump is and how the heart pumps blood. Have the children feel their heart beat before and after exercise, noticing how the heart must work faster when they exercise. Use a stethoscope to listen to their hearts.

- Take a clear plastic tube and water colored red to illustrate how the vessels take blood to all parts of the body. Have children look for veins on their body.
- Discuss how the stomach digests the food you swallow. Have children feel their stomach before and after they eat.
- Blow up a balloon to illustrate how the lungs fill up with air. Have the children feel their ribs and lungs as they breathe in and out.
- Bring in models of the human body for the children to examine.
- Have children trace the outline of their body on a large sheet of paper, then draw in their organs.

Growth—At the beginning and end of the school year, weigh the children on a bathroom scale and measure their height on a growth chart. Record weight and height and compare.

- Ask each child to bring in a baby picture. Discuss how they've changed and grown.

- Cut a piece of yarn their birth length and compare with their height now.

Staying Healthy—Discuss ways to stay healthy, and make posters of good health habits.

- Invite a dentist to visit the class and demonstrate proper flossing and brushing.
- Demonstrate how to wash hands with soap and water and how to dry them on a paper towel. Children should wash hands before and after eating, after playing, and after using the bathroom.
- Tell children you can't see germs, but they spread disease and make you sick. Cut a potato in half. Rub one half over a child's dirty hand, and the other half over a child's clean hand. Set aside and observe for several days. There should be noticeably more bacteria on the "dirty hand" potato.
- Discuss covering coughs and sneezes to prevent germs from spreading. Put powder in your hand, then cough and the powder will fly like germs being spread.

Seeds—Seeds produce like plants. Plant bean seeds, flower seeds, jelly beans, pennies, and a small toy. Which ones do you think will grow? Why?

- Have a "seed snack" with popcorn, sunflower seeds, and other seeds to eat.
- Ask children to go on a "seed hunt" around their house and see how many seeds they can find to bring to school.
- Make a sticky bracelet for each child by taping masking tape around their wrist with the sticky side out. Go on a nature walk and attach seeds to the tape to make a bracelet.
- Match up seeds with the fruit they come from.
- Sprinkle birdseed on a wet sponge and watch it sprout. Birdseed will also sprout on a pinecone if you mist it daily with water.
- Soak dry lima bean seeds overnight, then let the children open them and find the baby plant.
- Put a paper towel in a sandwich bag, then staple across the middle of the bag. Insert several bean seeds, water, and pin to a bulletin board. The children can watch their seeds grow daily and record the growth on a graph. (You

can also plant ordinary popcorn kernels between a glass and paper towel to observe the growth of a seed.)

- Give each child a styrofoam egg carton and let them fill each section with a small amount of potting soil. Plant different seeds in each section and label your mini-nursery.

- Discuss how plants can also grow from cuttings. Cut off the top of a carrot and place it in a saucer with a small amount of water. Root house plants in a clear glass to show how roots are formed. Take a sweet potato and suspend it in a clear glass with toothpicks. (Make sure the pointed end is down.)

Plant Growth—Ask children what they think plants need to grow. Try an experiment with bean seeds to test their ideas. Plant bean seeds in four cups: (1) with soil, water, sun; (2) with water and sun but no soil; (3) with water and soil but no sun; (4) with soil and sun but no water. Label the cups and observe their growth over several weeks, then summarize your results.

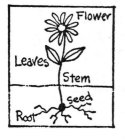

- Discuss different parts of a plant and their functions. Make a puzzle of the various parts by cutting apart a real turnip or carrot.

- Ask children to draw a plant and tell you the different parts. (You will need to write the words for younger children, but older children may enjoy doing their own labeling.)

- Put pictures of plant growth together in sequential order.

- Place a stalk of celery or a white flower (such as a carnation) in a glass of water. Add food coloring, and within a day the children will see how the water traveled up through the stem.

- Discuss the different parts of plants that we eat:
    leaves—cabbage, lettuce
    stems—celery, asparagus
    roots—carrots, sweet potatoes
    flowers—broccoli, cauliflower
    seeds—nuts, peas, beans, corn
    fruits—apples, tomatoes, oranges

- Plant a garden on your playground with vegetables that the children can harvest and eat.

- Make a terrarium from two clear plastic cups. In the bottom of one layer small rocks, sand, and soil. Put in several small plants, water, and tape the second cup on top. (A terrarium can also be made from a plastic liter soft drink bottle. Prepare the plants in the plastic section on the bottom of the bottle. Cut 7" from the bottom of the clear portion, invert it, and fit it inside the planter.)

- Brainstorm all the things we get from plants.

Trees—Trees are like people because you can look at them and tell what family they belong to from their bark, leaves, shape, size, etc.

- Have your class adopt a tree on the playground and observe it in the various seasons.

- Take a paper plate and divide it into fourths. Draw a picture of a tree in each of the four seasons and label it.

- Not all trees lose their leaves in the winter. Take a nature walk in the winter and look for evergreens.
- Ask parents to donate a tree for the playground in honor of their child's birthday. Label it as, "John's Tree."
- Hug a tree. How does it feel? Smell? Look? Sound? What would you do if you were a tree?
- Brainstorm all the things we get from trees.
- Take a slice of a tree and show children how to count the rings to tell how old the tree is.
- Collect leaves and make leaf rubbings, a collage, etc.
- Have children sort a bag of leaves by shape, then count the number of leaves in each set.
- Buy a bag of assorted nuts in the shell and ask children to categorize them.
- Press leaves by putting them between a napkin or paper towel. Place this between newspapers and stack several books on top for two or three days. You can also preserve leaves by ironing them between sheets of wax paper.

Plant Identification—Take children on the playground and teach them the names of trees, flowers, shrubs, grass, even weeds. Children love to impress others by saying, "That's an oak tree," or "That's a holly bush."

- Identify plants that grow in different habitats, such as a cactus in the desert, a palm tree at the beach, a water lily on the pond, etc.

Birds—Categorize feathers from different birds.
- Look at feathers with a magnifying glass.
- Identify parts of a bird, such as the beak, claw, wings, etc.
- Make "bird watchers" for observing the birds on the playground. Take two cardboard rollers from toilet paper and staple them together. Color and attach a string long enough to slip on and off the head.
- Learn the names of birds that frequent your playground. If you don't know what kind of birds they are, get a book and encourage the children to help you identify them.

- Take an old bird nest and try to identify all the materials the bird used to build it. Take it apart and then try to put it back together, or try building your own nest with mud, sticks, leaves, straw, and bits of trash.
- Help the birds build their nests by hanging bits of colored yarn on the branch of a tree in the early spring.
- Birds must protect the eggs they lay in their nest. Give each child a plastic egg (or real egg) to carry with them and be responsible for during the school day.

- Set up a bird feeding station in a secluded area of the playground or outside the fence.
- Make a bird feeder by cutting the sides off a plastic bottle or milk carton and filling it with bird seed.
- Roll suet (you can get this from the butcher) in birdseed and hang it in an old onion bag.
- Spread peanut butter or honey on a pinecone, then sprinkle with birdseed. Tie a piece of yarn on the top and hang it from a tree. (If you send this home with the children, be sure and put it in a plastic bag.)
- String cereal, cranberries, or popcorn and hang from a tree.

Mammals—Act out movements of different mammals or play "Guess what I am."
- Match up pictures of mother animals and baby animals and learn their names.
- Identify farm animals and their products.
- Sing songs about different animals.
- Make murals and paintings of mammals.
- Categorize mammals by their size—small, medium, or large.

Fish—Buy a whole fish at a fish market and identify the parts.
- Match up pictures of fish that are alike.

Insects and Spiders—Insects have six legs, while spiders have eight. Make insects and spiders from clay and pipe cleaners.

- Make a critter cage by cutting "windows" from the sides of a plastic bottle. Stretch old panty hose over this and tie a knot at the top. Collect insects and observe them for several hours, then let them go.
- Talk about how insects help us (bee and lady bug) and how they harm us (termite and mosquito).
- Observe dead insects, honeycomb, a wasp nest, etc. with a magnifying glass.
- Take a teeny, tiny walk on the playground and look for little insects. Turn over an old log or a rock and see what you might find.

- Observe a spider web and explain how spiders catch flies with their webs. Spray-paint a web, then gently catch it on a sheet of construction paper.

Pets—Rabbits, fish, gerbils, hamsters, and birds make good class pets. Children can learn about their care, nutrition, and habits from observing them.
- Have a Pet Show where children bring in their pets (dogs one day, cats the next, etc.), or ask children to bring in a picture of their pet.
- Talk about how pets and other animals help us.
- Make posters about being kind to pets.

• Make drawings, paintings, puppets, or stories about their pets.

Animal Growth—Let children sequence animal growth cards.

• Collect tadpoles and observe them as they change into frogs.
• Act out how caterpillars spin a cocoon, then turn into butterflies.
• Discuss what different animals need to grow.

Animal Habitat—Look for animal homes on the playground and around your school. Do not disturb them—just look! Be sure and look up in the air and down on the ground.

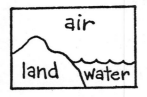

• Match pictures of animals and their homes. Describe what materials different animals use to make their homes.
• Classify animals and insects to the environment in which they live or travel.
• Make a mural of land, air, and water, then let the children draw or cut out animals and put them in the appropriate place.
• Discuss what animals do in different seasons, such as migrate and hibernate.
• Categorize pets, farm animals, zoo animals, and forest animals.
• What does "camouflage" mean? How do some animals blend in with their surroundings? Why is this necessary?

Extinct Animals and Fossils—Let children set up dinosaur figures in sand. Make paper plants and a volcano from cardboard.

• Make a dinosaur lotto game where children match up like dinosaurs.
• Make clay figures of dinosaurs or draw giant dinosaurs on butcher paper.
• Measure out the size of dinosaurs on the playground.
• Hide chicken bones or other bones in a box of dirt and let the children play "archeologist" and dig them up and try to put them together.
• Make fossils by pressing shells, leaves, and other objects in clay, plaster of Paris, or cookie dough.

Weather Reports—What is weather? Name different types of weather.

• Ask children to listen to a weather report on the television or radio or to bring in a newspaper clipping about the weather. Why is it important to know what the weather is?

- Have children keep a calendar of the weather for one month. Each day they should draw in a symbol for the weather that day, such as a sun for sunny, an umbrella for rainy, etc. After a month, make a graph of the different types of weather.
- Make a felt boy and girl for the flannel board, then cut out clothing for different types of weather from felt.
- Fill an old suitcase with assorted clothing, such as mittens, a bathing suit, umbrella, sweater, etc. Ask the children to tell you when they would need different items.
- Let children cut out clothing for different seasons and weather from old catalogs.
- Talk about jobs that are influenced by the weather, such as a farmer, baseball player, traffic officer, etc.
- Make a weather chart for your classroom like the one on the following page, or let each child make his or her own weather chart.

Thermometers—Take two thermometers and put one in hot water and one in cold water. Compare. Explain how the red mercury expands (or gets larger) when it gets hot and contracts (or gets smaller) when it cools.
- Make a paper thermometer and use elastic colored red for the mercury.
- Put a large thermometer on the playground and call the children's attention to it. Chart the daily temperature.

Rain—Explain the water cycle. When water in lakes and oceans is warmed, it evaporates and goes in the air. Large clouds form from the water vapor, and when they get dark and heavy it rains. The rain flows back into the lakes and oceans and the cycle begins again. Ask the children to draw a picture of the water cycle.
- Demonstrate how water evaporates by wiping a wet sponge on the bulletin board or placing a saucer of water in the window.
- Make it rain by holding a pan lid over boiling water. The steam will collect and fall back down into the pan like rain.
- Illustrate how clouds get heavy and cause rain by squeezing a sponge full of water.
- Place a rain gauge on the playground.
- To show what causes lightning, darken the room and rub two balloons together. The sparks you see are static electricity; the same thing happens when clouds rub together.
- Thunder is the noise made when lightning pushes the air away. Take a paper bag, blow it up, and hold the end tight. Push on the bag and make it pop like thunder.

Rainbows—Make a rainbow by squirting the hose in the sunlight on a hot day.
- Let children experiment making rainbows with a prism.
- Put a small mirror in a clear glass of water. Place the glass in a sunny window so the sun shines on the mirror, then look for the rainbow on the wall or ceiling.

Clouds—Clouds tell you what the weather will be, so look at the clouds when you are on the playground and predict the weather.
- Lay on your back and look for pictures in the clouds.

My Weather Chart

the weather song (tune: shortnin' bread)

Weather Song (Tune: Shortnin' Bread)

What will the weather, weather, weather,
What will the weather person say?
(One child is designated the "weather person" and reports
to the class if the weather is sunny, cold, rainy, etc.)
He/she says it's (*type of weather*), (*weather*), (*weather*),
He/she says it's (*weather*), (*weather*), today.

Wind—Wind is moving air. Can you see the wind? How can you tell if there's wind outside?

- Hang a wind chime on the playground, or make your own wind chime with pie pans.
- How do people use the wind?
- Make a pinwheel.
- Make a wind-tester by stapling a piece of ribbon or strip of cloth to a straw. Take it outside and see which way the wind is blowing.

Seasons—Categorize pictures of the four seasons.

- Have children draw or paint pictures of their favorite season.
- Fall is a "cool off" time. Discuss signs of fall. Pretend to be leaves falling off a tree and "dancing" around.
- We are farthest away from the sun in the winter, and that is why it is so cold. Catch snowflakes on your tongue or make tracks in the snow. What do animals and plants do in the winter? Catch snowflakes on dark paper and observe them with a magnifying glass. Melt snow and see if it's clean and clear or polluted. Take a full cup of snow, melt it, then measure the difference between when it was frozen and a liquid.
- Spring is a "warm up" time. Go on a nature walk and look for signs of spring. What do animals do in the spring?
- The earth gets close to the sun in the summer, and that is why it gets hot. What sports and outdoor activities can you do in the summer?

Rocks—Be "rock hounds" and start a rock collection in the science center.

- Group rocks that are alike by size, texture, color, weight, etc.
- Categorize rocks from large to small.

- Use rocks in art projects. For example, decorate a "pet rock," make rubbings of rocks, make a collage of small pebbles, etc.

- Compare rough rocks and smooth pebbles. What has made them different? Discuss the weathering of rocks.
- Take a hammer and crack open a rock. (Be sure and wear safety goggles and caution children not to do this alone.)

Dirt—Dig up a box of dirt. Have children smell it and feel it. Spread it out on a newspaper and sort through it. Play "detective" with a magnifying glass and try to figure out what the different particles are.

- Go on a nature walk and take a small shovel and several plastic bags. Collect dirt samples and compare when you return to the classroom.
- Play with mud without getting dirty. Put some dirt in a zip lock bag. Add a little water, zip the bag shut, and begin to squeeze and make designs.

Oceans and Streams—Collect a box of sand and shells from the shore and let children investigate and sort through.

- Group sea shells that are alike by shape, size, color, etc.
- Where do sea shells come from? Identify the various animals that live in shells.
- Make an "ocean in a bottle." Fill a plastic bottle with 1/3 baby oil and 2/3 colored water. Glue the top on and swirl and sway the bottle.

- Collect water samples from a stream, lake, or ocean. Can you drink the water? Why or why not?

Earth—The planet we live on is earth. Hold up a globe and talk about the shape of the earth. Discuss which colors represent land and which represent water.

Sun—The star closest to us is the sun. What does the sun do for us? What would happen if we had no sun?

Moon—The moon is a satellite that goes around the earth. The moon is always the same, but its shadow changes. Draw various phases of the moon.

Day and Night—Use a flashlight and a globe to illustrate how the earth's rotation causes day and night.

- Ask children to draw pictures of day and night on different sides of a sheet of paper.
- Have children take a walk at night with their parents. How is it different at night than in the day? Do you hear different sounds?
- What happens to different animals at night? Talk about nocturnal animals like the owl, bat, and opossum.

Solar System—Let children be various planets in the solar system and line them up in their order from the sun. This saying will help you remember the proper order:

"My very eager mother just served us nine pizzas."

> *My* – Mercury
> Very – Venus
> *E*ager – Earth
> *M*other – Mars
> *J*ust – Jupiter

Served – Saturn
Us – Uranus
Nine – Neptune
Pizzas – Pluto

Stars—What makes stars twinkle? The light from the stars must travel from far away, and when it goes through dust particles it makes them appear to twinkle.

- Have children draw a picture of the night sky.
- Hold a flashlight close to the children, then move farther away. What happens to the light as you move away? How large do you think the stars must be for their light to reach us on earth?
- Long ago people imagined groups of stars made pictures of animals, people, and things in the sky. Let children paste silver stars on black paper to resemble constellations.
- Punch holes in a sheet of black paper, then hold it up to the light.

Space Travel—Watch the launching of a shuttle on television.

- Bring in newspaper clippings of shuttle launchings.
- Count backwards and pretend to be rockets blasting off.
- Dramatize being astronauts in space. Move in "slow motion" as you walk on the moon.
- Use a model of a rocket to illustrate the different sections and their functions.
- What kinds of things do astronauts need to take with them in space?
- If you were an astronaut, where would you like to travel? Why?
- Make paper airplanes and fly them on the playground.

Valuing Nature—Be a rock on a beautiful day. Find a comfortable spot and sit and watch. What can you see? Hear? Feel? Smell?

- Read poems and stories about nature.
- Take a hula hoop or jump rope and place it on the ground and identify all the living and non-living things in that area.
- Take towels or blankets outside one day and have a rest or nap under the trees and clouds.
- Have children go on a treasure hunt outdoors. Ask each child to find one special item to share with their classmates.

- Plan a nature scavenger hunt for your class. You might include the following items for them to find in nature:
  - find something older than you
  - find something younger than you
  - find something alive
  - find something dead
  - find something that smells good
  - find something that feels soft
  - find something red
  - find something smaller than your thumb
  - find something that doesn't belong in nature (Pick it up and throw it away.)

Interdependence—How does nature help us? What can we do to help nature?

Pollution—

- What is litter? What can you do about it? Decorate trash cans for the school grounds. Make litter bags for their cars.
- Take a clean bottle of water. Pollute it by adding detergent, bottle caps, styrofoam scraps, paper scraps, etc.
- Hold a sheet of paper over a candle flame, then show children the smoke on the paper. How do people pollute the air?
- Make posters for the school about picking up trash.
- Organize a school clean-up day or neighborhood clean-up day.

Conservation—Make "turn it off" stickers for the light switches.

- Make a list to send home of ways to conserve energy and resources. For example, "turn the television off when you're not watching it," "close the doors to the outside," "walk or ride your bike instead of driving," "turn the water off while you brush your teeth," etc.
- Brainstorm ways to solve problems of dwindling resources.

Recycling—Recycle newspapers, aluminum cans, and other items at your school.

- Have the children do art projects with disposable containers and other items that are generally thrown away.

Air—How do you use air? Have the children breathe in and out. Can you see air?

- Turn a glass upside down and immerse it in water. Tip it to the side to let the bubbles up. What was in the glass?

- Blow up balloons or a paper bag. What happens to the shape? Air takes up space.
- Make your own bubbles by mixing 3 Tb. liquid detergent, 1 Tb. glycerine (you can buy this at the drug store), and 1 cup water. Use a berry basket, plastic six pack holder, pipe cleaner, and other unusual shapes to make your bubbles.

Water—Water comes in many forms. Fill a glass with water and mark the water line. Freeze it and mark the line where the ice goes to. What happens to water when it freezes?

- Give each child an ice cube to play with on a hot day. What happens to the ice? What makes it melt?
- Ask children what other things do they think will melt. Put the items they suggest on the playground and observe.
- Give children a pan of water and an assortment of items that will sink or float on the water. Let them predict what will happen, then put them in the water to find out. Have children categorize the objects that "sink" and "float" and summarize their results.
- Some materials dissolve in water. Give children a glass of water, a spoon, and salt, sand, sugar, pepper, oil, and other items to test. Let them predict what will happen and then try to dissolve the materials in the water.
- Some substances absorb water. Give children an eye dropper and colored water. Put a sponge, cotton, paper towel, foil, wax paper, and styrofoam on a tray and let children experiment to see which surfaces absorb the water.

Light—Some materials are transparent and some are opaque. Collect different types of fabric, paper, and objects that the children can hold up to the light to determine if they are transparent or opaque, or let them experiment with a flashlight.

- Make shadows with the light from a filmstrip projector.
- Make silhouettes of the children's shadows.
- Let the children draw each other's shadows on the sidewalk with chalk.
- Put several objects on blue or purple construction paper and set them in the sun. What does the sunlight do to the paper?
- Take a shoe box and cut a small peep hole in one end. Put a picture at the opposite end and ask the children to look in the box. Can they see anything? Open the lid of the box. Can they see anything now? Why?

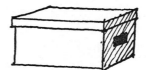

Mirrors and Lenses—Let children experiment with hand mirrors.

- Give children foil on the playground to experiment with.
- Ask children to write their names, then hold them up in front of a mirror. What happens?
- Give children old glasses. What happens when you look through them?
- Let children look at various objects in the classroom and on the playground with a magnifying glass.
- Take a clear glass of water and put a pencil in it. What happens?

- Give children a kaleidoscope to experiment with.

Color—Prepare the three primary colors (red, blue, and yellow) and let the children mix them at the easel.

- Give each child a small ball of red, blue, and yellow play dough. Let them pinch off small pieces and squeeze them together to make new colors.
- Make color paddles by gluing colored cellophane to cardboard cutouts. You can also tape cellophane to the ends of cardboard rollers to make color telescopes.
- Take clear plastic cups and fill them with water. Experiment making different colors with food coloring.
- Fix each child two small cups of vanilla yogurt for a snack. Put a drop of red, blue, or yellow food coloring in each cup. Give children a third cup and a spoon and challenge them to make a different color.
- What would the world be like if there were no colors?

Electricity—To make static electricity, darken the room and shuffle your feet across a rug, then touch metal. (This works better in cold weather.) You can also make static electricity by rubbing two balloons together.

Magnets—Look around the school and house for magnets. Give children a box of objects and let them separate those that the magnet will attract from those that the magnet does not attract. Can they generalize their results?

- Will magnets attract through other materials? Put a paper clip in water and see if the magnet will attract it. Move a paper clip through a sheet of paper with a magnet.
- Experiment with a bar magnet, horseshoe magnet, and refrigerator magnet to see which one is strongest.
- Sprinkle iron filings in a box of sand and let children separate them with a magnet.

Gravity—Why do things fall to the ground? Gravity is the force that pulls things to the earth. If you drop a feather and a rock, which one will land first? Why? Experiment by dropping various objects.

Chemical Changes—Do a little magic and grow a chemical garden. Put pieces of charcoal in an aluminum pie pan. Mix ¼ cup ammonia, ¼ cup non-iodized salt, and ¼ cup liquid bluing. Pour the mixture over the charcoal and watch the crystals start to form.

- How would you like to make old pennies look like new? Put a small amount of vinegar in a glass and add 1 tsp. salt. Drop in the pennies, stir, and watch them shine like new.

Materials—Collect an assortment of objects. Have children sort them by materials from which they are made, such as wood, plastic, glass, and metal.

Machines—Machines make our work easier. Brainstorm all the machines we use every day.

- Bring in kitchen machines (egg beater, sifter, tongs, etc.) for the children to experiment with.
- Let children take apart old radios, clocks, and appliances with a screwdriver. (Cut off the cord first and caution them not to do this at home.)

- Give children a flashlight to take apart and put back together.
- Let children experiment with simple machines (level, ramp, wheel) in the block center.
- Make a list of machines and their source of power.
- Provide children with workshop tools and wood scraps to make things.

Inventions—Let parents and children work together at home to make a new invention.

- Brainstorm things people should invent.
- Give children a box of junk and let them work in small groups to invent things.

How Do You Plan Field Trips for Children?

Whether you live in a rural area or the city, your community is overflowing with science field trips and experts just waiting to be discovered by you and your children. Field trips are an optimal way for children to learn and can be used to introduce, enrich, or culminate a science unit. These are some tips for successful outings:

1. Call well in advance to make reservations and get information about times, costs, etc. Request written information be sent to you, or visit the site yourself ahead of time.
2. Request permission from your administrator and check on transportation.
3. Notify the parents several weeks before your trip. Tell them the date, cost, special clothing (if necessary), and what the children will gain from the experience. Ask for volunteers to help chaperone the trip. (Some schools also require written permission from parents.)
4. Confirm your trip by phone the day ahead and send home a reminder to the parents.
5. Explain to the children what they will see and do; go over your expectations and rules.
6. Make a name tag with the school phone number for each child.
7. Assign children a "buddy" to be responsible for, or divide children up into manageable groups for chaperones.
8. Take a first aid kit for emergencies.
9. On your return, follow-up the trip with language experience stories, art projects, a class mural, etc.

10. Have children sign a thank you note or draw a picture expressing their appreciation.

Science field trips can be as near as your playground or as far as a museum:

nature hikes around the school	farm
zoo	grocery store
pet store	dairy
plant nursery	hospital
park	dentist office
museum	weather station
planetarium	factory
lake, river, pond, ocean	animal clinic

If you have difficulty traveling with your children, then invite one of these guest speakers to your room:

Cooperative Extension Service	forest ranger
doctor or dentist	weather forecaster
farmer	veterinarian
university professor or high school teacher	geologist
	archeologist
parent or grandparent with a hobby (flowers, rocks, fishing, etc.)	pharmacist
	engineer
Boy Scout or Girl Scout	architect
Public Health Service	ecologist

8

STORYTIME
MAGIC

In this section, you'll learn why reading to children is so important, and you'll be offered suggestions for the best times to read to children, where to find books, how to read aloud effectively, how to introduce stories and tell them in exciting ways, how to follow-up on storytime to keep the characters and plots alive, and how to integrate stories with the content areas.

Why Read to Children?

Reading aloud to children may be the single most important activity that you can do as a preschool teacher. In addition to the warm feelings that you and your students reap from sharing this special time, these are some other attitudes and skills that are enhanced when children are read to:

listening skills
attention span
language development
vocabulary
concept development—children can visit new places, meet exciting people, and learn new information through books
how to cope with emotions and feelings
creative thought and imagination
values and cultural expectations
appreciation of literature

Above all, reading to children is entertaining and pleasurable. It will create in children the desire to read and can spark a lifelong love of books.

When Should You Read to Children?

It is important to begin reading to children as soon as you can. With toddlers and very young children you will want to read and look at books individually or with a small group. Usually by the age of three, children are able to begin to sit and listen to stories as a group for a short period of time. The actual length of time you should spend reading will depend on your children's age and attention span. Always follow their lead and never force them to "sit still and listen." It's a good idea to try and stop before they get bored or restless so they will want to come back for more.

Storytime should be a regular, routine part of your day—a time both you and your children treasure and enjoy. Many teachers like to start the day with a story; others use a story for circle time; some teachers use stories to relax children before nap or to calm them down after play. In addition to a traditional storytime, keep books on hand to read to children if you finish an activity early or have a few minutes you need to fill in.

How Do You Choose a Story?

The secret of a good storytime is choosing the right book. Select books that both you and your children will enjoy, and don't worry about switching to another story if it's not interesting. Try to find stories that will fit your children's attention span, interests, and personal experiences. For example, a group of two-year-olds would enjoy nursery rhymes or picture books, while four-year-olds would prefer a story book. And, remember, little children love to have favorite stories repeated over and over again.

Children should be exposed to a broad variety of books at storytime and should have many different types of literature available to them in your classroom library, such as:

picture books (no words—just pictures)
story books
fairy tale books and folk tales
nursery rhyme books
magazines for children
reference books (children's encyclopedia)
picture dictionary
concept books (teach basic ideas)
manipulative books (books that pop-up and move)
sensory books (books that you can smell, touch, etc.)
information books (books about dinosaurs, shells, etc.)
alphabet books and number books
season and holiday books
books about feelings and emotions
homemade books

Where Do You Find Books for Children?

If you don't have many books in your school or center, then get a library card and make weekly trips to your public library. Your librarian can help you choose appropriate books for your children and can serve as a rich resource for you. Encourage your students to bring in books from home to share with the class, or look for old books at garage sales and flea markets. Joining a book club is another way to build up your classroom library.

What Are Some Tips for Storytelling?

How you read a story will depend to some extent on your individual style, personality, and the age of your students. These are some general tips to keep in mind when reading to children:

Reader's position—You should be relaxed and seated comfortably.
Position of book—Hold the book or visuals so that all children can see. Show the pictures very slowly all around the group.
Actions—Use actions that go with the story or add interest. Your body language will be an important factor in telling the story.
Eye contact—Use eye contact to relate to the children. Also, let your eyes and facial expression help tell the story.
Speed—Use a good, natural speaking voice and vary the pace according to the story. Take your time and never "rush" through a story.
Enunciation—Make sure your words are clear and understandable.
Expression—Be dramatic! Use your voice to convey the meaning of the story or change your voice for different characters.
Response of Children—Respect children's comments and reactions, yet retain control of the group. Many times you will need to say, "Let's wait and talk about that when I finish the story."

How Do You Introduce a Story?

You must set the stage for the story and capture the children's attention before you begin to read. First, make sure the children are seated comfortably and that they can all see. It works well to have children sit with their legs crossed on the floor and to have the reader seated in a low chair. State your expectations in a positive way and praise the children who are sitting quietly and are ready to listen.

Use one of these finger plays or songs to prepare the children for storytime:

Grandma and Grandpa

These are grandma's glasses.
    (make glasses with fingers over eyes)
Here is grandma's cap.
    (make triangle with hands and put on head)
This is the way she folds her hands
    (fold hands together)
and puts them in her lap.
    (put hands in lap)
These are grandpa's glasses.
    (make glasses with fingers over eyes)
And here is grandpa's hat.
    (pretend to pull down big hat on head)
And this is the way he folds his arms
    (fold arms over in front of body)
just like that!
    (shake head)
(Use a deep voice when you say grandpa's verse.)

Wiggle Them

Wiggle them, wiggle them, wiggle them so.
    (wiggle fingers in front of you)
Wiggle them high. Wiggle them low.
    (hold hands up high, then down low)
Wiggle to the left, and wiggle to the right.
    (move to left, then right)
Wiggle them, wiggle them, out of sight.
    (put hands behind your back)
(Variations: shake them, clap them, snap them, etc.)

Open Them—Shut Them (Tune: Shortnin' Bread)

Open them; shut them; open them; shut them; give a little clap.
    (open and shut fingers as you sing the song)
Open them; shut them; open them; shut them; put them in your lap.

Take Your Little Hands (Tune: The Wheels on the Bus)

You take your little hands and go clap, clap, clap.
    (clap hands)
Clap, clap, clap. Clap, clap, clap.
You take your little hands and go clap, clap, clap.
And put them in your lap.

The Finger Band (You can sing this to the tune of The Mulberry Bush or you
                can just say it.)

The finger band is coming to town, coming to town, coming to town.
    (put hands behind back, then bring them out marching)
The finger band is coming to town so early in the morning.

Second verse—This is the way we play our drums.
    (pretend to play a drum with hands)
Third verse—This is the way we twirl our hats.
    (pretend to twirl a hat)
Fourth verse—This is the way we play our horns.
    (pretend to play a horn)
Last verse—The finger band is going away.
    (make your voice get softer as you march with hands behind your back)

Storytime Friends

Put some small toy people or animals in an old purse, lunchbox, or school box.
Before you begin storytime, explain to your children: "I have some little friends that
would like to come hear the story with you today. They have teeny, tiny little ears,
so you will have to be very quiet during storytime. Do you think you can do that?
We don't want to hurt their little ears now. Okay, I'll take them out." Take your little
toys out and set them up so they can hear the story. When storytime is over, have
your little friends say good-bye to the children, then put them away until your next
storytime.

Begin by telling the children the title (or name) of the story, the author (or who
wrote it), and the illustrator (or person who drew the pictures). These are some other
fun ways to capture your students' attention and build their interest:

Story apron—Take an old apron with a pocket or make a special story apron like the one illustrated here. Hide a small toy or object in the pocket that relates to the story. Slowly pull it out of your pocket to build the children's curiosity about the story. For example, if the story has a mouse in it, hide a small toy mouse and have him pop up and introduce himself with a squeaky voice. A handful of dried beans could introduce Jack and his beanstalk; or a feather could be used to introduce a story about a bird.

Puppets—Puppets and stuffed animals love to introduce stories to children. Let the puppet whisper in your ear, then you can interpret for the puppet; or disguise your voice to talk like the puppet. The puppet could ask the children questions about their past experiences that relate to the story; such as, "Have you ever been lost? How did you feel?" Or the puppet could ask a riddle like, "This story is about an animal that has a shell on his back and pulls in his arms and legs when he is frightened. Do you know an animal like that?"

Props—Bring in a prop that relates to the story. It might be a cooking pot, a treasure map you've drawn, a suitcase, or even a tree branch. As long as it's real and it's in the story, the children will be interested and will want to listen to find out more.

Costumes—With a simple costume you can become a character in the story. A red scarf can turn you into Little Red Riding Hood; with a pair of glasses you will be grandma; or a paper crown could make you a king or queen. It doesn't take much to transform you into the character who would like to read to the children.

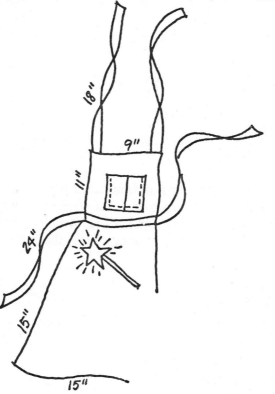

What Are Some Creative Ways to Tell Stories?

Using creative techniques with literature will increase the excitement and joy of storytime for you and your children. Most of these techniques can easily be adapted for folk tales, fairy tales, or other favorite stories. Use your imagination and see how many you can come up with.

Lunch box story—Get an old lunch box or bag. Make characters to tell your story from paper or hunt through an old toy box for little toys that could tell the story. This gingerbread boy would love to pop out of the lunch box and tell his story.

Color, cut out, and attach to a popsicle stick, straw, or wooden spoon. Let each child color and decorate their own little stick puppet gingerbread boy for a follow-up activity.

(You'll find a recipe for gingerbread in the nutrition chapter.)

Story mitt—Take an old glove or purchase a work glove and attach Velcro to each finger. Make various story characters out of pompoms and felt scraps. Glue Velcro to the back of your characters, attach to the glove, and you're ready to begin. Here are the Little Red Hen and her friends to tell their story.

Cat
(black pompom)

Dog
(brown pompom)

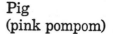

Red Hen
(red pompom)

Duck
(yellow pompom)

Pig
(pink pompom)

(You'll find the Little Red Hen's recipe for letter bread in the nutrition chapter.)

Flannel board—It's easy and inexpensive to make your own flannel board with some heavy cardboard, plywood, or styrofoam. First, cut your board to the desired size (24″×36″ works well). Second, cover the board with a piece of felt or flannel (white, beige, black, or navy make good background colors). Story pieces can be made from felt scraps, or you can draw directly on heavy pellon with crayons. A less expensive method is to make story pieces from construction paper, then glue felt strips to the back so they will stick on the board. An advantage of flannel board stories is that children can manipulate the pieces and "retell" the story as a follow-up activity. Goldilocks and these three bears will encourage children to match objects one-to-one, seriate by size, and repeat a story in sequential order.

Goldilocks
(pink felt with
yellow hair)

Baby Bear
(brown felt)

Mama Bear
(brown felt)

Papa Bear
(brown felt)

Draw and tell story—Here's a story that you can draw as you tell it. You can use the chalkboard, an overhead projector, or a large sheet of paper and markers.

The Pumpkin Man

Instruct children to make the following motions as you tell the story:

"rock"—rock body back and forth
"spin"—move hands around each other in circular motion
"knock"—tap fist on forehead and make a clicking sound with tongue
"come in"—put hand by mouth and say, "come in"

Once there was a little old lady, and all she did was sit and *rock* and *spin* and wait for someone to come in. Well, one day she was just sitting there and she'd *rock* and *spin* and wait for someone to come in. It wasn't very long until she heard a *knock* at the door. "*Come in,*" she called. And in came two big boots. (Draw big boots on the board). "I can't talk to two big boots," said the little old lady. So she would just sit and *rock* and *spin* and wait for someone to come in. It wasn't very long until she heard a *knock* at the door. "*Come in,*" called the old lady. And in came two skinny legs. "I can't talk to two skinny legs," said the old lady. . . . . . .Continue the story adding a little waist, two big shoulders, two long arms, two big hands, and finally, a big pumpkin head. When the pumpkin head comes in the little old lady says, "Well, I can talk to the Pumpkin Man." Sing "Do you know the Pumpkin Man?" to the tune of "Do you know the Muffin Man?"

The best part about this story is that you can change it for every holiday. For example, you could draw a turkey at Thanksgiving, Santa Claus at Christmas, a Leprechaun in March, etc. Your children will delight in hearing this story over and over.

Fold-and-cut story—Here is a story that you can cut out as you tell it. This is another one that your students will beg you to, "Do it again!"

The Little Bird

(Have in your lap before you begin a sheet of construction paper, scissors, and a marker or crayon.)

It was spring and time for mother and father bird to build a nest. They worked very hard carrying twigs, grass, and string to the top of the tree. What else do you think they might have used to build their nest? This is what it looked like when it was finished. (Fold paper in half lengthwise and cut.)

Now mother bird sat on the nest and she laid a beautiful egg that looked like this. (Unfold the nest and show the egg shape.) I bet you know what's inside this egg, don't you?

Mother bird tucked the egg down in the nest where it would be warm and safe. (Fold the egg into the nest shape again.)

Mother bird had to sit on the egg for a very long time. Sometimes it was hot and sometimes it rained, but she didn't give up. She made friends with two little bugs so she wasn't so lonely. (Make two dots, one on each side, one-third way from end.)

One day something very special began to happen. Mother bird heard a cracking sound. What could it be? There were some cracks in the egg, and then she heard a little pecking noise. (Cut lines as illustrated.)

At last the egg shell broke and out popped baby bird. Peep! Peep! Peep! (Fold top part of egg down and fold the bill up.)

How Can You Extend Stories?

Many of the characters and topics in books you read to children will naturally spark learning in other areas of your curriculum. Here are a few suggestions to get you started:

Cooking—Follow-up storytime with cooking experiences for your students. You'll find recipes for stone soup, peanut butter bears, and mud pies in the nutrition chapter.

Art—Stick puppets, paper bag puppets, paintings, paper crafts, etc. flow easily from stories. Use the techniques in the creative arts chapter and adapt them to your story.

Drama—Children love to act out favorite stories. A balance beam becomes the bridge in the THREE BILLY GOATS; paper hats can turn your class into the monkeys in CAPS FOR SALE; and music can turn you all into the butterfly in THE VERY HUNGRY CATERPILLAR.

Homemade books—Staple several sheets of paper together and encourage your students to draw pictures and "write" their own books. You can also make a class book, where each child draws one page of the book.

Story tree—Put a bare tree branch in a pot of dirt or secure it in a pot of plaster of Paris. (An old artificial Christmas tree works well, too.) With clothespins, attach small books, your story mitt, puppets, props, costumes, or hats. What a wonderful way to make a love of literature grow!

Field trips—Use literature to prepare children for field trips or build their enthusiasm. For example, read stories about CURIOUS GEORGE before going to the zoo; visit a bakery after telling the story about the Little Red Hen; or take a walk around your school and look for spiders after reading BE NICE TO SPIDERS.

Guest readers—Invite your principal or director, parents, grandparents, or older siblings to your classroom to read their favorite books.

9

ARTS AND CRAFTS

Arts and crafts are central to the early childhood curriculum. This section focuses on fostering creativity in children through art, and it includes suggestions for over 100 simple art projects that you can do in your classroom.

Why Is Art Important?

Probably nothing integrates all areas of the curriculum and stimulates children as much as art does. From finger painting with chocolate pudding to gluing leaves and flowers on paper, from making objects with clay to drawing with chalk on the sidewalk, art helps children grow creatively, socially, physically, emotionally, and intellectually. Through art experiences children also develop:

small motor control
eye-hand coordination
concepts about color, size, shape, form, texture
language skills
sensory perception
independence and confidence
cooperation and sharing
problem-solving and decision-making
planning and persistence
pleasure and satisfaction
aesthetics—the love of beauty in their own work and the work of others
self-expression

What Is Creativity and How Do We Foster It in Children?

C   Creativity is a spirit that cannot be taught, but it can be nurtured and cultivated in your classroom. Creativity is open, fresh, original, unique, and is a natural instinct in children. Creativity is also a powerful force that can help children develop their full potential.

R   Respect individual differences and never compare children. Display all children's artwork, not just "the best."

E   Encourage children and praise their efforts, not the finished product. Be enthusiastic about what they create—whatever it looks like, it's theirs!

A   Aesthetic appreciation and exposure to beautiful things is important. Take children on field trips to art museums, invite artists to your classroom, and display famous works of art and beautiful things.

T   Talent comes in many forms, sizes, and shapes. Some children may be creative in art, others in music, drama, or dance. Everyone possesses creativity to some degree.

I   Independence. Let the child do it! Allow children to make decisions, experiment, investigate, and explore on their own.

V   Variety is a key. Vary the materials, tools, projects, and the environment.

I   Imagination and curiosity should be challenged and valued. Ask children questions and make them think; then be willing to listen to their suggestions and ideas.

T   Time and space are essential. Give children the time they need and the freedom to create something unique and different.

Y   *YOU* are the catalyst for a creative classroom. You set the stage and provide

the atmosphere where wonderful things can happen—a place where children can freely express themselves and feel good as they create daily.

What Stifles Creativity?

Just as teachers can encourage creativity, they can also stifle it. Imposing your ideas and standards or correcting children's artwork can have a negative impact on creativity. Use of coloring books, dittos, and patterns to "copy" also limit creativity. Above all, an atmosphere of conformity, criticism, and competition will stifle the creative spirit in children.

How Do You Prepare for Art?

The best place to set up an art area is on a tile floor that is away from the flow of traffic. (If the floor is carpeted, just put down a shower curtain or newspapers before you do messy projects.) It's helpful if your art center is near a sink or source of water. There should be a low table and chairs for the children to sit on, as well as an easel. You can make an inexpensive easel from a cardboard box by cutting the top and bottom off and one of the sides. Bring the ends together to form a pyramid and tape. Use clothespins to attach paper. This easel can be used on a table, plastic crate, or taken outside for painting.

Store art materials in well-marked containers so children can easily get them out and clean them up. With so much "stuff," organization will keep your art area from looking like a disaster. Some materials should be available to children at all times, such as crayons, scissors, and paper, but other objects need to be stored in boxes, plastic tubs, or empty ice cream cartons and only taken out for particular projects. Empty juice cans and milk cartons are useful for storing brushes, crayons, markers, pencils, and chalk. (It will look neater if you cover cans and boxes with contact paper.) A rack for scissors can be made by poking holes in an empty tissue box. Paper stored in shallow cardboard boxes will keep shelves from looking messy and paper from getting ragged. Children will also enjoy a "junk box" in the art center with bits of this and that—like paper scraps, cotton balls, yarn, fabric, paper plates and cups, cardboard tubes, etc.

Here are some other "artful" hints:

1. Have all the materials set up ahead of time. Involve children in the preparation and clean-up.
2. State your expectations in a positive way. Set rules and limits that are clear and simple; such as, "Crayons are used only at the table."
3. Teach children how to use and care for basic tools and materials. For example, "Use one finger to glue," "Wipe your brush on the side of the container and then return it to the same color," "Put the top back on the marker when you're finished with it," etc.
4. Protect children's clothing when doing messy projects like painting or printing. (An adult's shirt buttoned in the back makes a great smock.)
5. Adapt art projects to the age, interests, and ability of your group. With young children you will want to do projects individually or in a small group. Older children can work much more independently.

6. Try not to force children to participate. Entice them by talking about how much fun it will be.
7. Give simple directions, and resist the urge to tell children exactly how to do things. One of the major benefits of art is for children to do some problem solving on their own.
8. Don't put up models or examples for children to copy. Remember, there is no right or wrong way to do art.
9. Provide children with a variety of materials and activities, yet don't overwhelm them with too many things at once.
10. Encourage children to think of titles for their pictures and paintings and to share their work with their classmates. Teach children to "sign" their art, or make sure that you write their name on it.

What Are Some Materials That You Can Use for Art?

You don't have to spend a fortune to have an exciting creative arts program in your school. Invest in some good, basic materials (crayons, paint, brushes, safety scissors, etc.), then "scrounge" around for other objects and tools. Send home the "save" list on the following page to parents at the beginning of each year so that they can help you collect these materials.

Here are some basic art supplies you should have:

crayons	scissors	newsprint
colored chalk	hole-punch	construction paper
colored pencils	stapler	ditto paper
markers (washable)	tape	butcher paper
powdered tempera	glue, paste	poster board
water colors	paint brushes	finger paint paper
water soluble ink	paper clips, brads	tissue paper

Super Art Ideas (That Are Super Simple, Too!)

Here is an art project for every day of the year. Most of them are open-ended to encourage creativity, and most are made from simple materials that are readily available. These projects have been tried and tested by little ones, and they all meet with their approval. Be creative and adapt these ideas to the age and ability of your students or to the unit or holiday that you are studying.

Crayons are widely accessible, inexpensive, and don't make a mess. Add a little variety with these new projects and techniques.

Crayon Rubbings

Materials: crayons, paper, textured objects (coins, combs, etc.)
Procedure: Tear outer paper from crayon. Place paper over textured object. Carefully rub the side of the crayon in one direction to make the image appear.

(Sample letter to parents.)

"SAVE" List

HELP! STOP! Before throwing anything away, look at the list below and see if we might be able to use it at school for art projects. Also, be on the lookout at your workplace for scraps or "junk" that we might be able to recycle.

margarine tubs
buttons
yarn
string
sponges
styrofoam packing
styrofoam meat trays
ribbon or lace scraps
egg cartons
seeds and nuts
lunch sacks or grocery sacks
tubes from toilet paper
cotton balls and Q-tips
straws
old beads and jewelry
feathers
pipe cleaners
wood scraps
clothespins
empty spray bottles

wallpaper scraps
fabric scraps
dried beans, rice, pasta
old magazines
newspapers
computer paper
paper plates
paper cups
shoe boxes
juice cans
aluminum foil or wax paper
wrapping paper or tissue paper
paper scraps
cupcake paper liners
cardboard boxes
coffee cans
plastic milk jugs
envelopes
popsicle sticks
wooden spoons

Thank you!

Variations: Make leaf rubbings; make rubbings of classroom puzzles; go on a walk outdoors and make nature rubbings; use chalk to make rubbings.

Crayon Resist

Materials: crayons, heavy paper, diluted tempera paint

Procedure: Draw a picture with crayons. Press hard. "Wash" over the entire page with paint. The areas covered by the crayon will resist the paint.

Variations: Color underwater pictures or sky pictures and "wash" with blue; make spooky Halloween pictures and "wash" with black; draw a picture with rubber cement and "wash" with paint when it dries.

Crayon Etchings

Materials: crayons, heavy paper or cardboard, paper clips

Procedure: Color over entire surface of paper with bright colors to look like a stained glass window. Now color on top of this with a black crayon. Unbend the paper clip and use one end to "etch" out a picture or design.

Musical Crayons

Materials: crayons, paper, music

Procedure: Play some music. Take your crayon and let it dance across the paper to the music.

Variations: Play different styles of music, such as classical, jazz, country, marches, etc.; close your eyes and let the crayon "dance."

Crayon Shavings

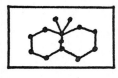

Materials: wax paper, old crayons, grater, iron

Procedure: Take one sheet of wax paper. Grate old crayons on top of it. Put a second sheet of wax paper on top of the crayon shavings. Iron and watch the crayons melt and make a design.

Variations: Put autumn leaves or tiny spring flowers in between the wax paper; cut the wax paper into holiday shapes and hang from the ceiling or window.

Dot-to-Dot

Materials: crayons, paper

Procedure: Make eight (or whatever number you're working on) dots on the paper. Can you connect them? What does it look like? Add details with crayons.

Variations: Tell children to make the dots, then exchange papers with a friend.

Self-Portrait

Materials: crayons, paper

Procedure: At the beginning of the year, ask children to draw a picture of themselves. Date and file. Toward the end of the year, again ask them to draw a picture of themselves. Can you see how much they've developed? This is always an interesting project to share with parents.

Body Art

Materials: crayons, butcher paper, scissors

Procedure: Spread paper out on the floor. Have child lay down. Trace around child's body with crayons. Child then colors and cuts out body.

Variations: Hang around the room or tape in chairs for open house; cut body into pieces to make a puzzle.

Half and Half

Materials: crayons, paper, paste, old magazines

Procedure: Take a magazine picture or a large object and cut it in half. Glue one half on one side of a sheet of paper. Now color the other half with your crayons.

Chunky Crayons

Materials: old crayons, muffin pan, non-stick spray

Procedure: Tear paper covering from crayons. Break crayons into several pieces and put in muffin cup. Continue until each muffin cup is full of a different color of crayon. Bake in 300° oven until crayons melt. Cool. Pop out and you're ready to color. (Hint: Use non-stick spray in pan.)

Variations: Use plastic candy molds.

Topsy-Turvey

Materials: crayons, paper

Procedure: Draw the outline of a picture. Color in "silly" colors, such as a purple dog or green sun.

Variations: Make the whole picture "silly" on April Fool's day.

Record Art

Materials: paper cut in 9″ circles, crayons

Procedure: Color your circle with a design or pattern. Punch hole in the middle. Put on a record player and watch your picture spin around.

Variations: Take three small crayons and wrap a rubber band around them. Use this to draw your record design.

Folded Art

Materials: paper, crayons

Procedure: Take a sheet of paper and fold it several times. Now open it up. Trace over the creases with a black crayon. Color in each shape with a different color, design, or pattern.

Variations: Close your eyes and scribble with a black crayon, then fill in sections with crayons.

Letter Camouflage

Materials: paper, crayons
Procedure: Draw a large letter in the middle of the paper. Turn the paper all around. What object, animal, person, or place does it look like? Use crayons to camouflage the letter to make it look like this.
Variations: Make pictures and objects from shapes and numerals.

Little to Large

Materials: large newsprint paper, crayons
Procedure: Make a very tiny object in the center of the paper. Take a different color of crayon and go around it, making it a little larger. Continue using different colors of crayons and making the object a little larger each time until it completely fills the page.
Variations: Use seasonal objects, such as hearts, shamrocks, eggs, flowers, etc.

Strange Surfaces

Materials: styrofoam meat trays, corrugated cardboard, paper plates, paper cut in shapes, paper sacks, etc.
Procedure: Give child unusual drawing surface and let them color with crayons.

Pass It On

Materials: crayons, paper
Procedure: Give everyone in the room a sheet of paper. He or she draws for 2 minutes, then passes it on to the next person. Stop and share pictures after 10 minutes.

Sidewalk Artists

Materials: colored chalk, cement surface
Procedure: Take children outside and give them colored chalk to draw with on cement pavement.
Variations: Tie in with your unit of study by having children draw with a certain color, make shapes, write names, etc.; decorate the sidewalk for special holidays like Valentine's, Mother's Day, or someone's birthday.

Color on Color

Materials: colored chalk, colored paper

Procedure: Draw with colored chalk on paper. How many different strokes can you make with the chalk? (Hint: For an inexpensive fixative, try hairspray.)

Chalk Rubbings

Materials: chalk, paper, paper stencils, paper towel
Procedure: Take paper stencil and draw around edge with chalk. Place on paper with chalk side up. Take paper towel and brush outward onto paper. Lift up stencil and you will see your design.
Variations: Let children cut out their own stencils; use shapes or seasonal patterns.

Wet Chalk

Materials: colored chalk, paper, cup of water
Procedure: Dip chalk in water and then draw on paper.
Variations: Dip chalk in buttermilk; wet paper and then use dry chalk.

Primary Colors

Materials: tempera paint, brush, easel, paper
Procedure: Start off with one primary color of paint (red, blue, or yellow). Add one new color each week and notice the children's excitement when they "discover" green by mixing blue and yellow, purple by mixing red and blue, and orange by mixing red and yellow. (Hint: a few drops of liquid detergent will make it easier to get paint stains out of clothing.)
Variations: Make pastels by adding white to paints; let children paint on different surfaces, such as newspapers, butcher paper, paper plates, grocery sacks, cardboard; cut paper into seasonal shapes, such as pumpkins, flowers, etc.

Sponge Painting

Materials: sponges cut up, tempera paint, paper, shallow container
Procedure: Dip end of sponge in paint and you're ready to create. (Hint: Use

styrofoam meat trays for paint, then just throw away when you're finished.)

Variations: Cut sponges into geometric shapes; cut sponges into holiday shapes and sponge-paint cards and wrapping paper.

Gadget Painting

Materials: feathers, forks, potato masher, spools, toys, etc., paint, shallow container, paper

Procedure: Dip end of object or gadget in paint and apply to paper.

Variations: Dip wheels of toy cars and trucks in paint and "drive" them across the paper.

Q-Tip

Materials: Q-tips, paint, paper

Procedure: Dip end of cotton swab in paint. Use a different swab for each color.

Variations: Mix food coloring in a small amount of water and paint with Q-tip on a paper towel.

Straw Painting

Materials: drinking straws, paint, paper, spoon

Procedure: Put a spoonful of paint on the paper. Take the straw and blow a design.

Variations: Drop several different colors and blow to make "fireworks;" add details to your design with crayons or markers.

Marble Painting

Materials: marbles, paint, spoon, paper, cardboard box

Procedure: Cut paper to fit into bottom of box. Put several marbles in the box. Add a spoonful of paint and roll the marbles around to make a design.

Variations: Cut paper to fit into coffee can or potato chip can, drop in marbles and paint, put top on and shake; use golf balls instead of marbles for younger children.

String Painting

Materials: string or yarn cut in 12″ or 18″ pieces, cups of paint, paper

Procedure: Hold yarn by one end and dip other end in paint. Lay on top of paper to make a design.

Variations: Fold paper in half on top of string with paint, then pull out string.

Eye Dropper Painting

Materials: eye droppers, food coloring, cups of water, coffee filter
Procedure: Mix food coloring with small amount of water. Using eye dropper, drip onto coffee filter. Dry.
Variations: Gather coffee filter together in the middle and twist around a pipe cleaner to make a butterfly.

Water Painting

Materials: water, containers, old paint brushes
Procedure: Take children outside on a sunny day and let them paint the building, sidewalk, and play equipment with water. Discuss what happens to the water when it dries.
Variations: Give children an ice cube to paint with on a hot day.

Bubble Painting

Materials: mixing bowl, food coloring, detergent, egg beater, paper
Procedure: Mix food coloring and detergent in a small amount of water. Beat with egg beater until the bowl is overflowing. Put paper on top of bubbles and they will pop and make a design.
Variations: Hang paper on a fence outside and blow bubbles onto the paper. (Make your own bubbles or buy commercial bubbles and add food coloring.)

Spray Painting

Materials: empty spray bottles, paint, paper, cardboard box
Procedure: Cut paper to fit in box. Put paint in spray bottle and squirt into box.
Variations: Lay stencils, leaves, shells, etc. on top of the paper before you spray to make a design.

Mud Painting

Materials: dirt, water, plastic container, brushes, paper
Procedure: Mix the dirt with the water to make mud. Paint a picture with a brush or with your hands.
Variations: Try to find different types of soil to create different shades.

Pine Needle Painting

Materials: pine needles, paint, paper
Procedure: Dip pine needles in paint, then apply to paper.
Variations: Use this to make wrapping paper; paint with sticks, rocks, and other objects found in nature.

Murals

Materials: butcher paper, crayons, paint, markers
Procedure: Capitalize on a unit of study by asking children to draw or paint a mural.

Variations: Follow-up on a field trip with a mural; have students make objects from construction paper and glue them to the mural.

Finger Painting

Materials: finger paint, finger paint paper, water, sponge

Procedure: Wet paper with a sponge. Put a tablespoon of paint on the paper. Make designs with fingers, knuckles, fist, etc. Another procedure is to paint directly on the table or in a plastic tray, then lay a sheet of paper on top of the design to make a print.

Variations: Cut finger paint paper into seasonal shapes or use seasonal colors; finger paint with hand lotion or shaving cream; finger paint with liquid starch, adding food coloring or sand for texture; finger paint with chocolate pudding; add food coloring to corn syrup and paint; finger paint with yogurt.

Homemade Finger Paint

Materials: 1 cup cold water
              1/2 cup cornstarch
              3 cups boiling water
              food coloring or tempera

Procedure: Dissolve cornstarch in cold water. Pour mixture into boiling water and stir until shiny. Cool. Add food coloring or tempera for color. Store in refrigerator.

Baggie Finger Painting

Materials: ziplock bags, finger paint

Procedure: Put 2 tablespoons of finger paint in the bag and zip it shut. Let children squeeze it to make designs and patterns.

Variations: Put a tablespoon each of two different primary colors. Let children squeeze them to make a secondary color.

Printing activities involve the transfer of an image from one surface to another. A basic technique children need to learn to print is "press down—lift up." You can use holiday patterns, objects in nature, or toys and gadgets that you have in your classroom or home to do these projects. Thick tempera, poster paint, or water-soluble ink all work well for printing.

Fingerprint Creatures

Materials: ink pad, paper, fine-tip markers
Procedure: Did you know that everyone's fingerprint is different? Take your index finger, press it on the stamp pad, then press it on the paper. Use fine-tip markers to make animals, people, flowers, insects, etc. out of your fingerprint.
Variations: Make notecards or gift tags with these; use thumbprints to make "Thumb-body loves you" or "You're thumb-kin special" cards.

Nature Prints

Materials: leaves, flowers, grass, and other objects from nature, paint, shallow tray, paper towels, paper
Procedure: Put paper towels in tray, then add a small amount of paint. Dip one side of leaf or object in paint, then press on paper.

Cookie Cutter Prints

Materials: cookie cutters, paint, tray, paper towels, paper
Procedure: Prepare tray with paper towels and paint. Dip cookie cutter into paint, then press on paper.
Variations: Use holiday cookie cutters to make wrapping paper; encourage children to make a pattern on their paper with cookie cutters.

Styrofoam Prints

Materials: styrofoam meat trays, paint, tray, paper towels, paper
Procedure: Cut patterns or shapes from styrofoam meat tray. Attach tab to the back for easy handling. Dip styrofoam pattern into paint and print.

Fruit and Vegetable Prints

Materials: oranges, apples, carrots, celery, green pepper, okra, and other firm fruit, tray, paint, paper towels, paper

Procedure: Cut fruit or vegetable in half diagonally. Drain on paper towel to remove excess juice. Dip in paint and press on paper.

Potato Prints

Materials: potatoes, plastic knives or spoons, paint, tray, paper towels, paper

Procedure: Cut potato in half. Carve a design into the potato or out of the potato. Drain. Dip in paint and print.

Clay Prints

Materials: modeling clay, toothpicks, paint, tray, paper

Procedure: Take a small ball of clay and form it into a cube or shape with a flat surface. Use a toothpick to carve a design, letters, or shape on the flat surface and you're ready to print.

Gadget Prints

Materials: spools, kitchen utensils, and other gadgets with interesting textures, paint, tray, paper towels, paper

Procedure: Ask children to bring a gadget or piece of junk from home. Dip into paint and print on paper. Take turns guessing what objects made different prints.

Variations: Make block prints with different-shaped blocks from your block center.

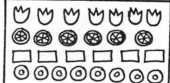

Styrofoam Etchings

Materials: styrofoam meat trays or styrofoam paper plates, paper clips, paint, tray, paper, brayer or roller

Procedure: On the back of the meat tray carve or "etch" out a design or picture with the end of the paper clip. Roll paint over etching, then press on paper.

Variations: Use this technique for holiday cards.

Sponge Prints

Materials: sponges, scissors, paint, tray, paper

Procedure: Cut sponge into shapes, letters, or holiday patterns. Dip in paint and press on paper.

Variations: Make wrapping paper or bulletin board borders with sponge prints.

Fingertip Prints

Materials: paint, tray, paper, crayons
Procedure: Draw a picture with crayons. Dip index finger in paint and fill in
             shapes.
Variations: Use white paint and make it snow; use green paint to add leaves
             to a tree; with pastel colors you can make a spring garden; add
             speckles to a frog or spots to a leopard with brown paint, etc.

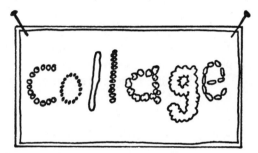

Children of all ages enjoy making collages. The materials you can use are prac-
tically limitless. As long as it's plentiful, inexpensive, and not too heavy, give it a
try. Although children enjoy seeing glue drip all over their paper, their collages will
be much more successful if you teach them to glue with "one finger," "one dot," or
how to "dip and put."

Torn Paper Collage

Materials: scrap paper, glue or paste, construction paper
Procedure: Use your fingers like scissors to tear scrap paper into small pieces.
             Glue them to your paper to make a design or picture.
Variations: Add detail with crayons or markers; cut construction paper into
             seasonal shapes, such as an egg or tree, and decorate with torn scraps;
             cut paper into small squares and glue to give the effect of a mosaic.

Cotton Collage

Materials: cotton balls, glue, construction paper
Procedure: Dip cotton balls into glue and arrange on paper to make a snowman, cloud, lamb, pussy willow, etc.
Variations: Cut construction paper into animal shape or holiday pattern before gluing on cotton balls.

Egg Shell Collage

Materials: egg shells, food coloring, glue, paper
Procedure: Dye egg shells with food coloring mixed with water. Dry. Glue shells to paper to make a design.

Popcorn Collage

Materials: air-popped popcorn, dry tempera, paper sack, glue, paper
Procedure: Put popcorn into paper sack. Add a small amount of tempera and shake. Glue to paper to make a picture.
Variations: Draw a picture with crayons and add detail with popcorn; use plain popcorn to make a snowman; draw a tree trunk, then add spring flowers with popcorn dyed pink.

Pizza Collage

Materials: oregano, thyme, bay leaves, or other seasonings, glue, crayons, paper plate
Procedure: Use crayons to draw a pizza with your favorite toppings on the paper plate. Glue on various seasonings.

Wallpaper Collage

Materials: wallpaper scraps or discontinued book of wallpaper samples, scissors, glue, paper
Procedure: Cut different shapes or patterns from wallpaper and glue to paper.
Variations: Glue to juice can to make a pencil holder or to ice cream cylinder to make a trash can; follow same procedure with wrapping paper scraps.

Fabric Collage

Materials: fabric scraps, ribbon and lace scraps, buttons, glue, scissors, paper
Procedure: Cut shapes from fabric and glue them to the paper. Add detail with ribbon, lace, and buttons.
Variations: Dress paper doll shapes with fabric; decorate Christmas tree shape with ribbon, sequins, etc.

Magazine Picture Collage

Materials: old magazine or sales catalogs, scissors, glue, paper
Procedure: Cut pictures from magazine and glue to paper.

Variations: Let children cut out pictures of their family members; make a collage of likes and dislikes; cut out things they are thankful for; use this project to reinforce basic concepts by having children cut out objects of a certain color, objects beginning with a consonant sound you are studying, sets, etc.

Tissue Paper Collage

Materials: tissue paper cut in 1″ squares, diluted glue (mix glue with equal parts of water), old paint brush, paper
Procedure: Brush paper with glue. Arrange tissue paper to make a design.
Variations: Use red, orange, and yellow tissue to make autumn leaves on a tree; glue seasonal colors to paper which has been cut into a holiday pattern, such as a flower, heart, etc.; crumple tissue paper and glue to make a three-dimensional picture.

Letter Collage

Materials: rice, beans, toothpicks, yarn, etc., glue, paper
Procedure: Have children draw the letter that you are studying on their paper with markers or crayons. (The teacher may need to do this for younger children.) Glue over the letter shape with a material that begins with that sound, such as rice for "R," beans for "B," toothpicks for "T," yarn for "Y," etc.
Variations: Use the same technique for teaching shapes, numerals, etc.

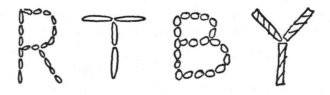

Soap Collage

Materials: Ivory soap flakes, water, spoon, bowl, paper
Procedure: Beat 1 cup of soap flakes with water until it is thick and fluffy. Let children cover the shape of a lamb, snowman, or rabbit with it.
Variations: Add food coloring to the mixture.

Mother Nature Collage

Materials: paper sack, objects from nature, glue, cardboard
Procedure: Go on a nature walk and encourage children to collect small objects, such as leaves, seeds, feathers, etc. Arrange them on the cardboard, then glue in place.
Variations: Arrange bits of bark, rocks, and heavier objects in a jar lid, smother with glue, and you'll have a paper weight that makes a great gift.

Food Collage

Materials: cereal, pretzels, raisins, glue, paper, crayons
Procedure: Glue small pieces of food to paper or add detail to a picture with food.
Variations: Decorate a Christmas tree shape with cereal; decorate the shape of a gingerbread boy with raisins; make a log cabin for Lincoln's birthday with pretzel sticks.

Spaghetti Collage

Materials: spaghetti, plastic bags, food coloring, paper
Procedure: Cook spaghetti, drain, and cool. Put in plastic bag and color with small amount of food coloring. (Store in refrigerator until you're ready to use it.) Take ends of spaghetti noodles and arrange on paper. As the noodles dry, they will stick to the paper.
Variations: Dip pieces of yarn or string in glue or liquid starch and arrange on paper in a similar manner.

Colored Sand

Materials: sand, dry tempera, plastic container, spoon, glue, paper
Procedure: Dye sand by mixing it with tempera. Make a design on paper with glue, then sprinkle with colored sand. Shake off excess sand and dry.
Variations: Color salt, grits, or cornmeal in a similar manner.

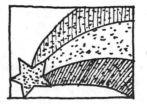

What Else?

There are many other different materials you can use for collages, including paper baking cups, styrofoam packing, wood scraps, old greeting cards, small shells, pasta, and popsicle sticks. Look in your closet, cupboards, basement, and attic to see what else you can find!

Uncooked Dough

Materials: 2 cups all-purpose flour, ¾ cup salt, ¼ cup oil, approximately ½ cup water, food coloring

Procedure: Mix dry ingredients together. Add oil. Add water until you get a nice consistency for molding. Store in airtight container.

Variations: Give each child a small ball and tell them to make a hole in it with their finger. Squirt a drop of food coloring into the hole and then let child squeeze it to mix the color.

Cooked Play Dough

Materials: 2 cups flour, 1 cup salt, 2 Tb. cream of tartar, 2 Tb. oil, 2 cups water, food coloring

Procedure: Mix dry ingredients together. Add oil, water, and food coloring and stir until smooth. Cook over medium heat until mixture thickens and sticks to spoon. Cool. Store in airtight container.

Variations: Make unusual colors like purple by mixing red and blue food coloring, orange by mixing yellow and red, etc.; roll and cut with scissors or cookie cutters.

Silly Putty

Materials: 1 cup liquid starch, 2 cups Elmer's Glue-All

Procedure: Slowly add starch to glue a little at a time. Mix well and refrigerate overnight in an airtight container. (Color with food coloring in color you desire.)

Ornament Dough

Materials: 2 cups flour, 1 cup salt, ½ to 1 cup water

Procedure: Stir flour and salt. Slowly add water, stirring well. Knead dough with hands until you get a nice consistency. Have children make ornaments, animals, beads, etc. Dry overnight or bake in a 300° oven until firm.

Variations: Dissolve ¼ cup instant coffee in warm water before adding to dry ingredients. This will make your dough a nice brown color like gingerbread.

Cut-Down Mobile

Materials: construction paper, scissors, yarn
Procedure: Fold piece of paper in half and cut out a shape. Go about 1″ inside that shape and cut a smaller one just like it. Continue as long as you can. Tie shapes together with yarn.
Variations: Use holiday shapes, such as hearts or shamrocks; hang from ceiling or window.

Coat Hanger Mobile

Materials: construction paper, crayons or markers, scissors, hole-punch, coat hanger, yarn
Procedure: Color pictures on construction paper. Cut out and punch a hole. Tie with yarn to coat hanger.
Variations: Cut out letters in name; use to illustrate a story, song, or rhyme; follow-up a unit of study with coat hanger mobiles.

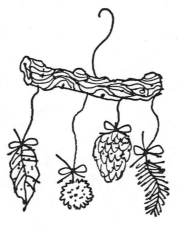

Mother Nature Mobile

Materials: sticks, pine cones, feathers, and other objects found in nature, yarn or string
Procedure: Go on a nature hunt, asking children to find an interesting stick and several other items in nature. Tie yarn to middle of stick to hang by, then tie other objects to hang down from the stick.

Paper Sack Puppets

Materials: lunch sacks, crayons, paper scraps, scissors, glue
Procedure: Using the bottom of the sack as the head, decorate with crayons, paper scraps, and other items to make a person or animal.
Variations: Make a favorite book character; make what you want to be when you grow up; create a seasonal puppet, such as a witch or leprechaun.

Sock Puppet

Materials: old sock, markers, yarn, buttons, fabric scraps, glue
Procedure: Ask children to bring in an old sock from home. Decorate with markers, buttons, yarn, etc.

Envelope Puppet

Materials: envelopes, scissors, crayons
Procedure: Glue down flap of envelope, then cut in half. Color a face with crayons, then insert your fingers.

Stick Puppet

Materials: popsicle stick, paper, crayons, scissors, tape
Procedure: Color a person or animal, then cut it out. Tape it to the stick and make it come alive.
Variations: Make a groundhog, bunny, or other animal that lives underground. Insert the stick in a paper cup, then make your animal "pop out" of its hole.

Spoon Puppet

Materials: wooden ice cream spoon, crayons
Procedure: Color a person or animal on the spoon with crayons. Encourage children to color the "front" and "back."
Variations: You can follow the same procedure on plastic spoons with permanent markers.

Tube Puppet

Materials: cardboard tube from toilet paper, crayons, paper scraps, scissors, glue
Procedure: Decorate tube with crayons and paper scraps. Insert your fingers in the bottom.

Coat Hanger Puppet

Materials: coat hanger, old hose, paper scraps, scissors, glue
Procedure: Bend ends of coat hanger to the middle to make a diamond shape. Stretch hose over this and tie at the bottom. Decorate with paper scraps and other items to make a character or animal.

Finger Puppet

Materials: paper, crayons, scissors, tape
Procedure: Color small characters and animals on the paper and cut out. Cut a ½″ by 2½″ strip of paper and tape to the back of the puppet to make a ring. Insert your finger.

Pin Wheel

Materials: pencil with eraser, paper cut in 8″ squares, crayons, scissors, straight pins
Procedure: Fold paper in half diagonally. Fold again. Open and draw a 1½″ circle around the center of the paper. Color both sides with swirls and designs. Cut in on the folded lines, stopping at the circle line. Take alternating points and bring them to the center. Insert a pin through the points and center, then stick the pin in the end of the eraser and blow.

Stuffed Animals

Materials: butcher paper, crayons, markers, or paints, stapler, newspaper, scissors
Procedure: Draw the outline of an animal on a sheet of paper. Cut out two identical shapes. Color or paint both sides. Staple the outside edges together, leaving a 6″ opening for stuffing. Tear strips of newspaper and stuff the animal. Close the opening and your animal is ready to be hung from the ceiling or bulletin board.
Variations: Make three-dimensional hot air balloons, houses, shapes, etc.

Sneaky Snake

Materials: paper, crayons, scissors
Procedure: Cut a large circle from your paper. With a crayon, draw a spiral line inside the circle. Color. Cut along the line, then gently pull the head and tail apart to make your sneaky snake grow long.

Paper Fan

Materials: paper, crayons, stapler
Procedure: Color the paper with designs, flowers, birds, etc. Fold the paper back and forth making 1″ creases. Staple at the bottom.
Variations: Attach your fan to another sheet of paper, turn upside down, and use for a dress, Indian teepee, or haystack.

Paper Chain

Materials: construction paper cut in 9″×1″ strips, glue
Procedure: Glue ends of a strip of paper together to make a circle. Loop a second strip through this one, and continue to make a chain.
Variations: Use seasonal colors, such as orange and black or red and white, to decorate the classroom; make a red and green chain for December with 25 links. Each day the children can remove a link to count the days until Christmas.

Paper Sculpture

Materials: construction paper, paper scraps, glue, scissors
Procedure: Take a piece of scrap paper. Fold it or bend it, then glue it to the construction paper. Cut springs, cones, stairs, and various three-dimensional shapes and glue to paper to make a sculpture.

Weaving

Materials: 12″×18″ construction paper, 1½″×12″ paper strips, scissors, glue, pencil, ruler

Procedure: Fold paper in half lengthwise. Using the ruler, draw 1½″ lines. Cut along these lines starting at the fold and stopping 1″ before the edge. (The teacher may need to do this step for younger ones.) Open. Take a paper strip and weave over and under. Secure ends in place with glue. Take a second strip and weave in the opposite direction by going under and over. Continue weaving strips in alternating patterns.

Variations: Weave seasonal shapes, such as turkeys or umbrellas, or weave animal shapes, such as fish or turtles.

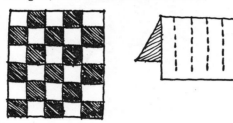

Swinging Animals

Materials: construction paper, crayons, scissors, straw, stapler

Procedure: Think of an animal that likes to swing from a tree or hang by its tail, such as a monkey or opossum. Draw that animal with crayons adding an extra inch to the arms or tail. Color and cut out. Bend the arms or tail over a straw, staple, and the animal is ready to swing.

Children will be so proud when they make one of these gifts for their parents, and their parents will treasure each one.

Pet Rock

Materials: rocks or stones (about the size of a fist), markers, felt, "googly" eyes, glue, scissors

Procedure: Go on a rock hunt and let each child find a special rock. Have children wash their rocks and set them aside to dry. Decorate the rocks with "googly" eyes and markers. Add a piece of felt to the bottom to make a paper weight.

Golden Shoe

Materials: old shoe, school glue, gold spray paint

Procedure: Ask each child to bring in one old shoe (tennis shoe, ballet shoe, baby shoe, any shoe will do). Dip the shoe in glue and then let it dry on wax paper for two days. Repeat the dipping and drying procedure. You can spray paint the shoe gold, silver, or bronze, or you can leave it natural.

Variations: Insert a small plant in the shoe to make a planter.

Pencil Can

Materials: juice or vegetable can, glue, pasta, spray paint

Procedure: Have each child bring in a can from home. Remove the label and glue different-shaped pasta around the can. Dry. Spray paint.

Variations: Put glue all over the can, wrap yarn around it, dry, and shellac.

Silhouette

Materials: filmstrip projector, black construction paper, white construction paper, pencil, scissors, glue

Procedure: Tape black construction paper to the wall. Have a child sit on a stool about 1 foot from the paper. Shine the light on the child's head and trace around the shadow. Cut the silhouette out and glue it to the white paper.

Recipe Book

Materials: ditto paper, construction paper, crayons, stapler

Procedure: Ask each child in the room to dictate the recipe for his/her favorite dish. Copy the recipes exactly as the children tell you, then run them off. Make a cover for the recipe books from construction paper and let the children decorate them with crayons. These are always funny, yet very special to parents.

Handprint

Materials: plaster of Paris or hardening clay, spray paint

Procedure: Prepare plaster of Paris according to directions and quickly pour it into a shallow plastic lid or dish that is slightly larger than the child's hand. The child places a hand on the plaster of Paris to make a print. Dry. Spray paint and attach a hanger to the back.

Coupon Book

Materials: ditto paper, construction paper, crayons, stapler
Procedure: Cut ditto paper into fourths and staple 8 sheets in construction paper to make a book. On each page write a different job that the child tells you they can do for their parents, such as get the mail, set the table, walk the dog, etc. Let the children decorate the cover and "coupons" with crayons.

Clothespin Magnet

Materials: spring clothespin, pompoms, felt scraps, glue, magnetic tape
Procedure: Give each child a clothespin and let them create a caterpillar or other creature by gluing pompoms and felt scraps to one side. Attach magnetic tape to the other side to make a refrigerator magnet.

Guest Soap

Materials: soap flakes (Ivory), food coloring, water, spoon, mixing bowl
Procedure: Mix 2 cups of soap flakes with a small amount of water and food coloring. Knead with hands until a nice consistency is achieved. Roll into balls or mold objects. Dry.

Each month and season suggest special projects for the art center. Many of the painting, printing, and collage projects previously described can easily be adapted for monthly themes, or try some of these activities.

September

Scarecrow: Make a scarecrow from construction paper, then glue on fabric scraps for patches and real straw for the arms and legs.
Leaf Art: Glue a leaf to a sheet of paper. Decorate with crayons to look like a person, tree, animal, etc.
Handprint Tree: Draw the trunk of a tree on a large sheet of paper. Dip one hand in red paint and one hand in yellow. Print on the trunk to make

leaves. Rub two hands together to make orange, then print on tree.

October

Glue Ghost: Squirt a glob of school glue on a sheet of wax paper. Dry. Peel off wax paper and decorate with markers to look like a ghost. Punch a hole and string on a piece of yarn to make a necklace.

Paper Sack Pumpkin: Take a lunch sack and draw a line 3″ down from the opening. Color with green above this line and orange below this line. Stuff the bottom with newspaper, then squeeze the top and tie with yarn where the two colors meet. Glue on eyes, nose, and mouth to make a jack-o-lantern.

Ghost Feet: Trace around the child's foot on white paper. Cut out. Draw a face on the heel, and you have a ghost. You can also make a ghost from the child's handprint.

November

Indian Costume: Each child can make his/her own Indian costume by coloring a large paper grocery sack. Fringe the bottom, and cut out holes for the arms and head. Make headdresses from construction paper, and drums from coffee cans or oatmeal boxes. String dyed pasta to make a necklace. (To color pasta, shake it in a plastic bag with alcohol and food coloring. Dry on wax paper.) Paint their faces with tempera mixed with liquid detergent.

Indian Village: Cut paper in the shape of a circle and decorate with Indian signs and symbols. Make a slit into the center, fold around, and staple to make a cone. Insert a few toothpicks in the top and cut a small opening for a door. Make canoes from construction paper and totem poles from toilet paper rolls. Indians can be made from clothespins and pipe cleaners. Set these objects on a board or small table. Build a campfire with small pebbles, add a lake made of blue paper, then stick tree twigs in clay for trees.

Handprint Turkeys and Indians: Make a turkey or an Indian from the child's handprint as shown.

December

Paper Plate Angel: Cut around the rim of a paper plate in each direction, stopping about 3 inches before you meet. Bend back the rim to make

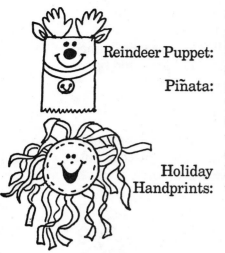

Reindeer Puppet:

Piñata:

Holiday Handprints:

wings and staple. Let the child decorate the plate to look like himself/herself. Add yarn for hair and glitter to the wings. Using the bottom of a lunch sack, color a reindeer's face. Add ears, then trace around the child's hands to make antlers.

Staple two paper plates together, leaving a 5″ opening. Decorate with markers and tissue paper. Fill with candy and staple the opening shut. Attach to the end of a broomstick with a thin wire. Roll up a piece of poster paper for a stick, blindfold the children, and let the fun begin.

Make a handprint Santa, a menorah, or a Christmas tree or wreath.

January

King Crowns:

Snowflakes:

Snowman:

Cut out a paper crown for each child. Ask them to draw their dreams for a better world on their crowns with crayons.

Take a sheet of paper and cut out a circle. Fold the paper in half, then fold into thirds to look like an ice cream cone. (Snowflakes have 6 points.) Cut little pieces out of your paper, open up, and you'll see a one-of-a-kind snowflake. (Tissue paper and coffee filters work well, too.)

Fold a dark sheet of construction paper in half and cut on the fold as shown. Open up. Glue wax paper on the back and decorate your snowman and picture with crayons.

February

Paper Plate Pouch:

Heart Creatures:

Take two paper plates. Cut one in half. Put the two plates together and hole-punch around the edges 1″ apart. Sew around the edges with yarn and decorate with crayons and stickers. Let the children use these to put their valentines in.

Cut a large heart out of construction paper. Bend four 12″×1″ strips of paper and attach to the heart for arms and legs. Trace around the child's hands and feet and attach for the heart creature's hands and feet. Decorate with crayons. (Use this same method on pumpkins, shamrocks, bells, etc.)

Sweetheart Tree: Cover a small juice can with paper. Stick a bare tree branch in the can and secure with clay or plaster of Paris. Add paper hearts and gumdrops to the branches.

March

Paper Sack Kite: Decorate a paper sack with crayons. Punch two holes opposite each other in the bottom and tie the end of a 6' piece of yarn or string through each hole. This is a kite even little ones can run with and fly.

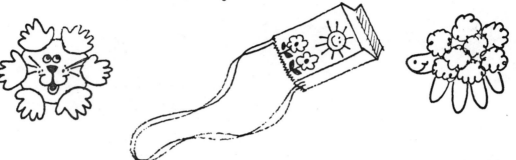

Lion or Lamb? Paint a paper plate brown. Cut out handprints from yellow paper and glue around the edges to make a mane. Decorate the face with paper scraps to look like a lion.
Trace around the child's hand on black construction paper and cut out. Glue cotton balls to the palm to make the lamb's body, and decorate the thumb for the face.

Handprint Bird: Cut a bird's body from construction paper. Trace around the hands, cut out, and attach to the body to make wings. Punch a hole, add a string, and make your bird fly.

April

Papier Maché Eggs: Blow up a small balloon. Dip strips of tissue paper in liquid starch or diluted glue, then wrap them around the balloon. Apply strips until the balloon is completely covered. When the papier maché has dried, pop the balloon.

Baggie Butterfly: Fill a small sandwich bag with torn pieces of tissue paper. Squeeze in the middle and wrap a pipe cleaner around to make the body and antennae. Attach a piece of yarn for flying or hanging.

Easter Berry Basket: Take a plastic basket that berries come in and weave yarn or small pieces of paper through the holes. Attach a pipe cleaner for a handle.

Foot Butterflies: Have children take off their shoes and trace around their feet. Decorate the wings and add a body and antennae. (It's also fun to paint the bottom of the feet, then step onto paper to make a butterfly.)

May

Sun Visor: Cut a moon-shape from a paper plate. Color. Staple the end of a long rubber band to each point.

Sunshine and Flowers: Use handprints to make the sun or May flowers.

Fishy Pictures: Cut out footprints and make a fish or a sail for a sailboat.

Mother's Day: Dip child's hands in mud or paint and apply to a sheet of paper. Let the child decorate the paper with crayons and attach this poem:

> "Here is a handprint made for you
> this Happy Mother's Day.
> It is one you can always keep,
> and not have to wash away!"

How Can You Display Children's Art?

Children are usually very proud when their artwork is displayed in the classroom. Your best area for displaying the children's art will be bulletin boards. First, choose a background material for covering your board. You can use butcher paper, construction paper, burlap or other fabric, wallpaper, wrapping paper, or newspaper. Second, put a contrasting border around your bulletin board. Try ribbon, small cutouts, colored tape, or use one of the attached patterns to make your own border. Third, think of a short, "catchy" title and cut out your letters. You can get ideas for titles from books, songs, greeting cards, the newspaper, advertisements, or ask the children to help you think of a title. Now you're ready to add the children's artwork.

You may want to pin the children's pictures directly on the bulletin board, or you may want to frame them first. Try one of these framing techniques:

- take a sheet of construction paper and make a fold 1″ in on all sides to create a frame
- mount pictures on styrofoam meat trays
- use a shoe box lid or gift box for a frame

Patterns for Bulletin Board Borders

Use construction paper, wallpaper, wrapping paper, wide ribbon, fabric, or any other suitable material.

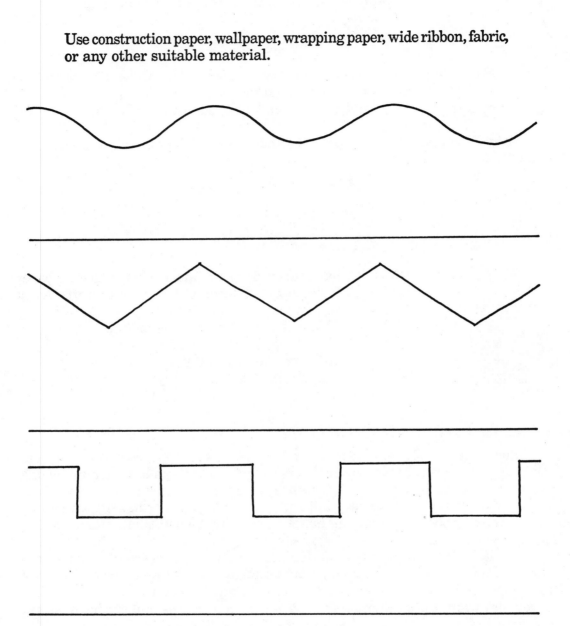

- plastic lids from food containers are handy for framing small pictures
- mount pictures on colored cardboard

In addition to bulletin boards, these are some other ways to turn your classroom into an "art gallery":

1. Tape pictures to the door.
2. Hang three-dimensional art from the ceiling. (Tie a paper clip to each end of a piece of fishing line that is a yard long. Unbend one paper clip and hang on the light fixture or from the ceiling tile. Unbend the other paper clip so you can easily hang up and take down projects.)
3. Stand three-dimensional projects on a table or book shelf.
4. Paint a large appliance box and hang children's pictures on it.
5. Take children's pictures and put them together to make an art book for your classroom.
6. Use empty wall space to display children's art.
7. Stretch a piece of ribbon or clothesline between two nails and hang pictures up with clothespins. (This is a good method to use in the hall outside your room.)
8. Save children's art and have an art show. Invite parents and make it a party with goodies that the children have made to eat. (One school sells the artwork to raise money.)

A bad habit that many teachers fall into is leaving artwork up too long. A good rule-of-thumb to remember is that you should rotate bulletin boards and displays at least every two weeks. The children will enjoy the variety and you will, too!

10

MUSIC
AND MOVEMENT

Music can be a powerful teaching tool in your classroom. This section will provide you with simple songs, finger plays, creative movement activities, ideas for homemade instruments, and other music experiences that will give children the opportunity to explore and enjoy music in a personal way.

191

How Does Music Impact the Lives of Young Children?

Music is more than a frill; it is basic to early childhood and is a natural expression of children. Music should not be limited to a specific time, but should be spontaneous and interrelated to other activities during the school day. Music involves the whole child and can contribute to children's learning in the following ways:

(do) Music develops listening skills and auditory awareness.

(ti) Music contributes to speech and language development.

(la) Music involves both large motor skills and small motor skills.

(so) Music encourages creative expression and offers a release for feelings and frustrations.

(fa) Music can teach basic concepts, such as colors, numbers, animal sounds, etc.

(mi) Music gives children opportunities for social interaction and cooperation.

(re) Music can be used to guide, calm, and comfort children.

(do) Music sets the tone for your classroom, adding joy and pleasure.

What Music Concepts Should You Introduce to Children?

These are some basic music concepts that are fun for children to learn and can increase their understanding and enjoyment.

Listening—Listening is more than hearing. Active listening involves paying attention to sounds.

- Encourage children to listen to sounds in the classroom and outside. Have them close their eyes and identify sounds that you make around the room.
- Invite guests to your classroom to share a musical talent. This might be a grandparent, parent, friend, sibling, or another child in your school.
- Take a field trip to hear a live performance of a symphony or high school band.
- Have a music show and tell where children bring their favorite tapes or records for the class to listen to.
- Expose children to a wide variety of music, such as classical, country, jazz, and folk. Ask children if they like or dislike different pieces and why.
- Allow children to rest to music, paint to music, eat lunch to music, or dance to music.

Fast and slow—Sing a familiar tune, such as "I'm a Little Teapot" at a normal speed. Sing it fast, then slowly.

- Sing one line of a song fast, then sing the next line slowly.
- What animals move fast? Move like a rabbit or pony. What animals move slowly? Move like a tortoise or elephant.

- Tell the story of the tortoise and the hare, then let the children act it out.
- Play a record on different speeds and let the children move their bodies to show fast and slow.
- Compare pieces of music, such as a lullabye and march, and talk about the tempo.
- Clap your hands or play a drum fast and slowly while the children walk or run as the tempo changes.

Loud and soft—Some sounds are loud, while others are soft. Sometimes there is no sound at all. What makes a loud sound? What makes a soft sound? What makes no sound?

- Sing the "Eensy-Weensy Spider" and other favorite songs loudly and softly.
- Let one child sing a song with a loud voice or soft voice, while others try and identify which type of voice they used.
- Play musical instruments loudly, then softly.
- Play music on a record player and vary the volume. Ask children to move their arms to show you if it is loud or soft. (Arms stretched out mean loud, while close together mean soft.)
- Compare pieces of music that are loud and soft, such as a string quartet and brass band.
- Clap your hands loudly, then softly.
- Talk about when you should use a loud voice or a soft voice.

High and low—Music has high and low sounds, and so do other things in our environment. Birds sing high, while bears growl low. What instruments make a high sound? A low sound?

- Play a xylophone, bells, or other instruments from high to low. Let children guess if a note you play is high or low.
- Start a song on a high pitch, then start it on a low pitch.
- Say a rhyme or finger play with a regular pitch. Say it with a high "baby" voice, then say it with a low "daddy" voice.
- Put your hands on your toes and sing a low note. As you move up the scale, move your hands up your body until your arms are extended with a high pitch.
- Be an elevator and move your bodies up and down as you go up and down the scale.

Beat—Talk about the steady beat of a clock, your heart, or the wipers on a car.

- Clap, tap, snap, walk, sway, or swing your arms to the beat of the music.
- Give each child two paper plates, two blocks, or two pencils and let them hit them together to the beat of the music.
- Clap to the beat of nursery rhymes and simple songs.
- Have children march to the beat of a drum, then stop and freeze when the drum beat stops.
- Ask children to repeat a clapping pattern. Do this as a group or individually.

What Are Some Familiar Songs to Sing?

Young children love to sing, and you will, too, with these favorite songs and rhymes. In choosing songs, pick those with a simple tune, steady beat, limited range, repetition of words and phrases, and those with a content interesting to children. Encourage your class to choose songs they like to sing, to teach new songs to each other, or to make up their own songs to sing. Get together with other groups in your school for sing-alongs and share new tunes and records among the staff. Never force children to sing, but, if you enjoy singing, chances are your children will want to join you.

Many of these songs can be enhanced by simple visuals and props. For example, by showing illustrations of letters, numerals, and colors when singing the learning songs, you will reinforce those concepts. Felt cutouts, stick puppets, paper sack puppets, paper hats, and simple costumes can easily be made for many of the songs. (Use the patterns in the Appendix for these.) Also, children will enjoy acting out many of the songs and finger plays after they learn them. Feel free to change the words, tune, or motions to any of the songs to suit the needs and abilities of your class.

Good Morning Songs

Start your day with a song by singing one of these tunes to greet your children or open your circle time.

GOOD MORNING (Tune: Lassie & Laddie)

Good morning to (_____child's name_____),
to (_____child's name_____),
to (_____child's name_____).
Good morning to (_____child's name_____),
How do you do?
(Go around the room and sing this song to each child. Encourage children to describe how they're feeling with words.)

GOOD MORNING TO YOU (Tune: Traditional)

Good morning to you.
Good morning to you.
Good morning dear freinds.
We're glad to see you.
Good morning to (_____first child's name_____),
Good morning to (_____second child's name_____),
Good morning to (_____third child's name_____),
Good morning to (_____fourth child's name_____).
(Use each child's name in the group.)

ANIMAL MORNING SONG (Tune: Farmer in the Dell)

When cows get up each day,
When cows get up each day,
"Moo, moo, moo, moo,"
Is what they say.
(Insert other animals and their sounds.)

I'M SO GLAD (Tune: In my Heart There Rings a Melody)

I'm so glad I came to school today, came to school today, came to school today.
I'm so glad I came to school today. I came to be with all my friends.

WHERE IS JOHN? (Tune: Frere Jacques)

Where is (_____child's name_____)?
Where is (_____child's name_____)?
Please stand up.
Please stand up.
How are you today (_____child's name_____)?
"Very well, I thank you." (child answers)
Please sit down.
Please sit down.
(Sing to all children.)

WHERE, OH, WHERE? (Tune: Paw Paw Patch)

Where, oh, where is dear little (_____child's name_____),
Where, oh, where is dear little (_____child's name_____),
Where, oh, where is dear little (_____child's name_____),
There he/she is wearing (name color or type of clothing).
(Use each child's name).

TODAY IS (Tune: Jimmy Crack Corn)

Today is Monday,
I'm so glad,
Today is Monday,
I'm so glad,
Today is Monday,
I'm so glad,
We'll (activity) today.
(Insert a special activity or ask children to tell you something they are looking forward to doing at school, such as painting, riding trikes, eating a snack, etc.)

DAILY SONG (Tune: She'll Be Coming Round the Mountain)

If you're glad it's (day of the week),
Clap your hands. (clap, clap)
If you're glad it's (day of the week),
Clap your hands. (clap, clap)
If you're glad it's (day of the week),
If you're glad it's (day of the week),
If you're glad it's (day of the week),
Clap your hands. (clap, clap)

WEATHER SONG (Tune: Shortnin' Bread)

What will the weather, weather, weather?
What will the weather person say?
(One child is designated the "weather person" and looks out a window and reports to the class.)

She says it's _____ , _____ , _____ ,
She says it's _____ , _____ today. (Insert the word sunny, cold,
windy, rainy, etc.)

Transition Songs

Try one of these songs to capture children's attention and to guide them from one
activity to the next.

Clean up the room with these tunes:

A HELPER I WILL BE (Tune: The Farmer in the Dell)

A helper I will be. A helper I will be.
There's work to do, there's work to do.
A helper I will be.

A picker-up I'll be. A picker-up I'll be.
It's time to put the toys away.
A picker-up I'll be.

THIS IS THE WAY (Tune: Mulberry Bush)

This is the way we clean up our room,
Clean up our room, clean up our room.
This is the way we clean up our room
At school every day.
(Change the words to "put on our coats," or "lay down to rest," or any command
you want the children to follow.)

CAN YOU? (Tune: Skip to My Lou)

I can clean quietly how about you?
I can clean quietly how about you?
I can clean quietly how about you?
How about you, my darlin'?
(Change words to "push in my chair," "pick up trash," "walk quietly," etc.)

TIDY UP (Tune: Jingle Bells)

Tidy up, tidy up, put the toys away,
Tidy up, tidy up we're finished for today.
Tidy up, tidy up, put the toys away.
For we'll get them out again the next time that we play.

Here is a song to sing when the children wash their hands:

HANDY GAME (Tune: Row Your Boat)

Wash, wash, wash your hands,
Play the handy game.
Rub and scrub and scrub and rub.
Germs go down the drain.

Sing these songs to get the children's attention before an activity:

LISTENING (Tune: Frere Jacques)

Are you listening, are you listening,
Boys and girls, boys and girls?
It is time to listen. It is time to listen,
Boys and girls, boys and girls.
(Teach the children to sing the second line, "Yes, we are. Yes, we are.")

WHO IS READY? (Tune: The Bear Went over the Mountain)

(child's name) is ready.
(child's name) is ready.
(child's name) is ready.
To go out and play.
(Reinforce children who are doing the right thing by singing their names.)

LOOK AT ME (Tune: If You're Happy and You Know It)

If you're ready for a snack look at me.
If you're ready for a snack look at me.
If you're ready and you know it then your face will surely show it.
If your ready for a snack look at me.
(Change the words to fit what you want the children to do; such as, "If you want
to hear a story sit down please," or "If you want to go outside line up at the door.")

I LOVE SOMEBODY (Tune: Farmer in the Dell)

I love somebody, I do.
I love somebody, I do.
I love somebody,
And I'll tell you who.
(Find a child doing the correct thing and say their name.)

TWO LITTLE HANDS (Finger Play)

Two little hands, clap, clap, clap.
Two little feet tap, tap, tap.
Two little hands thump, thump, thump.
Two little feet jump, jump, jump.
One little body turns around.
One little child sits quietly down.

SNAP—SNAP!

(Snap your fingers or clap your hands four times.)
Snap—snap—snap—snap!
If you want to *hear a story* (go outside, or another activity) this is what you do.
You've got to *sit down on the rug* (line up at the door, etc.) like the soldiers do.
You've got to listen to your teacher,
raise your hand.

You've got to let her know
that you understand.
That's right! That's right! That's right! That's right!

Closing Songs

Sing these at the end of your day just before the children go home.

WE HAD A GOOD DAY (Tune: Good Night, Ladies)

We had a good day, we had a good day,
We had a good day, we had a good day at school.
See you tomorrow, see you tomorrow,
See you tomorrow, see you tomorrow at school.

(wave good-bye)

THE MORE WE GET TOGETHER (Tune: Lassie & Laddie)

The more we get together, together, together.
The more we get together, the happier we'll be.
For your friends are my friends, and my friends are your friends.
The more we get together, the happier we'll be.

Anytime Songs

These songs will delight your youngsters on the bus, while waiting for lunch, before a story, or anytime!

I AM SPECIAL (Tune: Frere Jacques)

I am special.
I am special.
Take a look,
You will see.
Someone very special,
Someone very special,
And it's me!
And it's me!

TONY CHESTNUT (Tune: London Bridge)

Tony Chestnut knows I love you.
Knows I love you, Knows I love you.
Tony Chestnut knows I love you.
I do love you!
Point to sound alike body parts: Toe, knee, chest, nut (head), nose, eye, love (cross arms over chest), you (point).

IF YOU'RE HAPPY (Traditional Tune)

If you're happy and you know it, clap your hands. (clap, clap)
If you're happy and you know it, clap your hands. (clap, clap)

If you're happy and you know it, then your face will surely show it.
If you're happy and you know it, clap your hands. (clap, clap)

2. Stomp your feet. (stomp, stomp)
3. Honk your nose. (beep, beep)
4. Shake your head. (nod, nod)
5. Pat your tummy. (yum, yum)
6. Say "I love you." (I love you)
7. Shake a hand. (shake, shake)

(When you talk about feelings, change the words and sing, "If you're sad and you know it rub your eyes," or "If you're mad and you know it stomp your feet," etc.)

WHEELS ON THE BUS (Tune: Mulberry Bush)

The wheels on the bus go round and round, (move hands in circular motion) round and round, round and round.
The wheels on the bus go round and round, all through the town.
2. Wipers go swish, swish, swish. (move arms like wipers)
3. Horn goes beep, beep, beep. (honk horn)
4. Doors go open and shut. (move arms open, then close together)
5. Children go up and down. (bounce body)
(Make up your own verses of things that happen on the bus.)

EENSY-WEENSY SPIDER (Traditional Tune)

The eensy-weensy spider (use fingers and pretend to climb up in the air)
went up the water spout.
Down came the rain (make raining motion with fingers)
and washed the spider out. (swish arms to the side)
Out came the sun and (make circle above head)
dried up all the rain.
And the eensy-weensy spider (pretend to climb fingers up in air)
went up the spout again.
2. The big fat spider (use loud voice and large movements)
3. The teensy-weensy spider, (use a high, baby voice and small motions)

JACK AND JILL (Traditional Tune)

Jack and Jill went up the hill   (hold thumbs up and pretend they are
                                                  Jack and Jill climbing a hill)

To fetch a pail of water.
Jack fell down and broke his crown   (drop down right thumb)
And Jill came tumbling after.   (bring left thumb down in circles)
2. Then up got Jack and said to Jill   (hold up right thumb)
As in his arms he took her.   (have right thumb pick up left thumb
You're not hurt, brush off that dirt.   and brush off)
Now let's go fetch that water.
3. So Jack and Jill went up the hill   (hold thumbs up and pretend to climb
To fetch a pail of water.   the hill)

They brought it back to mother dear,   (have thumbs climb down the hill)
Who thanked her son and daughter.   (clasp hands as in prayer)

HICKORY DICKORY DOCK (Traditional Tune)

Hickory, Dickory Dock
The mouse ran up the clock. (run hands up in air)
The clock struck one. (clap hands above head one time)
The mouse ran down. (run hands down)
Hickory, Dickory Dock.
2. The clock struck two (clap twice), the mouse said, "Boo!"
3. The clock struck three (clap three times), the mouse said, "Wee!"
4. The clock struck four (clap four times), the mouse said, "No More!"

CLAP YOUR HANDS (Tune: Row Your Boat)

Clap, clap, clap your hands,
Slowly as can be.
Clap, clap, clap your hands.
Do it now with me.
2. Stomp your feet.
3. Flap your arms.
4. Snap your fingers.
5. Nod your head.

A SAILOR (Tune: Pretty Little Dutch Girl)

1. A sailor went to sea-sea-sea (put hand over eyes as if looking)
   To see what he could see-see-see
   And all that he could see-see-see
   Was the bottom of the ocean sea-sea-sea.
2. A sailor went to chop-chop-chop (move hand in chopping motion)
3. A sailor went to knee-knee-knee (touch knee)
4. A sailor went to tap-tap-tap (tap foot)
5. A sailor went to Oo-washy-wa (put hands on waist and wiggle hips)

SWIMMING (Tune: Sailing, Sailing over the Bounding Maine)

Swimming, swimming (move arms in stroking motion)
In the swimming pool. (make imaginary square in front of body)
When days are hot (fan self with hands)
Or days are cold (grasp arms and shiver)
In the swimming pool. (make imaginary square)
Back stroke, (move arms backwards)
Side stroke, (move arms on side)
Fancy diving, too. (clasp hands in diving motion)
There's no place I would rather be (shake head, "no")

than in the swimming pool. (make imaginary square)
2. Hum the first line and do the motions.
3. Hum the first two lines and do the motions.
Continue until you hum the entire song.

HEAD, SHOULDERS, KNEES, AND TOES (Traditional Tune)

Head, shoulders, knees and toes, knees and toes,
Head, shoulders, knees and toes, knees and toes,
And eyes and ears and mouth and nose,
Head, shoulders, knees and toes, knees and toes.
(Point to each body part as you come to it.)
2. Hum the word "head" each time you come to it.
3. Hum the words "head" and "shoulders" each time you come to them.
Continue until you hum the entire song.

FISHING SONG (Tune: Do Your Ears Hang Low?)

Have you ever been a fishin' (clasp hands and pretend to throw out a line)
On a bright and sunny day (make circle above head with arms)
When you see those little fishes (wiggle hands like fish)
Swimming up and down the bay? (make hands go up, then down)
With their hands in their pockets (pretend to put hands in front pockets)
And their pockets in their pants (pretend to put hands in back pockets)
All the little fishes (put hands on hips)
Do the hoochie-coochie dance. (wiggle hips)
(Sing this song several times, each time a little faster. You can also omit one
verse at a time and just do the motions.)

HUGS AND KISSES (Tune: Baby Bumblebee)

Oh, I'm bringing home a big surprise for you.   (clasp hands and swing from
One that says, "I love you true."   side to side)
Oh, I'm bringing home a big surprise for you.
It's a great big hug   (hug self with arms)
And a (kiss) (kiss), too.   (kiss in the air twice)

I WISH I WERE (Tune: If You're Happy and You Know It)

Oh, I wish I were a little foreign car.
Oh, I wish I were a little foreign car.
I'd go zoom, zoom, zoom over everybody's room.
Oh, I wish I were a little foreign car.
2. Oh, I wish I were a little piece of orange...
   I'd go squirty, squirty, squirty over everybody's shirty.
3. Oh, I wish I were a little piece of cake...
   I'd go yummy, yummy, yummy down in everybody's tummy.
4. Oh, I wish I were a little soda pop...
   I'd go down with a slurp and up with a burp.

5. Oh, I wish I were a little bar of soap...
   I'd go slidey, slidey, slidey over everybody's hidey.
6. Oh, I wish I were a little baby fish...
   I'd go swimming in the nudey without a bathing suity.
7. Oh, I wish I were a little motorcycle...
   I'd go speedy, speedy, speedy over everybody's feety.
8. Oh, I wish I were a little radio...
   I'd go click. (Just say this one time as if turning off the song.)

Learning Songs

Incorporate these songs into learning activities or change the words to reflect the skills and concepts that you are working on.

FIVE LITTLE DOUGHNUTS (Tune: Five Little Ducks That I Once Knew)

Five little doughnuts   (hold up five fingers)
In a bakery shop
Round and fat   (stretch arms out in front as if fat)
With sugar on top.   (pat hands on head)
Along came (child's name)
With a penny one day.
He/she bought a doughnut
And he/she took it away.
(Continue until all the doughnuts are gone using a different child's name for each verse. Make doughnuts out of paper and let each child put down a real penny as they take a doughnut away.)

MONKEYS (Finger Play)

Five little monkeys hanging from a tree,   (hold up 5 fingers)
Teasing Mr. Alligator,
"Can't catch me!" (point finger and say teasingly)
"Can't catch me!"
Along comes Mr. Alligator   (put arms together and move hands like an
Slow as slow can be   alligator)
And SNAP! (clap)
(Continue until all the monkeys are gone.)

HOT DOGS (Finger Play)

Five little hot dogs frying in the pan,   (hold up five fingers)
The grease got hot and one went BAM!   (clap hands)
Four little hot dogs...etc.
No little hot dogs frying in the pan,
The pan got hot and it went BAM!

PHONE NUMBER (Tune: Twinkle, Twinkle Little Star)

931–2912
931–2912
931–2912
931–2912
931–2912
I can say my phone number for you.
(Help each child learn his/her phone number, address, etc., with this tune.)

THREE BLUE PIGEONS (Tune: Row Your Boat)

Three blue pigeons sitting on the wall.
Three blue pigeons sitting on the wall.
One flew away, OHHH!
(Say this line and pretend to cry.)
2. Two blue pigeons. . . . .
3. One blue pigeon. . . . .
4. No blue pigeons sitting on the wall.
   No blue pigeons sitting on the wall.
   One flew back—Yeah! (Say this verse and pretend to cheer.)
5. One blue pigeon. . . . .
6. Two blue pigeons. . . . .
7. Three blue pigeons. . . . .

(You can change the pigeons' color to reinforce the color you are working on.
Children also enjoy acting this out by being the pigeons.)

MY SCHOOL (Tune: Mary Had a Little Lamb)

The name of my school is (school name) _____ , _____
The name of my school is _____ .
That's the name of my school.
(Use this song to learn the teacher's name, cook, director, etc.)

WRITING (Tune: Mulberry Bush)

This is the way we make a (letter)
Make a (letter), make a (letter)
It is easy as can be,
To make a _____ .
(Sing as you practice writing letters and numerals.)

COLOR SONG (Tune: I'm a Little Teapot)

If you're wearing (color) stand up quick.
If you're wearing (color) stand up quick.
If you're wearing (color) stand up quick.
Take a bow and then you sit.
(Sing various colors while children wearing that color stand up and bow.)

LITTLE BOX (Tune: Polly-Wolly Doodle)

I wish I had a little (<u>color</u>) box to put my (<u>name child wearing that color</u>) in.
I'd take her/him out and go kiss, kiss, kiss. (kiss in air)
And put them back again.
(Continue using different colors and children.)

COLORS (Tune: Bingo)

There was a girl who had a bird and "Green" was her name-o.
G–R–E–E–N (clap on each letter)
G–R–E–E–N
G–R–E–E–N
And "Green" was her name-o.
2. Boy who had a cow and Brown was his name-o.
3. Girl who had a cat and Orange was her name-o.
4. Boy who had a horse and Black was his name-o.
5. Girl who had a pig and White was her name-o.
6. Make up your own verses.
(You can also spell children's names with this tune.)

MARY' LETTERS (Tune: Mary Had a Little Lamb)

Mary had a little (<u>b</u>).
Little (<u>b</u>), little (<u>b</u>).
Mary had a little (<u>b</u>).
" <u>b</u> ", " <u>b</u> ", " <u>b</u> ".
(Sing for various letters making the letter sound in the last line.)

NAME SONG (Tune: Frere Jacques)

<u>S</u> is for <u>Susan</u>
<u>S</u> is for <u>Susan</u>
<u>S</u> <u>S</u> <u>S</u>, <u>S</u> <u>S</u> <u>S</u>.
<u>S</u> is for <u>Susan</u>
<u>S</u> is for <u>Susan</u>
<u>S</u> <u>S</u> <u>S</u>, <u>S</u> <u>S</u> <u>S</u>.
(Insert different letters and children or objects that begin with that sound.)

COMMUNITY HELPERS (Tune: Do You Know the Muffin Man?)

Do you know the dentist
the dentist, the dentist?
Do you know the dentist
Who keeps your teeth so clean?
(Use other helpers and the job they do.)

DAYS OF THE WEEK (Tune: The Bear Went over the Mountain)

There are seven days in the week,

Seven days in the week,
Seven days in the week,
And I can name each one.
There is Monday, Tuesday, and Wednesday, Thursday, Friday, and Saturday.
The last day is Sunday,
And I have named each one.

Finger Plays and Chants

These rhymes will keep little ones entertained and little hands busy!

TWO APPLES

Way up high in the apple tree (point up in the air and look up)
Two little apples smiled down at me. (hold up two fingers and look down)
I shook that tree as hard as I could. (pretend to shake)
Down came the apples, (move arms downward)
Mmmmmmmmmmmmmmmmmm, they were good! (pat stomach)

TEDDY BEAR

Teddy bear, teddy bear, turn around. (turn around)
Teddy bear, teddy bear, touch the ground. (touch ground)
Teddy bear, teddy bear, tie your shoes. (pretend to tie shoe)
Teddy bear, teddy bear, read your news. (hold up hands as if reading)
Teddy bear, teddy bear, go upstairs. (lift knees as you walk)
Teddy bear, teddy bear, say your prayers. (fold hands)
Teddy bear, teddy bear, turn out the lights. (pretend to turn off switch)
Teddy bear, teddy bear, say good night. (fold hands and lay down head)

A LITTLE MOUSE

A little mouse hid softly in a hole, (hold up right thumb)
A little mouse hid softly in a hole. (make a fist with left hand and insert right
                                        thumb)
When all was quiet as quiet can be,
Sh! Sh! Sh!
Out popped he. (pull out right thumb)

THE ELEPHANT

Elephants walk like this and that. (bend over and sway)
They're terribly big and terribly fat. (stretch out arms)
They have no hands, they have no toes, (shake head "no")
But goodness gracious, what a nose. (extend one arm to make a trunk)

CAPTAIN AND HIS MEN

One, two, three, four, five in a row   (hold up fingers on right hand)
A captain and his men.
And on the other side you know
Are six, seven, eight, nine, ten. (hold up fingers on left hand)
They marched to the left, they marched to the right, (move left, move right)
Then they all marched out of sight. (march behind your back)

CATERPILLAR

A caterpillar crawled (extend left arm and crawl right index finger up it like
To the top of a tree.   a caterpillar)
"I think I'll take a nap," said he. (wiggle right index finger)
So under the leaf he began to creep. (move under left hand)
He spun a cocoon and he fell asleep. (make fist around index finger)
For six long months he slept in that cocoon bed,
Till spring came along and said,
"Wake up! Wake up! You sleepy head." (shake arms)
Out of the leaf he did cry, (hook thumbs and spread fingers to make a butterfly)
"Lo, I am a butterfly."

FISH

One, two, three, four, five (hold up fingers on right hand)
I caught a fish alive. (clap hands as if catching something)
Six, seven, eight, nine, ten. (continue counting fingers on left hand)
I let it go again. (extend hands as if letting go)
Why did you let that fishy go?
Because he bit my finger so.
Which finger did he bite?
My little finger on the right. (hold up little finger on right hand)

THE BUNNY HOLE

Here is a bunny (hold two fingers up on right hand)
With ears so funny, (wiggle two fingers)
And here's his hole in the ground. (put left hand on hip)
At the slightest noise he hears
He pricks up his ears, (straighten two fingers)
Then hops to his hole in the ground. (hop bunny into hole)
2. Here is daddy bunny. (say with deep voice)
3. Here is baby bunny. (say with high, soft voice)

TEN IN THE BED

There were ten in the bed (hold up ten fingers)
And the little one said,

"Roll over, I'm crowded."
So they all rolled over and one fell out.   (move to left in arch)
There were nine in the bed   (hold up nine fingers)
And the little one said,
"Roll over, I'm crowded."
So they all rolled over and one fell out.
There were eight in the bed,
(Continue until there is one left.)
There was one in the bed   (hold up little finger)
And the little one said,
"I'm sleepy!"   (rub eyes)

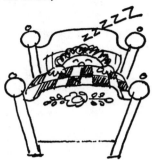

BEAR HUNT (Children repeat each line)

Going on a bear hunt....	(slap thighs to beat)
I'm not afraid....	(slap thighs)
There's a tall tree....	(put hand over eyes and look)
We can't go under it....	(shake head "no")
We can't go through it....	(shake head)
Let's climb up it....	(extend arms and pretend to climb)
There's some tall grass....	(slap thighs)
We can't go over it....	(shake head)
We can't go around it....	(shake head)
Let's go through it....	(brush hands together)
There's a river....	(slap thighs)
We can't go over it....	(shake head)
We can't go around it....	(shake head)
Let's swim across it....	(move arms as if swimming)
There's a cave....	(slap thighs)
Let's go in it....	(slap thighs)
It's dark in here....	(crawl on hands and knees)
It's cold in here....	(shiver)
I feel something furry....	(stretch out hands as if feeling something)
I feel a cold nose....	
I feel some long claws....	

I feel some teeth....
Oh! It's a bear!....
(Quickly reverse motions swimming across the river, going through the grass, climbing the tree, going in the house, and shutting the door.)
Whew!....
I went on a bear hunt....
And I wasn't afraid!.... (shake head and point thumbs at self as if boasting)

WHO STOLE THE COOKIE?

Class says: Who stole the cookie from the cookie jar?
(child's name) stole the cookie from the cookie jar.
Child says: Who me?
Class says: Yes you.
Child says: Couldn't be.
Class says: Then who?
Child says: (names another child) stole the cookie from the cookie jar.
(Continue going around the room using each child's name. The last person answers, "Possibly!" when asked if they stole the cookie.)

CHICA-BOOM, CHICA-BOOM (Children repeat each line of this chant)

I said a boom chica-boom....
I said a boom chica-boom....
I said a boom chica-roca, chica-roca, chica-boom....
Uh huh!....
Oh yeah!....
One more time....
2. Baby version—say in baby talk with fingers in mouth.
3. Prissy version—say sophisticatedly.
4. Underwater version—put forefinger between lips and gently move up and down.
5. Make up your own silly verses.

HICKLETY-PICKLETY BUMBLEBEE

Hicklety-picklety bumblebee,   (slap thighs to the beat of the chant)
Who can say their name for me? (slap thighs)
(say child's name)—(repeat name)
Clap it. (say child's name in two syllables) (clap twice)
Whisper it.   (whisper child's name with two beats)
No sound. (mouth child's name)
Hicklety-picklety bumblebee....
(begin again slapping thighs and using another child's name)

HI! MY NAME IS JOE (children join in saying this)

Hi! My name is Joe.
I've got a wife and three kids and I work in a button factory.

One day my boss came to me and said, "Joe, are you busy?"
I said, "No,"
"Then work with your right hand." (start moving right hand up and down)
2. "Work with your left hand" (move left hand up and down with right)
3. "Work with your right foot" (add right leg motion with hands)
4. "Work with your left foot" (add left leg motion to others)
5. "Work with your head" (nod head as well as moving hands and legs)
6. "Joe, are you busy?" I said, "Yes!" (shout out "Yes!" and stop other movements)

APPLES AND BANANAS

I like to eat. I like to eat.
I like to eat, eat apples and bananas.
I like to eat. I like to eat.
I like to eat, eat apples and bananas.
2. Use the long A sound for each vowel in the chant.
3. Use the long E sound.
4. Use the long I sound.
5. Use the long O sound.
6. Use the long U sound.

PEANUT BUTTER

Refrain: Peanut—peanut butter—and jelly   (shake arms to the
         Peanut—peanut butter—and jelly   right in the air on
                                              "peanut butter" and
                                              down to the left on
                                              "jelly")

First you take the peanuts and you pick 'em,   (pretend to pick)
you pick 'em, you pick 'em, pick 'em, pick 'em.
    Refrain
Then you take the peanuts and you crack 'em,   (pretend to crack)
you crack 'em, you crack 'em, crack 'em, crack 'em.
    Refrain
Then you take the peanuts and you crush 'em,   (rub hands together)
you crush 'em, you crush 'em, crush 'em, crush 'em.
    Refrain
Then you take the peanuts and you spread 'em, (spread on one hand)
you spread 'em, you spread 'em, spread 'em spread 'em.
    Refrain
Then you take the jelly and you spread it,   (spread on one hand)
you spread it, you spread it, spread it, spread it.
    Refrain
Then you take the sandwich and you smush it,   (rub hands together)
you smush it, you smush it, smush it, smush it.
    Refrain
Then you take the sandwich and you eat it...   (close your mouth as
(mumble, mumble, mumble, mumble.)   if stuck together
    Refrain   with peanut butter)

MR. SMITH AND MR. BROWN

Here's Mr. Smith. (hold up right thumb)
And here's Mr. Brown. (hold up left thumb)
One day Mr. Smith opened his door (open fingers on right hand)
and he went outside and closed his door. (stick out right thumb and close
It was so beautiful outside he decided   fingers into fist)
to take a walk to Mr. Brown's house.   (move thumb and arm up and
He walked up the hills and down the hills.   down, up and down)
When he got to Mr. Brown's house he knocked (knock on left fist)
on the door and said, "Oh, Mr. Brown. Oh, Mr. Brown."
"I guess he's not home."
So Mr. Smith walked up the hills and down the hills. (move right hand up and down)
When he got home he opened his door and   (open fingers and tuck in right
he went inside.   thumb)
On the second day. . . (This is repeated with Mr. Brown going to visit Mr. Smith.)
On the third day. . . (They both go visit each other and run into each other on
the way. They dance around and play and have fun, then they both go home, shut
their doors, and go to sleep.)

Change the characters in this story for some fun.

How Can You Guide Children Through Creative Movement?

Creative movement gives children an outlet for their energy and encourages them to use their bodies to express their feelings and imagination. Since there is no right or wrong way, there is total success with creative movement. Creative movement can be spontaneous, or you can guide it with one of these activities:

Space—Children need to learn how to find their own space and stay in it. Carpet squares, hula hoops, jump ropes, or tape on the floor can help children establish boundaries.

Warm-up—Do stretches and deep breathing exercises before you begin. "Stretch your arms as wide as you can. As high as you can. Can you be stiff like a soldier? Now be floppy like a rag doll. Be a balloon and fill yourself up with air. Now slowly let it all out."

Animal Movements—Challenge children to imitate animals.
Can you. . .fly like a butterfly?
    swim like a fish?
    waddle like a duck?
    gallop like a horse?
    jump like a kangaroo?
    hop like a bunny?

Feelings—Ask children to show you different feelings with their face, body parts, and whole bodies.
Show me. . .a happy face. A happy arm. A happy body.

a sad face.
an angry face.
a surprised face.
a scared face.

Nursery Rhymes—Have children say and act out nursery rhymes and songs, such as:

Jack and Jill
Humpty Dumpty
Mary Had a Little Lamb
Three Blind Mice
Hey, Diddle, Diddle

Pantomime—Pantomime is like watching television with no sound because you use your body to talk instead of words. Ask children to pantomime the following actions:

waking up in the morning
getting dressed
picking flowers
climbing a tree
laughing
eating spaghetti
riding a tricycle

Pretend—Pretending comes natural for children because they are much less uninhibited than adults. Pretend you are:

fairies
monsters
twinkling stars
rain
sunshine
astronauts on the moon
robots
seeds growing

Guess What I Am—One child at a time acts out an animal or thing while classmates try and guess.

Mirror—Divide children into pairs. One child is to be the mirror and do exactly what the other person does. Switch places after a few minutes. (This is also fun to do to music.)

Touch—Children find a partner. Ask them to touch various body parts with their partner, such as hand to hand, back to back, ear to ear, etc.

Statue—This activity can be done individually or in small groups. Give children several minutes to decide what kind of statue they would like to create for their classmates. The groups then form their statues and hold it while classmates observe.

Dance—Put on music and let children move spontaneously. Play music and tell children to freeze when the music stops. Ask children to make different parts of their body dance to the music, such as their head, arms, shoulders, feet, etc.

Role-Play—Assign children to different roles and have them act out various life situations such as:

> going to a birthday party
> getting lost in a store
> finding $100
> having a toy taken away
> finding your house on fire

What Musical Instruments Can Children Make and Play?

Children need to experiment and explore with instruments to see how sounds are made and how they can be changed. You can purchase musical instruments or you can make your own.

Body Instruments—How many different sounds can you make with your body?

> clap your hands
> snap your fingers
> slap your thighs
> brush your hands together
> stamp your feet
> whistle
> sing
> What else? What else?

Drums—Cover a coffee can or oatmeal box with a child's drawing or yarn.
- Use wooden bowls, pots, or pans.
- To make drumsticks cover the end of a pencil with cotton, wrap it in fabric, and secure it in place with a rubber band.

Shakers—Put beans or a bell between two paper cups and tape them where they join.
- Put beans or popcorn kernels between two paper plates and staple the edges together.
- Place beans or buttons in a coffee can or margarine tub.
- Color a toilet paper roll. Insert beans and tape the ends.
- Make a slit in a tennis ball and fill it with pebbles.
- Put popcorn kernels in a paper sack and shake.

Kazoo—Color a toilet paper roll. Stretch wax paper over one end and secure with a rubber band. Punch a hole in the tube 1 inch from the end and hum.

Glasses and Bottles—Take several glasses or soft drink bottles and fill them with

different amounts of water. Tap with a spoon to make a sound. (The more water you use, the higher the sound will be.)

Rhythm Sticks—Use two pencils, or a broom handle or dowel rod cut in 12″ lengths.

Spoons—Hit two metal spoons together.

Bells—String jingle bells on a 6-inch piece of elastic and tie the ends.

Cymbals—Pot lids and pie pans make a loud sound, but two paper plates make a soft sound. Thimbles on fingers make tiny cymbals.

Banjo—Stretch several different-sized rubber bands over the bottom of a shoe box and strum.

Sand Blocks—Glue sandpaper to two pieces of wood.

Once you have constructed your instruments, you can sing "Old MacDonald Had a Band," naming and playing instruments. You can sing "This is the way we play our instruments" to the tune of "Mulberry Bush." Children will also enjoy playing their instruments to records or pretending they are a marching band in a parade.

How Can You Purchase Records, Tapes, and Videos?

There is a wealth of quality music produced especially for children. Most of the records and tapes are reasonably priced and will give you and your children years of pleasure and entertainment. The following distributors carry a wide selection and will be happy to send you a catalog if you call or write them:

Children's Book and Music Center
2500 Santa Monica Boulevard
Santa Monica, CA 90404
800–443–1856

Educational Record Center
Building 400/Suite 400
1575 Northside Drive
Atlanta, GA 30318–4298
800–438–1637

Kimbo Educational
10 North Third Avenue
Long Beach, NJ 07740
800–631–2187

These are some of the most popular recording artists for the younger set. Their music is fun, up-beat, and educational.

Steve and Greg	Ella Jenkins
Raffi	Hap Palmer
Sharon, Lois, and Bram	Tom Glazer
Burl Ives	Fred Penner
Rosenshontz	Wee Sing
Sesame Street	Disney

11

SMALL MOTOR SKILLS

The small muscles in children's fingers and hands need a great deal of practice and exercise in the preschool years. This section will provide you with a variety of interesting activities for developing small motor skills, including prewriting skills and eye-hand coordination.

What Are Small Motor Skills?

Small motor skills are often referred to as fine motor skills, manual dexterity, manipulative skills, or perceptual motor skills. The purpose of small motor activities is to develop the small muscles in the fingers and hands, as well as to improve eye-hand coordination. Development of small muscles will contribute to the child's ability to write and read in future years. Further, small motor activities can increase the child's attention span, encourage persistence in a task, foster independence, and develop problem-solving and thinking skills.

How Do Small Motor Skills Develop?

Observe the hands of a two-year-old, then observe the hands of a five-year-old. The difference in their physical appearance clearly suggests the different levels of ability and maturation. Small motor activities must be geared to the child's age and level of development. The two-year-old simply does not have the small muscle development and motor control to cut, color, or write as the five-year-old child does.

Small muscle development takes a great deal of practice and exercise during the preschool years. Capitalize on children's interests and give them daily experiences that are fun, yet challenging. Start off with large objects, such as big paint brushes and crayons, large beads to string, and big puzzles with just a few pieces. As children master these activities, move to increasingly smaller objects. In addition to going from large to small, remember to go from simple activities to more complex tasks. Children should progress from tearing paper with their fingers, to snipping with scissors, cutting on lines, cutting curves, and finally, cutting out shapes and objects. They should move from scribbling, to drawing simple lines and circles, to making more complex shapes and writing letters.

What Activities Will Promote Small Motor Development in Children?

Children need experiences with a wide variety of manipulative materials and projects. "Please touch" and "hands-on" are key principles underlying all small motor activities. Children will develop muscles in their hands and fingers through carefully planned centers, as well as while participating in art projects and music, building with blocks, cooking, playing in the dramatics area, and many other activities during the school day.

These are some simple activities with familiar objects that will interest children while developing their small muscle coordination:

Puzzles—There are many wooden, cardboard, and plastic puzzles that you can purchase for your classroom, or you can make your own from food boxes. First, cut off the front of a cereal box or detergent box. Next, cut the box into 3–10 pieces (depending on the ability of your students). Finally, put the pieces in a ziplock bag.
- Another way to make puzzles is to glue colorful magazine pictures to cardboard, then cut them into puzzle pieces.

- Make puzzles of each child's name. Write the child's name on a sentence strip or sheet of paper, then cut between the letters. Put the pieces in an envelope on which you have written the child's name.

To make puzzles more difficult, ask children to do them with their eyes closed or with a blindfold on. Can they put the puzzle together outside the frame or upside down?

Clay and Play Dough—Modeling materials provide excellent opportunities for children to exercise small muscles. (Make your own mixture with the recipes in the creative arts chapter.) Old plastic placemats or lunch trays will help children keep their dough in a specific area. Add rolling pins and cookie cutters, gadgets that make prints (such as spools, straws, forks), or toy dishes for variety. Children will also enjoy cutting the dough with scissors or a plastic knife.

Sewing—Make your own sewing cards from styrofoam meat trays, paper plates, plastic lids, or cardboard. Draw a picture with permanent markers, then hole-punch around the edges. Use shoelaces, plastic cord, or yarn whose ends have been dipped in glue to sew with. Children can also sew on burlap with a large plastic needle.

Stringing—Young children are capable of stringing large beads, cardboard tubes cut in 1-inch rings, spools, or pretzel twists. Older preschoolers can string buttons, straws cut in ½-inch pieces, or cereal and pasta with holes.

Hammering—Cut a stump of wood 12 inches high. Lightly tap 2-inch nails into the stump, then allow children to pound them in the rest of the way. Younger children can hammer golf tees or push pins into styrofoam with plastic hammers.

Twisting and Turning—Collect several sizes of plastic jars and lids. Children can fit the lids to the appropriate jars and screw them on and off. Buy plumber's pipes and fittings or nuts and bolts at a hardware store for other twisting experiences.

Hole-Punching—A fun way to develop muscles in the hand is with a hole-punch. Just give children a shoe box to punch in, some scrap paper, and they're ready to begin. (Save the holes for art projects.)

Cutting—Scissors also provide exercise for hands and fingers. Supervise young children with scissors and talk about how to use them safely. Offer right- and left-handed scissors to children and color code them so they can tell the difference. Start by teaching children how to snip, then how to cut straight lines, curves, and more complicated shapes. Vary the paper they can cut by using newspaper, construction paper, wrapping paper, magazines, wallpaper, paper sacks, etc.

Construction—Have children duplicate construction patterns with unit blocks, colored cubes, Legos, or other building toys. Build bridges, towers, stairs, and other designs and challenge children to copy them. Make cards with patterns that children can reproduce with blocks.

Inserting—Little ones think it's fun to put things in, then take them out. Make a simple game by cutting a hole in the lid of a shoe box. Children can insert small objects, then take off the lid and retrieve them. You can also cut an opening in the plastic lid of a coffee can and use poker chips, pennies, or golf tees to drop in.

Pinching—It's a good small motor exercise to pinch clothespins and attach them to a hanger. Children will also enjoy hanging up doll clothes or artwork on a clothesline in the classroom.

Flannel Board—Little fingers can put felt pieces on a flannel board and tell stories, make sets, or complete a pattern.

Put Together—Children can make necklaces and chains by hooking paper clips together. Older children can hook large safety pins together.

Dressing—Stuffed animals, dolls, and old baby clothes will provide children with dressing activities. Nail an old sneaker to a wooden board to practice tying and

lacing. You can also make your own dressing board by cutting out the zipper, buttons, snaps, and buckles from old clothing and tacking them to a heavy board or sheet of cardboard.

Pegboards—Initially, children will be challenged simply by putting pegs in holes. As they advance, ask them to reproduce shapes, letters, or other color designs and patterns.

Tongs and Tweezers—Children can use ice tongs to move nuts, sweet gum balls, or small toys from one tray to another. They can also fill up an ice cube tray or egg carton with small objects using the tongs. Use tweezers and smaller objects, such as birdseed or buttons, as children develop more coordination.

Pouring and Spooning—Children can practice pouring with small plastic pitchers and cups in the classroom sink or at a water table. For variety, have them pour beans or rice over a plastic tub. Give them a spoon and ask them to fill up a margarine tub or jar with the beans or rice. (These activities can also be done at a sand table or outside in a sandbox.)

Basters and Eye Droppers—Fill a container with colored water. Using a baster, have children transfer the water to another container. Do the same activity with an eye dropper and ask children to fill up a small bottle.

Templates and Patterns—Make cardboard patterns and templates for children to trace around or inside. Plastic lids from margarine tubs and styrofoam meat trays can also be used to make patterns and templates. (Use the shape and holiday patterns in the Appendix for these.)

Washing and Scrubbing—Fill a tub with soapy water and allow children to wash doll clothes and toy dishes. They will also enjoy scrubbing rocks or toys with a small brush.

When Should Children Begin Writing?

Children need to scribble and should have many experiences with crayons, pencils, and unlined paper before presenting them with formal writing instruction. It is common for them to switch back and forth from the right to the left hand as they begin writing. Allow them to choose which is more comfortable for them. Children should never be pressured, and you certainly should not criticize their work or expect perfection and neatness. However, you can encourage them to participate and advance at their own rate with these pre-writing activities:

Writing Area—Set up a writing center in your room with lined and unlined paper, blank books, a chalkboard, letter stencils, pencils, crayons, markers, a magic slate, picture dictionary, words to copy, etc.

Finger Exercises—Hold your fingers in the air. Can you make them stiff? Floppy? Make it rain with your fingers. Make your fingers roll like a ball. Can they hop like a frog? Practice making imaginary strokes, letters, and numerals in the air with your fingers.

Tracing—Use sentence strips or file folders to make a tracing game with lines similar to those below. Laminate or cover with clear contact. Children can trace over the lines from left to right with an erasable marker or crayon.

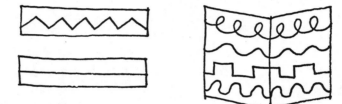

Copy Cat—Ask children to reproduce simple shapes and objects on paper, the chalkboard, or on laminated game boards.

Follow the Dots—Have children connect dotted lines to make objects.

Name Games—Print the child's name in dotted lines at the top of a page. The child traces over it, then continues to practice writing it underneath.
- Write the child's name with glue, then sprinkle with glitter or have the child trace over it with beans, yarn, crumpled tissue paper, etc.
- Have the child write his/her name in a sand tray, with finger paints, with chalk on the sidewalk, on the chalkboard, with colored pencils, and other media.

Strokes—Provide children with practice making these simple strokes used in manuscript writing.

/ / / / /   O O O O o o o o

| | | | | | | | — — — —

Writing Numerals—These poems will make numeral writing more fun and will help children remember the proper strokes.

One is easy,
one is fine.
Pull down straight
and make a line.

Go around and slant down
to make a two.
Then push back straight,
is what you should do.

Make half a circle,
make another half you see.
That's the way
to make a three.

Straight down and push over,
Then pull down some more.
There you have
the numeral four.

For five pull down,
then go around.
Make a line on top
and then you stop.

Circle to the left,
then make a loop.
Six looks like
a cowboy's hoop.

First push over,
then slant down straight.
Seven comes before
the numeral eight.

Make an "s" that
looks like a snake.
Curve back up
and you have an eight.

Make a circle,
then a line.
Now you've made
the numeral nine.

A straight line and a circle
will make a ten.
Go back to one
and start again.

Manuscript Writing—Manuscript writing is the style most frequently presented to young children. All letters are made from basic strokes (lines and circles), and this is the style most often seen in books and print. As a teacher, you should model good writing for children on everything you do. Many adults print all words for children in capital letters, but this is incorrect. You should only capitalize the first letter of names and other proper nouns, as well as the first letter in each sentence. Use the accompanying letter chart for proper letter formation, or contact the school system where your students will attend for a copy of their letter style.

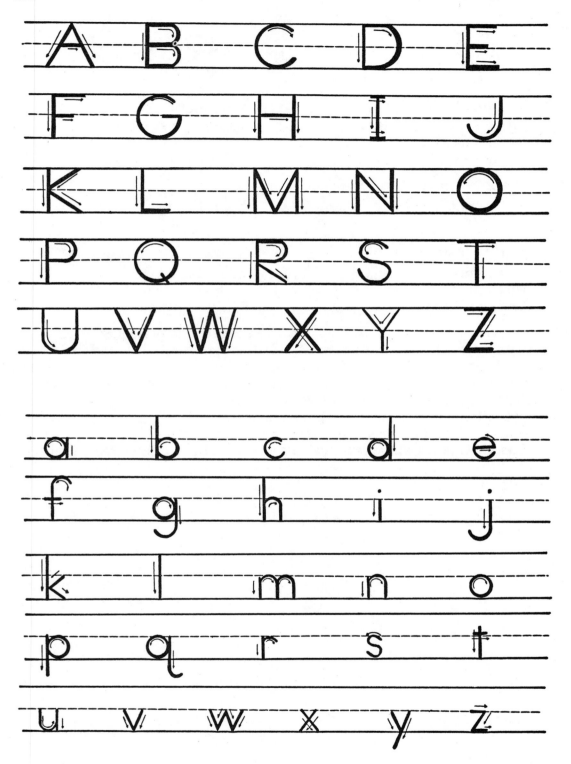

12

LARGE MOTOR SKILLS

This section focuses on the importance of developing large motor skills and physical fitness in young children. Favorite indoor and outdoor games are described, as well as ideas for making and using simple homemade equipment.

Why Should Motor Development and Fitness Be Stressed in Preschool?

Although adults are increasingly involved in exercise and sports, the percentage of children who are overweight and out-of-shape is growing dramatically. Television is a major factor in children's lack of fitness, as are machines which do so much of our work for us. Adult models (parents and teachers) who have an inactive life style and poor health habits also have a negative impact on children. Even though there is a current emphasis on academics, teachers should remember that it is equally important to develop children's physical skills.

It is natural for young children to move, and to derive a great deal of pleasure from doing so. As they move they develop strength, coordination, body awareness, self-control, and confidence. Movement activities can make children healthier and happier; can relieve stress; can serve as an outlet for energy; and can help children concentrate and perform better. Movement activities also provide opportunities for social interaction and can be a vehicle for teaching major concepts.

What Large Motor Skills Should Be Developed and Practiced?

Large motor skills, often referred to as gross motor skills, develop in children more rapidly than small motor skills. All children progress through the same steps and stages, although their individual rate of development will vary greatly. For example, most children will not skip until the age of four or five, but there will often be three-year-olds who master this skill. Further, advanced academic ability does not necessarily parallel motor achievement. A five-year-old may be able to read a book, but he or she may not be able to skip or catch a ball. What this means to you as a teacher is that every child has different strengths and weaknesses. You should assess children to determine which skills they have acquired, then build on these skills while providing them with experiences to improve or develop new skills. Observe, demonstrate, offer suggestions, and praise their efforts. It is often effective to work with small groups of children or individuals on a specific skill, or try to make up a game that involves that skill. Many times children are their "own best teachers" and will learn from each other.

In early childhood years, children will master motor skills that will provide the foundation for all future movement and exercise. They will progress from simple movements to more complex tasks and combinations. These are some fundamental skills that children will acquire during their first six years:

walk (forward and backward)
run
climb stairs (alternating feet)
tiptoe
march
jump on two feet
balance on right foot; on left foot
hop on right foot; on left foot
walk on a balance beam

Life is not a spectator sport!

gallop
skip
kick a ball
throw a ball and catch a ball
swing
ride a tricycle

Children need a variety of experiences, activities, equipment, and practice to master these skills. They need *time* to play—time alone, with friends, and in structured and unstructured activities; they need *space* to play in—safe and challenging areas indoors and outside; they need *equipment*—different types of toys and sports equipment to play with and climb on; and they need to be allowed to make *choices.*

Why Play Games?

You should provide children with many opportunities for free time and spontaneous play, as well as planned activities and games. Games encourage children to cooperate, develop motor skills, and are fun. Teachers who enjoy playing with their children and make games fun usually do not have any trouble getting children involved. You will remember some of the games described here from your own childhood, while others will be new to you. Many of these games will need to be adapted to the abilities and interests of the group you teach.

Here are a few suggestions for introducing games to children:

1. Choose simple group games with a lot of active involvement.
2. Tell children the name of the game and explain it as briefly as possible.
3. Point out the boundary lines and demonstrate the use of the equipment involved.
4. Keep the rules few and flexible.
5. Walk through the game several times before playing it.
6. Work on playing one game at a time until children are familiar with it and feel confident playing it.
7. Accept the children's input as to how the game should be played.
8. Emphasize the fun of participating, not winning and losing.

What Indoor Activities and Games Do Children Enjoy?

It's raining again! You can't go outside and the children are restless and bored. HELP!

Jack Be Nimble

Place a candlestick (plastic bottle or block) in the middle of the circle. Children take turns jumping over it while the rest of the class says the nursery rhyme:

> Jack be nimble,
> Jack be quick.
> Jack jump over the candlestick.

Follow the Leader

The class lines up behind a chosen leader. Whatever the leader does, the rest of the class must follow. The leader may hop, march, skip, crawl under a table, or perform other actions. Give several children a turn to play leader. (This is also fun to play outdoors.)

Simon Says

The leader (teacher or a child) is Simon. Simon gives various commands to the class which they must follow exactly if it is introduced by "Simon Says." If "Simon Says" does not come before the command, the children should not act. If they do, they are out of the game and must sit down. The last one standing becomes the new "Simon."

Muffin Man

One child is blindfolded and stands in the middle of the circle. The other children walk around and sing, "Do you know the Muffin Man?" The teacher taps one child who walks up to "it." "It" must try and identify him/her by feeling their face.

Doggie and Bone

One child is selected to be the Doggie. The Doggie sits with his/her back to the rest of the class and covers his/her eyes. A bone (eraser or block) is placed behind the Doggie. The teacher taps one child who sneaks up behind the Doggie, steals the bone, barks several times, then returns to their seat. The class says, "Doggie, Doggie, where's your bone? Somebody stole it from your home." The Doggie gets three guesses to identify who stole the bone.

Huckle Berry Beanstalk

Choose two or three children to leave the room. The teacher hides a small object in plain sight. When the children return to the room the others give clues by saying "cold" (far away from the object), "warm" (getting close to the object), and "hot" (right next to the object). The first one to spot it yells "huckle berry beanstalk" and becomes the next person to hide the object.

Hot Potato

Children stand in a circle and pass around a beanbag or toy (hot potato). Music is played, but when the music stops the one who is holding the beanbag must sit down. The game is played until there is only one child left standing.

Cats and Kittens

One child is selected to be the mother cat and three others are chosen to be her kittens. Mother cat leaves the room while her kittens hide. When mother cat returns, her kittens "meow." She then goes around the room and finds them.

Going on a Trip

The children sit in a circle. The first one says, "I'm going on a trip and I'm taking (names anything)." The second repeats what the first person said and adds one new item. This continues until a child forgets the items, and then the game starts over. (For older children, have them name items in alphabetical order, such as A–apples, B–books, C–cap, etc.)

Gossip

Children sit in a circle. The leader or teacher whispers a sentence in one child's ear. He or she whispers what they have heard to the next person and so on around the circle. The last child must tell everyone what he/she has heard. The leader then repeats what was really said.

I Spy!

The teacher starts the game by picking out an object in the room and saying, "I spy something (names a color)." Children take turns guessing what it could be. The first one to guess becomes "it." (Besides spying objects of different colors, you can use beginning sounds or shapes.)

Detective

The children sit in a circle. One child is "it" and leaves the room. The child changes one thing on their person before returning to the room. For example, the teacher can suggest that they could roll down a sock, unbutton a button, take off a bracelet, etc. When "it" returns to the room the other children play "detective" and try to guess what is changed or missing. The first one to do so then becomes "it."

Lost Child

The teacher plays the mother and one child is the police officer. The mother pretends to cry and says, "Oh, dear! I've lost my child! Can you help me find my child?" The police officer says, "What does your child look like?" The mother describes the child's clothing, hair color, etc. The police officer walks around the room, picks out the child based on the description, and returns the lost child to the mother.

Roll Ball

Children sit in a circle with their legs stretched out. The teacher takes a beach ball or sponge ball and rolls it to a child saying, "I roll the ball to _____ , and he rolls it back to me." Continue rolling the ball to all the children in the circle. The children then take turns calling a name and rolling the ball to that person. (You can play a similar game outside by throwing a ball or beanbag.)

Cinderella

All children take off one shoe and put it in the middle of the circle. The children then hide their eyes while the teacher or "it" hides their shoes in plain sight around the room. When the teacher claps his/her hands 12 times, the children try to find their shoe, put it on, and return to their seat.

Mousie–Mousie

One person is "it" and stands while the other children sit in a circle. "It" says, "Mousie–Mousie, how quiet can you be? When I clap my hands, one-two-three, we shall see." "It" claps his/her hands three times, then looks around the room for the person who is sitting the most quiet and still. "It" taps that person, who becomes the next "it."

Dont' Topple the Tower

Give each child a block and ask them to sit in a circle. Start by putting one block in the middle of the circle. As you go around the circle, each child adds his or her block to the top of the tower. When the tower "topples," begin again.

Four Corners

Number each of the corners in your room. One person is "it" and hides his/her eyes and slowly counts to 10. As "it" counts the other children quietly tiptoe to a corner. "It" says "freeze" and calls out the number of one corner. The children who are in that corner are out of the game and must sit in the middle of the room in the stew pot. "It" begins counting to 10 again as the rest of the children tiptoe to a new corner. The game continues until there is one child left who then becomes "it."

Musical Chairs

Place chairs in two rows back-to-back facing outward. (There should be one more player than chairs.) When the music starts, all the children march in a circle around the chairs. When the music stops, all the children find a chair and sit down as quickly as they can. The child left standing is out of the game and another chair is removed. The game continues until there is only one child and one chair left. (Vary this game by using carpet squares or construction paper and calling it "Magic Carpets.")

Quiet Touch

The first player quietly touches an object in the room. The second player touches that object and one other object. The third child touches the first two in sequence, then touches a third object. The game continues until a player misses, then the game starts over.

Win, Lose, or Draw

Divide the class into two teams. Let the children take turns drawing simple objects, nursery rhymes, songs, book titles, etc. while their teammates try and guess what it is.

Preschool Trivia

Divide the class into two teams. Alternate asking them simple questions, such as, "How many blind mice were there?" "What state do you live in?" "What color do you get when you mix blue and yellow?" "What day comes between Tuesday and Thursday?"

London Bridge

Two children join hands and raise their arms to make a bridge. The following song is sung as the rest of the class makes a line and walks under their hands:

London Bridge is falling down,
falling down, falling down.
London Bridge is falling down,
My fair lady.

A child is captured in the last line of the song and gently swung back and forth as the second verse of the song is sung:

Take the keys and lock them up,
lock them up, lock them up.
Take the keys and lock them up,
My fair lady.

The captured child takes the place of one child forming the bridge and the game continues.

Did You Ever See a Lassie?

The children stand in a circle and one child is the "lassie" (girl) or "laddie" (boy). The lassie or laddie stands in the center of the circle and leads the others in a motion, such as jumping jacks, hopping, etc., while this song is sung:

Did you ever see a lassie, a lassie, a lassie?
Did you ever see a lassie go this way and that?
Go this way and that way,
And this way and that way.
Did you ever see a lassie go this way and that?

The child in the center then chooses another child to be the lassie or laddie.

Stunts

Children will be challenged and will develop new skills with the following stunts:

rocket   —child squats down then jumps up after counting to 10 backwards
seesaw   —child extends arms and spreads feet apart, then bends body from side to side
airplane —child balances on one leg, then extends arms while moving the body forward

elevator	—child slowly squats down then comes back up saying first floor, second floor, etc.
robots	—child stiffens body and bends and moves like robot
crab	—child sits and places hands on the floor behind the body, lifts trunk, and walks backwards on all fours
inch worm	—child wiggles on floor by bending and stretching body
log roll	—child lays on floor and extends arms above head, then rolls body

frog	—child squats with hands touching the floor and jumps
duck	—child grabs ankles, squats, and waddles
bear	—child stiffens legs, puts hands on the floor, and walks on all fours
seal	—child extends legs on the floor behind him/her and drags body forward with stiffened arms

What else?—Let children take turns thinking up new stunts for others to imitate.

What Outdoor Games Can You Play with Children?

Life is not a spectator sport! Get your youngsters and yourself involved outdoors with these games.

Obstacle Course

Set up an obstacle course on your playground using cardboard boxes, ropes, tricycles, climbing apparatus, and other equipment. The teacher explains what the children should climb over, crawl under, run around, etc. The class then lines up single file and goes through the course from one obstacle to the next.

Squirrels in Trees

Two children form a tree by facing each other and placing their hands on each other's shoulders. Another child is a squirrel and gets in between their arms. The rest of the class forms trees with squirrels. There should be one extra squirrel in the center of the trees. When a whistle is blown, all the squirrels hurry to another tree. The one left over then goes to the center and the game continues.

Jump the Creek

Place two ropes on the ground to form a creek a few inches wide. The children line up single file and jump over the creek one at a time. After every child has jumped, move the ropes farther apart to make the creek wider. When a player can no longer jump the distance they are out of the game. The object is to see how wide a distance the children can jump. (You can also play this game by drawing lines in the dirt or sand.)

Build the Castle

Two people hold a jump rope so that it is touching the ground. The children line up single file and jump over the rope one at a time. After every child has jumped, the rope is lifted a few inches above the ground. Continue lifting the rope as the children jump over it. When a player can no longer jump the height, they are out of the game.

Relays

Divide the class into teams with five or six players each. Have players line up single file, and one at a time run to a designated point and back. The first player tags the second player who then runs the distance. The first team to have all players run is the winner. You can also do ball relays, animal relays, hopping or skipping relays, a back-to-back relay using partners, a dressing relay where children put on and take off clothes, etc.

Stoop Tag

One child is "it." "It" chases the other children and tries to tag them before they stoop to the ground. If "it" does tag someone, that person becomes the next "it." You can also play tag with shadows, by naming a color when you stoop down, by freezing when tagged and hugging someone to "unfreeze" them, etc.

Mother May I?

Children line up with their backs to a wall. One person is chosen to be "mother" and stands about 20 feet in front of them. One at a time "mother" names a child and tells them a motion they must perform, such as three baby steps, or four scissor steps, or two giant steps. The child must remember to ask, "Mother May I?" before performing the movement or they must go back to the starting line. The first one to reach "mother" becomes "it."

Wolf and Chickens

Two lines are drawn approximately 40 feet apart. The children are "chickens" and line up behind one of the lines. The teacher or another child is the wolf and stands between the two lines. The wolf pretends to be a chicken and says, "Cluck-cluck, cluck-cluck." But when the wolf shouts, "Wolf," all the chickens must run to the other line.

If the wolf tags them in the process, they must then become wolves, too, and help the wolf catch the others. The game continues until all the chickens are caught. The last one caught becomes the first wolf in the next game.

Red Light

Two lines are drawn 30 feet apart. The children stand on one line, while "it" stands on the opposite line. "It" turns his or her back to the other players and calls, "one-two-three red light!" The players run toward "it," but must stop on the word "red light." On this signal, "it" turns and faces the players. If anyone is caught moving, the player is sent back to the starting line. The first one to tag "it" becomes the new leader.

Call Ball

The children form a circle. The teacher stands in the middle with a ball. The teacher throws the ball in the air and calls out a child's name. That child must run forward and try to catch the ball after one bounce. If he/she is successful, they may come to the center and throw the ball.

Ground Basketball

The children stand in a circle and a basket or box is placed in the center. The children take turns trying to throw a ball into the basket.

Circle Kick Ball

The children stand in a circle and join hands. One child begins by trying to kick a ball between the legs of another player or two players. The children continue to kick the ball around the circle. If the ball is kicked out of the circle, the player or players who let it out are eliminated. If a child kicks the ball over the heads of other players, the child who kicked the ball is eliminated. The game continues until there are only two children left.

Duck-Duck-Goose

The children form a circle and squat down. One child is "it" and walks around the outside of the circle saying "duck" as he/she touches each player. When "it" touches a child and says "goose," that child must chase "it" around the circle before "it" can get back to "goose's" place. If "it" is caught, he/she must sit in the center of the circle. "Goose" then becomes "it" and the game continues.

Cat and Mouse

Children form a circle and hold hands. One child stands in the center and is the "mouse." Another child stands outside the circle and is the "cat." On a given signal, the "cat" must chase the "mouse." They may enter or leave the circle only if the other players hold up their arms to form an arch. (Vary this game for holidays by having the farmer chase the turkey, cupid chase the valentine, etc.)

Dodge Ball

Mark a circle or square playing area. Have all the children get in the circle. The teacher takes a rubber ball and rolls it into the circle while the children try and "dodge" it. If a child is touched by a ball, he/she comes out of the circle and helps the teacher roll the ball and get others out. The game continues until one child remains.

How Can You Make Your Own Equipment?

Supplement the equipment at your school with some of these homemade materials.

Bean bags—Take an old sock and cut off 4 inches from the toe. Fill the toe with beans and securely stitch the top. For younger children, fill it with styrofoam packing so it won't hurt them if they are hit with it.
- Toss it alone, play catch with a friend, play relays with it, throw it at a target, or toss it in a box.

Jump ropes—Buy a clothesline and double the distance from the child's shoulders to the floor. Tape the ends or tie knots.
- Besides jumping, you can make shapes, letters, or numerals with your rope. Use it to mark off your own space for creative movement. Tuck it in your pants to make a tail, or slip it around a friend's waist and play horsie.

Wands—Staple one yard of ribbon or crepe paper to a straw.
- Spin your wand around you, above your head; with your right hand, throw it up and catch it; do a dance with it; etc.

Bowling pins—Save plastic soft drink bottles. Arrange them in a triangle and let children take turns knocking them down with a ball or beanbag.

Balance beam—Put a piece of masking tape on the floor or place a 2"×4" board directly on the floor.
- Can you walk forwards, backwards, sideways, turn a somersault?

Balls—Wad up a piece of newspaper. Wrap masking tape all around it and you'll have a safe and inexpensive ball. (Older children can make these themselves.)

- Make a stocking ball from old pantyhose. Cut 12 inches off of one foot. Stuff this with the rest of the pantyhose. Twist and turn it inside out until it becomes a small ball. Stitch the ends down.
- Yarn balls can be made with a 3-inch strip of cardboard and medium weight yarn. Wrap the yarn around the cardboard approximately 100 times. Gather the yarn together and tie it tightly with another piece of yarn. Cut the yarn loops apart and fluff it.

Frisbies—Styrofoam paper plates can be colored and then thrown as frisbies.
- Play catch or see who can throw theirs the farthest.

Balloons—Who can keep their balloon in the air the longest? Kick it, toss it, play catch with it, tie a string to it, or play balloon volley ball.

Chalk—Use chalk on pavement to make hop scotch, an obstacle course, roads and signs for riding toys, or a balance beam.

Tin can stilts—Take two large juice cans, punch a hole in each side, and insert a piece of cord or rope. Bring the ends together and tie at the child's waist. (Use tuna cans for the little ones.)

Blanket toss—An old sheet or blanket is almost as good as a parachute for tossing balls and playing games.

13

NUTRITION
AND COOKING

There is a strong connection between what children eat and how they behave. This section suggests ways you can help children develop healthy eating habits. Included are guidelines to help you conduct successful cooking experiences with children, as well as many simple recipes preschoolers can make and enjoy.

Why Is Good Nutrition Important for Young Children?

What children eat can have implications on their physical and mental growth, as well as their future health. Have you ever heard the saying, "You are what you eat?" This is particularly true for children. Many times they don't feel well or act right because they are not eating proper foods. We live in a world of "fast food," additives, and sugar. Further, many children have parents with poor diet patterns. It is up to preschool teachers to give children alternatives and to teach them positive eating habits. The more children learn about nutrition, the better choices they will be able to make.

Follow these guidelines to help children eat right and feel and act their best ("Dietary Guidelines for Americans," 1985):

1. Encourage children to eat a variety of foods from the four food groups: (1) fruits and vegetables; (2) milk, cheese, and milk products; (3) breads and cereals; (4) meat, fish, poultry, eggs, dry beans.
2. Never force children to eat, but do encourage them to try all foods.
3. Offer children nutritional snacks, such as fresh fruit, yogurt, vegetable sticks, popcorn, etc.
4. Avoid processed foods and serve foods as close to the natural state as possible.
5. Remember, all things in moderation! (Especially watch sodium and sugar.)
6. Limit fried foods and foods high in cholesterol.
7. Make sure children drink plenty of water.
8. Don't reward children with sweets or food.
9. Involve children in the cooking and preparation of food.

The teacher's attitude about food will influence the children's attitudes. If the teacher acts like fresh fruit is a treat, the children will, too. If the teacher sits with the children and enjoys the food served with them, the children will be positive about the meal, too. On the other hand, a teacher's negative attitude about certain foods can also rub off on the children. And what are children to think if the teacher has a soft drink and eats a package of potato chips and doughnuts for lunch? Be a good model, for your actions speak louder than your words!

How Can Cooking Be a Learning Experience?

Cooking is more than making something good to eat; it is an ideal way to learn because it involves all five senses. Children are enthusiastic about cooking and feel a real sense of accomplishment and independence from it. These are a few skills that children can develop by relating food experiences to other areas of the curriculum:

math—measuring, counting, fractions
language—following oral directions, vocabulary, communicating
reading—decoding symbols, reading a recipe, sequential order
science—chemical changes, problem solving, plant and animal products
nutrition—four food groups, increased awareness of good nutrition
social studies—foods from different countries, careers with food

small motor—pouring, stirring, and mixing build small muscles
health—cleanliness, safety in using equipment
social—cooperation, taking turns, group projects
emotional—self-confidence, success

How Do You Prepare for Cooking Activities?

Cooking can be pleasurable for you and your students if you are well-prepared and organized. Here are some suggestions for successful experiences:

1. Choose recipes that are simple and involve a few ingredients. Children do not like to wait, so select things that are immediately edible. Also, make sure the cooking activities fit the abilities and interests of the children you teach.
2. Relate cooking experiences to seasons and topics being studied. For example, serve roasted pumpkin seeds around Halloween; make mud pies when you're studying the letter "m"; make cup gingerbread after reading "The Gingerbread Boy."
3. Select a place to cook where you will not disturb others. A sink, electrical outlet, and washable surface are advisable. Children will be more comfortable if they sit around a table with low chairs.
4. Work with a small group at a time. (You might want to let children eat at a place different from where you cook.)
5. Have all utensils and ingredients assembled before you begin. Use paper disposables whenever possible to cut down on clean-up.
6. Always start by *washing hands*!
7. Display the recipe on a chart, poster, or large card. Use picture symbols, as well as words.
8. Go over the entire recipe, explaining the names of ingredients and cooking terms like "chop," and "beat." Demonstrate step-by-step what children are to do.
9. Remember, children should do the major amount of the work. Help them be successful by doing difficult steps ahead of time.
10. Teach children how to use utensils safely.
11. Make cooking a learning time by encouraging children to use their five senses. Ask questions and keep the conversation going.
12. Allow children to taste various ingredients raw or alone.
13. Be open to their suggestions.
14. Praise children's efforts and make cooking and eating a happy time.
15. Encourage children to use good manners, including chewing with their mouths closed, using proper utensils, etc.
16. Involve children in the total process, from setting the table to cleaning-up.
17. Send copies of recipes home to parents, or save recipes and make a class cookbook for the end of the year.
18. Cost? Cooking ingredients can add up. Most parents are willing to send ingredients if you notify them in advance. You can also ask each child to contribute money to cover cooking expenses.

What Equipment and Materials Do You Need?

You don't need a fancy kitchen in your classroom to make foods that children will enjoy. Most of the recipes in this chapter require no cooking, or can be made with a simple appliance, such as an electric skillet. If you don't have the items below available to you, look around at garage sales or solicit donations from parents.

mixing bowls	grater
measuring cups	aluminum foil, wax paper
measuring spoons	paper plates, cups, utensils
spatula	pot holders
wire whisk	cookie sheet
serrated knives	large and small pot
vegetable peeler	cookie cutters

These appliances are necessary for some recipes:

electric skillet
toaster oven
electric blender
iron
hot plate

What Simple Recipes Can Children Cook?

Get ready for some big smiles from your youngsters with these cooking experiences. All of these recipes have been tested, tasted, and approved by children. In fact, your children will have almost as much fun making them as they do eating them. These recipes are simple, nutritional, and economical. Be a "preschool gourmet" by changing the names of these recipes, varying the ingredients, or experimenting with new combinations. You will find the recipes organized under the four food groups: (1) fruits and vegetables; (2) milk and milk products; (3) breads and cereals; (4) meats.

Terms: Tb.=tablespoon
        t. =teaspoon

Ants on a Log

Ingredients: celery, peanut butter, raisins

Procedure: Spread peanut butter in the hollow of the celery (log). Put raisins (ants) on top.

Variations: Use cream cheese or pimento cheese.

Smiles

Ingredients: red apples, peanut butter, miniature marshmallows

Procedure: Slice the apple into eighths. Spread peanut butter on one slice, then place four marshmallows on top. Add another slice of apple, and you'll have a big smile.

Fruit Kabobs

Ingredients: bananas, grapes, apples, pineapple chunks, toothpicks

Procedure: Slice bananas, wash grapes, and cut apples into chunks. Take one of each kind of fruit and stick it on the toothpick.

Frozen Bananas

Ingredients: bananas, popsicle sticks

Procedure: Peel the banana and cut it in half. Insert a popsicle stick in the end, place on wax paper, and freeze.

Variations: Dip in honey or yogurt and roll in chopped nuts or wheat germ before freezing

Tossed Salad

Ingredients: lettuce, carrots, cucumbers, croutons, salad dressing, zip lock bag

Procedure: Wash lettuce and tear into small pieces. Wash and slice carrots and cucumbers. Take a handful of lettuce and put it in the bag. Add several pieces of carrot, cucumber, and croutons. Put in 2 teaspoons of salad dressing, zip, and shake.

Potato Latkes (Traditional Food Served for Hanukkah)

Ingredients: 4 potatoes, 1 small onion, 1 egg (beaten), dash of salt, 1 Tb. flour, margarine

Procedure: Grate potatoes and onion. Stir in egg, flour, and salt. Pour a heaping spoonful in a skillet and fry in margarine until light brown.
Variations: Serve with applesauce or sour cream.

Corn on the Cob

Ingredients: fresh corn, salt, pepper, margarine
Procedure: Give each child an ear of corn and let them shuck it and wash it. Cook in boiling salted water for 15 minutes or until tender. Serve with salt, pepper, and margarine.

Veggie Dip

Ingredients: 1 cup sour cream, ½ package dry vegetable soup mix, carrots, celery, cucumbers, green pepper, and other raw vegetables
Procedure: Stir vegetable soup mix into sour cream. Wash and slice vegetables into small pieces. Dip and eat.

Banana Sandwich

Ingredients: bananas, peanut butter
Procedure: Take half a banana and slice it in half lengthwise. Spread peanut butter on one half, then top with the other half.
Variations: Put a slice of banana between two vanilla wafers to make a dessert sandwich.

Apples, Apples, Apples

Ingredients: raw apples, dried apples, apple sauce, apple juice
Procedure: Give each child a small sample of each form of apples. Make a bar graph of their favorite.

Pumpkin Seeds

Ingredients: pumpkin seeds, margarine, salt
Procedure: Wash and dry pumpkin seeds. Melt 2 Tb. of margarine in an electric skillet. Stir in 2 cups of pumpkin seeds and cook until they are slightly brown and toasted. Sprinkle with salt.

Carrot Cars

Ingredients: celery, carrots, toothpicks
Procedure: Wash celery and cut into 4″ lengths. Wash and scrape carrots, then cut into diagonal slices ½″ thick. Put a carrot on either side of the celery and secure in place with a toothpick. Put back wheels on your car the same way.
Variations: Fill the celery with peanut butter or cheese.

Bunny Salad

Ingredients: canned pear halves, lettuce, raisins, cottage cheese, carrot sticks
Procedure: Lay down a leaf of lettuce, then put the pear half on top for the bunny's body. Add raisins for nose and eyes, a cottage cheese tail, and carrot sticks for ears. (Super Easter treat!)

Cinnamon Applesauce

Ingredients: canned applesauce, cinnamon red hot candies
Procedure: Put ½ cup of applesauce in a small cup. Count out 10 cinnamon candies and put them in the cup. Stir, stir, stir. The applesauce will turn a pretty pink and have a cinnamon flavor. (Especially good around Valentine's Day.)

Fruit Pops

Ingredients: fruit juice, (orange, grape, apple), popsicle sticks, cups
Procedure: Pour fruit juice into cups or ice cube trays. Insert popsicle sticks and freeze. (Children can really go through these on a hot day, so make plenty.)

Johnny Appleseed Salad

Ingredients: apples, peanut butter, raisins
Procedure: Halve apples and cut out the seeds. Spread peanut butter and top with raisins.

Stone Soup

Ingredients: potatoes, carrots, celery, can of corn, five beef bouillon cubes, tomato juice, clean stone, water
Procedure: Read the story of "Stone Soup" to your class. Ask each child to bring one of the above ingredients or another vegetable to school the next day. Retell the story beginning with the stone and let the children add their vegetables to the soup. Cook for several hours until the vegetables are tender. (The best part about this soup is smelling it cook!)

Finger Jello

Ingredients: 2 pkg. unflavored gelatin, 2 (3 oz.) pkg. fruit-flavored gelatin, 2½ cups boiling water
Procedure: Mix dry gelatins together. Add boiling water and stir well. Pour into jelly roll pan and refrigerate. Cut into small squares.
Variations: Pour onto a cookie sheet to make a thin layer. Cut out cookie cutter shapes after it hardens.

Apple Cider

Ingredients: apple juice or cider, cloves, cinnamon stick
Procedure: Heat apple juice in a pan. Pour into a cup, add one clove, and stir with the cinnamon stick. (This will warm you up on a cold day.)

Orange Jubilee

Ingredients: 6 oz. can orange juice concentrate, 1 cup milk, ½ cup sugar, 1 tsp. vanilla, 1 cup water, 10 ice cubes
Procedure: Put ingredients in blender and mix until smooth.

Tutty-Fruity Salad

Ingredients: bananas, apples, pineapple chunks, grapes, orange slices
Procedure: Put two or three pieces of each fruit in a small cup. Stir and eat.

Grape Surprise

Ingredients: seedless grapes, cups
Procedure: Count out 10 to 15 grapes (or however high the children can count). Wash and dry the grapes, then put them in a cup. Freeze several hours. (Frozen grapes really hit the spot on a summer day.)

Banana Shake

Ingredients: ½ banana, 1 cup milk, 1 Tb. honey
Procedure: Put all ingredients in a blender and mix well.
Variations: Add 2 Tb. peanut butter.

Carrot Salad

Ingredients: carrots, raisins, mayonnaise
Procedure: Grate ½ carrot in a small bowl. Add 12 raisins and 1 t. mayonnaise. Mix well.
Variations: Substitute pineapple juice or yogurt for the mayonnaise.

Baked Potatoes

Ingredients: baking potatoes, salt, pepper, margarine, sour cream, grated cheese, bacon pieces, foil
Procedure: Scrub potatoes, then wrap with foil. Bake in 450° oven approximately 1 hour or until tender. Eat with your favorite toppings.

Cheese Popcorn

Ingredients: popcorn, oil, salt, margarine, Parmesan or grated American cheese
Procedure: Pop popcorn, then add salt, margarine, cheese, and shake well.

Baked Apples

Ingredients: apples, raisins, cinnamon sugar, margarine
Procedure: Core apples and fill the center with raisins. Sprinkle with cinnamon sugar and put a pat of margarine on top. Bake covered in an electric skillet at 350° until tender (20–30 minutes).

Butter

Ingredients: 1 pint whipping cream, 1 t. salt
Procedure: Set whipping cream out at room temperature for one hour. Pour in a glass jar, add the salt, and seal tightly. Take turns shaking the jar as you pass it around the group. After about 10 minutes it should become yellow and thick. Pour off the excess liquid and serve on crackers.
Variations: Pour ¼ cup whipping cream and a dash of salt into a baby food jar. Screw the lid on tightly and shake. This way each child can make his or her own butter.

Mud Pies

Ingredients: 1 package instant chocolate pudding, 2 cups milk, flat bottom ice cream cones
Procedure: Tell the children a few days ahead about the wonderful mud pies you are going to make. Put the pudding (dirt) in a sealable plastic container. Add milk and stir well. Cover and take turns shaking the container. Serve the "mud" in ice cream cones. (This cooking experience is fun to do outside.)

Hot Chocolate Mix

Ingredients: 8 qt. package dry milk, 6 oz. jar non-dairy creamer, 2 lb. box Nestle's Quik, 1 lb. box confectioner's sugar, ½ tsp. salt
Procedure: Mix all ingredients well. Mix 3 or 4 heaping teaspoons to 1 cup boiling water.
Variations: This makes a great gift for parents or school helpers.

Individual Homemade Ice Cream

Ingredients: milk, sugar, vanilla, soup can, 28 oz. can, foil, crushed ice, ice cream salt, spoon

Procedure: Pour ⅔ cup milk, 4 t. sugar, and ¼ t. vanilla into the soup can and cover with foil. Place this can inside the larger can and fill the space with layers of crushed ice and salt. Remove the foil and stir mixture with a spoon for 15 minutes or until ice cream thickens.

Berry-Berry Yogurt

Ingredients: vanilla yogurt, fresh strawberries or blueberries

Procedure: Put ½ cup yogurt in a small bowl or cup. Slice strawberries or add whole blueberries, stir, and eat.

Variations: You can also use bananas or other canned fruits.

Cheese Toys

Ingredients: cheese, pretzel sticks

Procedure: Cut cheese into small cubes. Insert pretzel sticks into cubes to make an edible structure.

Ice Cream Sandwich

Ingredients: ice cream, graham crackers

Procedure: Soften ice cream. Put a heaping tablespoon of ice cream between two graham crackers. Wrap in plastic wrap or wax paper and freeze for one hour.

Variations: You can make mini-ice cream sandwiches using vanilla wafers or other cookies.

Pudding Pops

Ingredients: 1 large (4 oz.) package of regular pudding mix, 3½ cups milk, popsicle sticks, cups, foil

Procedure: Stir pudding mix and milk until well-blended. Pour into cups, cover with foil, and insert popsicle sticks. Freeze and enjoy.

Miss Muffet's Delight

Ingredients: cottage cheese, crushed pineapple

Procedure: Mix ½ cup of cottage cheese with ¼ cup crushed pineapple in a small bowl. Watch out for spiders as you eat!

Frozen Yogurt

Ingredients: 2 cups plain yogurt, 1 can (6 oz.) frozen orange juice concentrate, 2 t. vanilla

Procedure: Thaw orange juice. Mix well with yogurt and vanilla and freeze in small cups. Serve with a spoon.

Variations: You can also use puréed strawberries or other fruit.

Baby Cheese Balls

Ingredients: cream cheese, cheddar cheese, chopped nuts or crushed cereal
Procedure: Soften cream cheese and grate cheddar cheese. Put 1 Tb. cream cheese and 1 Tb. grated cheddar cheese in a paper cup and mix well. Form a small ball and roll in nuts or cereal. Serve with crackers.

Trail Mix

Ingredients: dry cereal (Cheerios), pretzel sticks, peanuts, raisins, zip lock bag, ice cream cone
Procedure: Add ¼ cup of each to the bag, seal, and shake. Take along on a hike or pour into an ice cream cone which you can eat when you finish your trail mix.
Variations: Add carob chips or M&M's for a treat. Make this at Halloween and call it witch's stew. The cereal can be frog eyes, the pretzel sticks bones, the peanuts stones, and the raisins worm pieces. The children will love it!

Ironed Sandwiches

Ingredients: bread, margarine, cheese, foil
Procedure: Place cheese between two slices of bread. Spread softened margarine on each side. Wrap foil around sandwich and place on cutting board or suitable surface. Using medium heat, iron both sides of the sandwich until the cheese melts and the bread browns.
Variations: Add a slice of ham or cooked bacon. Grilled peanut butter sandwiches are good, too.

Cracker Creations

Ingredients: crackers with different shapes, peanut butter, plastic knives
Procedure: Using peanut butter like glue, make houses, cars, and other objects you can eat.

Cooked O's

Ingredients: Cheerios, margarine, cinnamon sugar

Procedure: Melt 2 Tb. margarine in an electric skillet. Add 3 cups Cheerios and sprinkle with cinnamon sugar. Stir over low heat until cereal is toasted and tasty.

MMMMM Muffins

Ingredients: English muffins, margarine, sliced cheese

Procedure: Spread margarine on ½ muffin and top with a slice of cheese. Broil in toaster oven until the cheese melts.

Variations: Put slices of hard-boiled egg or pieces of bacon on the muffin before topping it with cheese.

Little Red Hen's Letter Bread

Ingredients: bread, milk, food coloring, Q-tips, margarine

Procedure: Mix a small amount of milk with a few drops of food coloring. Using a Q-tip, paint letters or designs on the bread with the colored milk. Toast in a toaster. Serve with margarine.

Pocket Sandwiches

Ingredients: pita bread, cheese, sprouts, tuna fish, or other favorite sandwich filling

Procedure: Cut pita bread in half. Fill the "pocket" with your favorite filling.

Patty Cake Biscuits

Ingredients: canned biscuits, flour, wax paper, jam

Procedure: Flour your hands and pat a biscuit until it is flat. Put ½ t. jam in the middle, fold it over, and press the edges together. Bake in a 400° oven until lightly browned.

Gingerbread Treats

Ingredients: gingerbread mix, wax-coated paper cups (5 oz.), water

Procedure: Mix 3 Tb. gingerbread mix in the cup with 1 Tb. water. Place in an electric skillet, cover, and bake on 400° approximately 12–15 minutes.

Oatmeal Balls

Ingredients: 2 Tb. softened margarine, ½ cup peanut butter, ¼ cup honey, 1 cup raw oatmeal, ¾ cup powdered milk

Procedure: Blend butter and honey. Stir in oatmeal and dry milk. Roll into balls. (Store leftovers in the refrigerator.)

French Toast

Ingredients: bread, 1 egg, ¼ cup milk, ½ t. vanilla, dash of cinnamon, margarine, syrup or powdered sugar

Procedure: Beat egg, then stir in milk, vanilla, and cinnamon. Dip bread in egg mixture, then fry in margarine until light brown. Serve with syrup or powdered sugar.

Letter Pancakes

Ingredients: pancake mix, egg, oil, margarine, syrup, squeeze bottle (similar to those used for ketchup)

Procedure: Make pancake mix according to directions. Heat oil in skillet. Fill squeeze bottle with pancake mix, then form letters or numerals with it on the hot surface. Serve with margarine and syrup.

Variations: For St. Patrick's Day, add green food coloring to the pancake mix.

Happy Face Sandwiches

Ingredients: bread, peanut butter, raisins, sunflower seeds, grated carrot

Procedure: Cut a large circle from the bread with a cookie cutter. Spread peanut butter on the circle. Use raisins and sunflower seeds to make eyes, nose, and mouth. Add grated carrot for hair.

Wheaty Snacks

Ingredients: mini-shredded wheat squares, margarine, salt, parmesan cheese

Procedure: Melt 2 Tb. margarine in skillet. Add 3 cups cereal and sprinkle with salt and cheese. Stir and cook until toasty.

Variations: Substitute dry ranch dressing for cheese and salt.

Paint Brush Cookies

Ingredients: egg yolk, food coloring, roll of refrigerator sugar cookie dough, Q-tips

Procedure: Slice sugar cookie dough into ¼-inch slices. Mix small amount of food coloring with egg yolk and paint a design on the cookie dough with Q-tips. Bake on cookie sheet according to package directions.

Nachos

Ingredients: corn chips, jar of salsa, cheese (cheddar or mozzarella)

Procedure: Spread chips out on a cookie sheet. Spoon on several Tb. of salsa, then grate cheese on top. Bake in 375° oven until cheese melts or heat in a microwave.

Fluffer Nutter Sandwiches

Ingredients: bread, peanut butter, marshmallow creme

Procedure: Spread peanut butter on one slice of bread and marshmallow creme on the other piece of bread. "Smush" them together, take a bite, mmmmmm!

Variations: Peanut butter and marshmallow creme on graham crackers makes a tasty snack.

Mini-Pizzas

Ingredients: English muffins, jar of pizza sauce, sliced pepperoni, mozzarella cheese

Procedure: Split muffin and spread sauce on each half. Add pepperoni and grated cheese. Broil until cheese melts.

Variations: Vary the toppings or make mini-mini-pizzas using crackers.

Green Eggs and Ham

Ingredients: eggs, green food coloring, sliced ham, margarine

Procedure: Beat five eggs. Cut two slices of ham into small pieces and add to the eggs. Stir in several drops of food coloring. Cook in 1 Tb. margarine in a skillet.

Porcupine Balls

Ingredients: 1 pound ground beef, 1 cup instant rice, oil, ketchup

Procedure: Mix ground beef and instant rice together in a bowl. Form small balls and fry in 1 Tb. oil. Drain. Insert a toothpick in balls and serve with ketchup.

Pigs in a Blanket

Ingredients: 1 package crescent rolls, hot dogs, cheese

Procedure: Slice hot dog about halfway through and stuff with cheese. Roll hot dog up in one section of crescent roll dough. Bake in 375° oven approximately 12 minutes.

Variations: Use canned biscuits or omit the cheese.

Homemade Peanut Butter

Ingredients: shelled peanuts (for fun buy roasted peanuts and let the children shell them), oil

Procedure: Put 1 cup of shelled peanuts in the blender. Add 1 Tb. oil and blend until smooth. Add salt if you desire and serve on crackers.

Sausage Balls

Ingredients: 1 pound bulk sausage, 1 pound cheddar cheese, 3 cups biscuit mix

Procedure: Grate cheese and mix well with other ingredients. Form small balls and bake on ungreased cookie sheet in 375° oven until slightly brown.

Cookie Cutter Sandwiches

Ingredients: bread, sliced meat, cheese slices, cookie cutters

Procedures: Cut bread, meat, and cheese with a cookie cutter. Put together and eat.

Variations: Use seasonal cookie cutters such as bells, hearts, shamrocks, etc.

Peanut Butter Play Dough

Ingredients: smooth peanut butter, honey, instant nonfat dry milk

Procedure: Mix 1 cup peanut butter, 1 cup dry milk, and ¼ cup honey together until smooth. Roll on wax paper into balls, snakes, bunnies, etc.

14

PUTTING IT
ALL TOGETHER WITH
A TEACHING THEME

Teaching themes can provide you with a variety of interesting topics
to use as springboards for organizing learning activities and integrating
content areas.

255

What Is a Teaching Theme?

The "teaching theme" or "unit" approach provides the content and a framework for organizing learning activities and integrating the different areas of the curriculum. Through a broad range of subject matter, a variety of experiences, and active involvement, children are able to develop skills as well as learn information about the topic being studied. Units should be based on children's interests and should be appropriate to their background experiences and developmental level. Seasons, holidays, community events, and children's cultural backgrounds will often spark a unit of study.

After you have selected your topic, choose informational objectives and skill objectives that you will focus on during the course of study. Use this book as a resource and brainstorm all the activities and experiences you could include from different areas of the curriculum. Consider how different methods and materials could be adapted for your theme. Select the most meaningful activities for your children and write lesson plans for the unit. Next, collect materials and develop learning centers that will achieve your objectives. As you implement your unit, you will want to make changes and adaptations to accommodate the interests and needs of your students.

Many teachers choose a different theme or unit for their classroom each week, while other teachers plan units that last two to four weeks. These are some possible topics for units of study:

Africa
All About Me
Apples
Babies
Balloons and Bubbles
Bears
Birds
Birthdays
Black Americans
My Body
Boxes
Butterflies
Camping
Career Awareness
Caring
Christmas
Christmas Around the World
Circus
City Life
Clothing
Colors
Columbus Day
Communication
Community Helpers
Cooking
Corn
Cows

Day and Night
Dental Health
Dinosaurs
Easter

Ecology
Emotions/Feelings
Eskimos
Exercise
Fairy Tales

Family and Friends
Fall
Farm Animals
Father's Day
Fire Fighters
Food
Forest Animals
Friends Around the World
Frogs
Fruits and Vegetables
Garden
Ghosts

Gift Making
Grandparents
Groundhog Day
Halloween
Hanukkah
Hats

Health
Helpers We Will Be
Holidays
Homes
I Like Myself
Insects
Instruments
Japan
Jewelry
July 4th
Knights and Dragons
Magnets
Mail Carriers

Manners
Math and Measurement
Mexico

Money and Stores
Mother's Day

Musical Instruments
Native Americans
New Year's
Nursery Rhymes
Nuts
Oceans
Opposites
Oriental Culture
Our School
Patriotism
Personal Hygiene
Pets

Pigs
Plants
Poetry
Police Officers
Pond Life
Pumpkins
Puppets
Reptiles and Amphibians

Safety
Self-Concept
Senses
    Hearing
    Seeing
    Tasting
    Touching
    Smelling
Sesame Street
Shapes
Shoes

Soil and Rocks
Space
Sports and Games
Spring
St. Patrick's Day
Summer Fun
Thanksgiving
Tools and Machines
Toys
Trains
Transportation
Trees
Vacations
Valentine's Day

Washington and Lincoln
Water
Weather
Wheels
Wild West
Wildlife
Winter
Witches
Zoo

The following is an example of a unit on bears for four-year-olds. Note how the theme is adapted to provide children with a broad variety of experiences that will enable them to develop the desired skills and objectives.

Information Objectives:

1. The child will identify a bear from pictures of animals.
2. The child will be able to identify various parts of the bear's body (head, ears, nose, tail, eyes, etc.)
3. The child will be able to name two places where bears can be seen: zoo, circus, forest, Arctic.
4. The child will be able to sort pictures of real bears from pretend bears.

Skill Objectives:

1. The child will retell a story in sequence.
2. The child will categorize objects by size (small, medium, large).
3. The child will make sets of five objects and orally count to five.
4. The child will identify the letter "b".
5. The child will balance on one foot for 10 seconds.

Activities

Story Time

Goldilocks and the Three Bears

Brown Bear, Brown Bear by Bill Martin
Corduroy by Don Freeman
Ask Mr. Bear by Marjorie Black
Berenstain Bears by Stan and Jan Berenstain
Ranger Rick and Poems about Bears

Reading Readiness

Dictate a story about a bear
Language development story about their teddy bears
Act out the story of THE THREE BEARS
Visual memory game of what's missing on a bear
Visual discrimination game of matching like bears
Letter recognition game of matching upper and lower case letters
Act out opposites
Match up rhyming pictures
Sequence pictures of THE THREE BEARS
Act out words that begin with "b"
Select objects of things that begin with "b" for Bear's basket
Recite bear finger plays and poems

Math

Make sets of objects on the flannel board and count
Seriate bears by size
Make a teddy bear bar graph
Match sets and numerals
Identify bears by ordinal position
Categorize objects by size (small, medium, large)

Science

Discuss the difference between real bears and pretend bears
Identify types of bears
Look at pictures of bear habitats
Name foods bears eat
Act out habits of bears (growling, fishing, climbing, etc.)
Point to body parts on bears and body parts on self
Field trip to a zoo

Small Motor Skills

Make bears from play dough
Put together bear puzzles
Sew lacing cards of bears
String a cereal necklace
Trace around stencils of bears

Large Motor

Play follow the bear
Follow a bear obstacle course
Do bear relays
Play bear-hug tag
Do bear exercises
Play jump the creek

Art

Make bear puppets from paper sacks or make stick puppets
Paint bears
Make paper plate bears
Sponge-paint the shape of a bear
Make a tissue paper bear

Music and Movement

Baby Bumblebee
The Bear Went over the Mountain
Going on a Bear Hunt
Teddy Bear, Teddy Bear
I Wish I Were
The Fishing Song
Ten in the Bed
Hokey-Pokey

Blocks

Make caves for bears or cages for bears
Make a house for their teddy bear
Stack blocks as tall as their teddy bear
Use toy bears as accessories

Dramatics

Play with a Goldilocks doll and three sizes of bears in housekeeping
Play with their teddy bears in housekeeping
Dress up in clothes and act out THE THREE BEARS

Nutrition

Ants on a Log
Honey Bear Bread
Apple Salad
Berry Bear Yogurt
Peanut Butter Play Dough Bears
Animal Picnic of Raw Vegetables

Age Group Four-year-olds

Date January 15–19

Theme Bears

Concepts Parts of a bear's body / bear habitats / real and pretend bears

Objectives Sequence a story / make sets of 5 and count to 5 / identify the letter "b"

	Monday	Tuesday	Wednesday	Thursday	Friday
Circle Time	Identify bears from other animals	Name parts of a bear's body	Discuss bear habitats	Sort pictures of real and pretend bears	Bring a teddy bear from home for Teddy Parade
Language/ Reading Readiness	Select objects that begin with "b"	Put 3 BEARS pictures in sequence	Match pictures of like bears	Put rhyming picture puzzles together	Tell story about their teddy bear on tape recorder
Math	Categorize objects by size	Make sets 1–5 on flannel board	Seriate bears by size	Match sets and numerals 1–5	Make a teddy bear bar graph
Science	Watch a filmstrip about bears	Label body parts of bears	Act out habits of bears	Field trip to the zoo	Identify objects by smell and taste
Art	Make bear puppet from a paper sack	Make a tissue paper bear	Sponge-paint a bear shape	Make a paper plate bear	Paint a picture of their teddy bear
Music & Movement	Bear Went over the Mountain / Baby Bumblebee	Fishing Song / 10 in the Bed	Bear Hunt / Hokey-Pokey	I Wish I Were / Ten Little Bears	Teddy Bear, Teddy Bear / Class choice
Small Motor/Manipulatives	Make bears from play dough	Put a bear puzzle together	String a cereal necklace	Sew a lacing card of a bear	Trace around stencils of bears
Blocks	Build caves and cages for bears	Construct a house from Lincoln Logs	Play with toy bears in blocks	Build with unit blocks	Stack blocks as high as their teddy bear
Dramatic Play	Play with bear puppets in theater	Play GOLDILOCKS and 3 BEARS	Dress-up clothes	Use blankets and boxes to make bear caves	Play with teddy bears in housekeeping
Sand/Water	Trace letters in the sand	Blow bubbles with cups and straws	Pour and measure water	Wash plastic dishes in water	Play with funnels and pipes in sand
Outdoor Play/Large Motor	Play Bear-Hug Tag	Balance on one foot	Follow an obstacle course	Do bear exercises	Play Jump the Creek
Special Activities (Field trip, cooking, etc.)	Make honey bear bread	Prepare ants on a log	Make peanut butter bears	Field trip to the zoo	Teddy Bear Picnic and Teddy Bear Parade

15

THE PROFESSIONAL
TEACHER

Being a professional is an integral part of your job. Try to be a positive member of the teaching team in your school, participate in professional organizations, and seek to grow and learn. Work with families to make them feel comfortable, wanted, and needed.

Why Is It Important to Be Professional?

Professionalism is a critical component of teaching young children. For many years preschool teachers hid in their classrooms, but now they are coming out and shouting, "Yes, I teach children and I'm proud of it!" Across the United States and around the world early childhood educators are joining hands to work together to improve the quality of programs for children. Professionalism means commitment, upholding ethical principles, being informed, joining and working in teacher organizations, and demanding what is best for children. *Together we can make a difference!*

What Professional Organizations Can Early Childhood Teachers Join?

ASSOCIATION FOR CHILDHOOD EDUCATION INTERNATIONAL (ACEI)
11141 Georgia Avenue, Suite 200, Wheaton, MD 20902
COUNCIL FOR EXCEPTIONAL CHILDREN (CEC)
1920 Association Dr., Reston, VA 22091
DAY CARE AND CHILD DEVELOPMENT COUNCIL OF AMERICA (DCCDCA)
1401 K Street, NW, Washington, DC 20005
EDUCATIONAL RESOURCES INFORMATION CENTER (ERIC/ECE)
805 W. Pennsylvania Avenue, Urbana, IL 61801
NATIONAL ASSOCIATION FOR THE EDUCATION OF YOUNG CHILDREN (NAEYC)
1834 Connecticut Avenue, NW, Washington, DC 20009 (800–424–8777)
SOUTHERN ASSOCIATION FOR CHILDREN UNDER SIX (SACUS)
P.O. Box 5403, Brady Station, Little Rock, AR 72215

What Professional Behaviors Are Necessary for Preschool Teachers?

Take a look at yourself! Are you the kind of employee you would enjoy working with? Do you model the kind of behavior you wish your children would have? These are some skills and attitudes that are important for everyone who works with children.

- *Attendance*—You can't do your job if you're late or if you are not there. Little children are counting on you.
- *Appearance*—Working with children does not require a suit and heels, but you do need to take pride in your appearance and always be neat, clean, and appropriately dressed.
- *Attitude*—Keep a positive attitude about your job, the children you teach, and the people you work with.
- *Communication*—Keep communication open with other school staff and parents. Share your thoughts and feelings with those with whom you work.
- *Avoid Pettiness*—If there is a problem, deal directly with the person involved. Ignore minor grievances, don't overreact, and be forgiving.
- *Flexibility*—Mistakes, problems, spills, and scheduling crises are a routine part of the school day. Do try to be resilient and adaptable when problems occur.
- *Follow-Through*—Follow through on assignments, reports, and other responsibilities. Don't wait to be reminded.

- *Confidence*—Don't share private information and avoid gossip. Never discuss children, teachers, or school matters with outsiders.
- *Ethics*—Model a high code of ethics. Be the type of person others look up to.
- *Carry More than Your Share*—"It's not my job," will not work in our profession. We must all do more than is expected of us, including cleaning, cooking, nursing, and whatever else needs to be done.
- *Willingness*—Be willing to try new things and to make changes that will improve your program for children.
- *Teamwork*—Be a part of the professional team in your school by working closely with and supporting other teachers and administrators.
- *Organization*—Keep your room organized and clean, write and follow-through on lesson plans, use an appointment calendar, set up a file system, and maintain records on each child in your room.
- *Growth*—Attend professional meetings, conferences, and workshops. Take classes, read articles, and continue to learn all you can about children and teaching.
- *Fairness*—Treat all children fairly and don't have biases or prejudices. Look for the best in each child, focus on their strengths, and accept their differences.
- *Honesty*—Honesty is always the best policy. Lying merely chips away at your credibility, so don't do it.
- *Excuses*—No one wants to hear them. Do the best you can and you won't have to make them.
- *Humor*—Keep a sense of humor, laugh, smile, and enjoy your job.

ADMINISTRATORS—Please remember that teachers need good role models, support, positive feedback, training, time for planning, salaries commensurate with the work they do, and a positive working environment.

How Can You Deal with Job Stress?

As wonderful as teaching may be, there will also be many stressful moments. By maintaining good physical health and well-being, teachers can avoid a great deal of stress. Here are a few other suggestions to help you maintain your "cool" and keep a positive attitude:

1. Accept those things that you are incapable of changing. Children will cry, make messes, and forget the rules—but that's okay.
2. Don't be too hard on yourself. Think about all the good things you do every day for children.
3. Find pleasure in the simple things in your job—a child's smile, a word of thanks, a hug, a success.
4. Don't procrastinate. Do your least favorite tasks first, then you can enjoy the rest of the day.
5. Eat nutritional foods.
6. Get plenty of sleep and rest.
7. Exercise is one of the best remedies for stress, so participate in some form of exercise regularly.

8. Don't let stress build up. Vent your feelings to someone you can trust and slow down.

9. Take time to relax each day and do something you enjoy.

10. Doing something nice for someone else or saying something nice to someone else is another simple way to reduce stress.

THINK POSITIVE THOUGHTS, SMILE, AND ALWAYS LOOK FOR THE BEST IN YOURSELF AND YOUR SITUATION!

Why Is It Important to Work with Parents?

Parents are a child's first and most important teacher, and they are a valuable partner in the child's education. Research suggests that the more involved families are, the greater the child's academic success in school will be. Let parents know how much you care about their children, keep communication open, respect them, encourage them to participate, and together you can create what is best for children.

How Can You Nurture the Home/School Partnership?

These are some of the many ways to help parents feel needed, appreciated, and to get them on your "team."

1. Develop a handbook with information about your school's philosophy, goals, policies, procedures, etc.

2. Offer an orientation program for parents before their child enters. Tour the building, introduce them to teachers, and answer their questions.

3. Invite parents to serve on a board and include them in decision-making.

4. Be open to parents' comments and input. Make a suggestion box and encourage parents to evaluate your program.

5. Make a home visit before school begins.

6. Communicate daily with parents through conversations and written reports about the child's eating habits, sleep, mood, etc.

7. Send home a weekly or monthly newsletter telling about what the children have done, upcoming events, recognizing special parents, etc. Parents will also enjoy words to songs, recipes, games to play, toys and books to purchase, field trips to take, and community activities.

8. Have a special bulletin board for parents with the weekly lesson plan, pertinent articles, photographs of the children, things to remember, etc.

9. Offer workshops and seminars for parents on discipline, stress management, storytelling, how to make homemade materials, preparing nutritious snacks, and other topics of interest.

10. Invite parents into the classroom to observe. They might want to come for group time, lunch, or center time.

11. Encourage parents to volunteer in the classroom by teaching an art activity, cooking with the children, reading to the class, or sharing a hobby.

12. Plan parties for parents, such as "muffins with mom," "dessert with dad," "grandparents' day," etc.

13. Arrange an open house, family field trip, pot luck dinner, play, or a social once a month for families.

14. Say positive things about each child to his or her parents. Send home "happy grams" and notes of praise.

15. Schedule conferences with parents several times a year.

16. Make telephone calls to update parents on their child's progress.

17. Display examples of the children's work in the classroom and send home work for the parents to see.

18. Provide babysitting for parent meetings and conferences.

19. Encourage parents to borrow games, books, and materials to use at home with their children.

20. Listen to parents!

How Can Parents Get Involved?

These are just a few of the many ways parents can get involved and contribute to their child's education:

Attend meetings, seminars, and conferences.
Chaperone field trips, make phone calls, plan parties, etc.
Collect free items for projects, such as fabric, scrap paper, etc.
Type the newsletter, activity calendar, and other information.
Assist with clerical work.
Make games and materials for the class.
Plan service projects, fund raisers, or carnivals.
Participate in a support group for parents.
Share their culture, trips, career, or hobby with children.
Volunteer to tell stories, play a musical instrument, assist with a project, or teach
    a special activity.
Tutor children with special needs.
Participate in clean-up days.
Repair broken toys or equipment.
Loan materials to the school.
Compile a class scrapbook with photos, stories, and children's drawings.

An activity calendar such as this one is a good way to involve parents in the learning process.

OCTOBER

OCTOBER LEARNING CALENDAR

SUN	MON	TUE	WED	THU	FRI	SAT
						1 CLAP AND SNAP A PATTERN FOR YOUR FAMILY
2 THROW A BALL WITH A FRIEND	**3** HOW MANY BEDS ARE IN YOUR HOUSE?	**4** BRING YOUR PARENTS TO OPEN HOUSE AND THE BOOK FAIR	**5** WHAT IS A COMMUNITY HELPER?	**6** HOW DO FIRE FIGHTERS HELP US?	**7** WHERE IS THE NEAREST FIRE STATION?	**8** MAKE A SANDWICH AND CUT IT INTO SQUARES
9 PLAN A HOME FIRE DRILL WITH YOUR FAMILY	**10** WHAT IS THE EMERGENCY PHONE NUMBER?	**11** NAME ONE FIRE SAFETY RULE	**12** WHO WAS CHRISTOPHER COLUMBUS?	**13** WHO ARE THE COMMUNITY HELPERS AT OUR SCHOOL?	**14** WHICH COMMUNITY HELPER WOULD YOU LIKE TO BE?	**15** WHAT COLORS ARE THE LEAVES ON YOUR TREES?
16 WHY DO THE LEAVES TURN COLOR IN THE FALL?	**17** BRING ONE FAVORITE LEAF TO SCHOOL TO GRAPH	**18** DESCRIBE ONE PERSON IN YOUR FAMILY	**19** CAN YOU RECITE "PETER, PETER, PUMPKIN EATER?"	**20** NAME ONE THING THAT IS FUN TO DO IN THE FALL	**21** CAN YOU SAY THE DAYS OF THE WEEK?	**22** HOW MANY TIMES CAN YOU HOP ON ONE FOOT WITHOUT LOSING YOUR BALANCE?
23 SING A HALLOWEEN SONG FOR YOUR FAMILY	**24** HOW MANY LETTERS ARE IN HALLOWEEN?	**25** HOW MANY MORE DAYS UNTIL HALLOWEEN?	**26** WHAT IS A STRANGER?	**27** WHAT IS SCAREY TO YOU?	**28** HOW DOES A PUMPKIN BECOME A JACK-O-LANTERN?	**29** WHAT ARE THE RULES FOR SAFE TRICK-OR-TREATING?
30 TEACH YOUR FAMILY YOUR FAVORITE HALLOWEEN POEM	**31** BRING YOUR HALLOWEEN COSTUME IN A PAPER BAG WITH YOUR NAME ON IT. HALLOWEEN! ! ! ! ! !					

Source: Huntsville City Schools, Huntsville, Alabama.

How Do You Conduct a Parent Conference?

Conferences are a time for both parents and teachers to share information about the child. By sending home a questionnaire similar to the one on the following page before the conference, the parent will feel more involved and will have more input. The teacher should have examples of the child's work, a written assessment, and other observations compiled before the conferences. "Be prepared," "be professional," and bear in mind the following:

1. Be friendly, relaxed, and smile.
2. Sit beside the parent at a table, rather than behind a desk.
3. Keep the conversation focused on the child. (This is not the time to talk about siblings or a class party.)
4. Start off with positive comments about the child.
5. Go over the questionnaire the parents have brought to the conference. Encourage them to share their feelings about their child and school.
6. Listen, listen, then listen some more. Be accepting of what the parent says. Being defensive or arguing will not help the child or your relationship.
7. Review the child's work and your assessment, including intellectual, physical, social, and emotional development.
8. Discuss goals and future plans. Give the parents specific ideas for how they can help their child at home.
9. If there is a problem, brainstorm solutions and develop a plan for action.
10. End the conference on a positive note by reassuring parents and thanking them for their support.
11. Follow-up with parents on their child's progress.

Send the questionnaire on page 273 home several days before your conference for the parents to complete. This will give you a smooth transition into the conference and encourage parent participation.

PARENT QUESTIONNAIRE FOR CONFERENCES

Child's Name _____ Date _____

1. My child's favorite activity at school is _____
   _____

2. My child expresses concern about _____
   _____

3. My child's strong qualities are _____
   _____
   _____

4. Areas I feel my child needs to work on are _____
   _____
   _____

5. Something my child would like to do at school is _____
   _____

6. Something I would like to see my child do at school is _____
   _____

7. Is there any special information about your child that you think we should
   know about? _____
   _____

Appendix A
PATTERNS

Use a copy machine to enlarge or reduce these patterns for games, projects, and visuals.

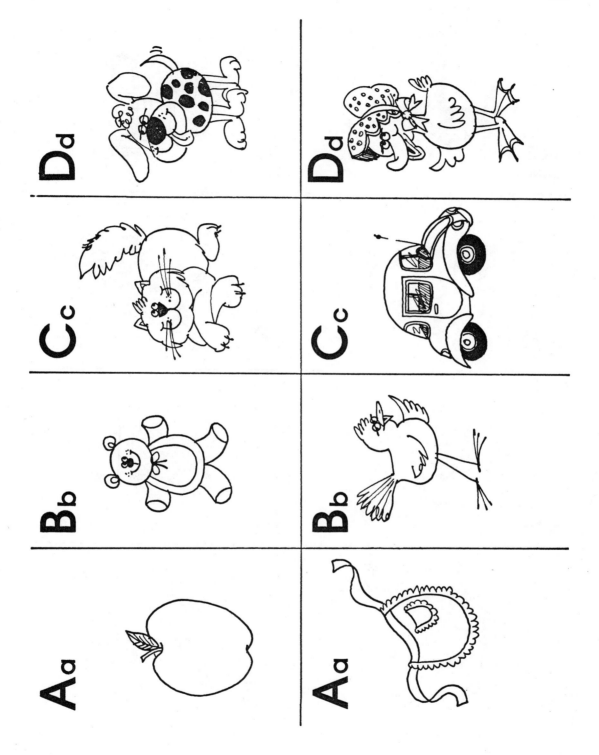

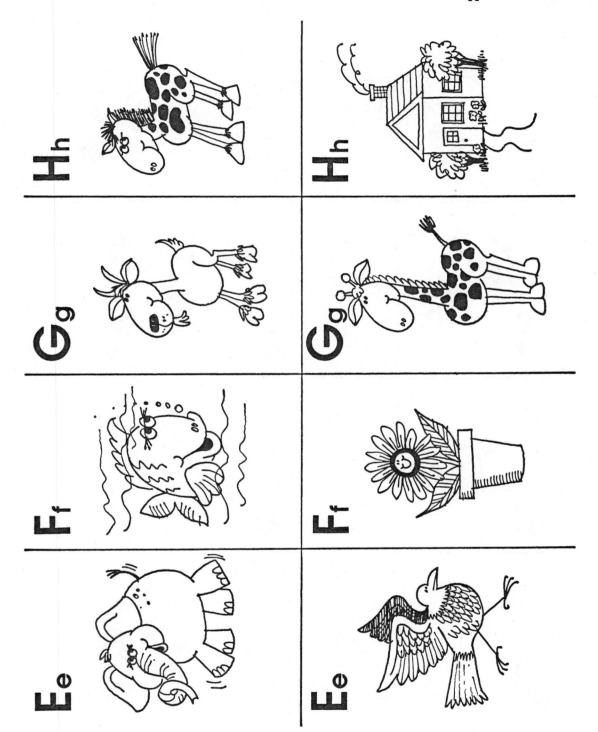

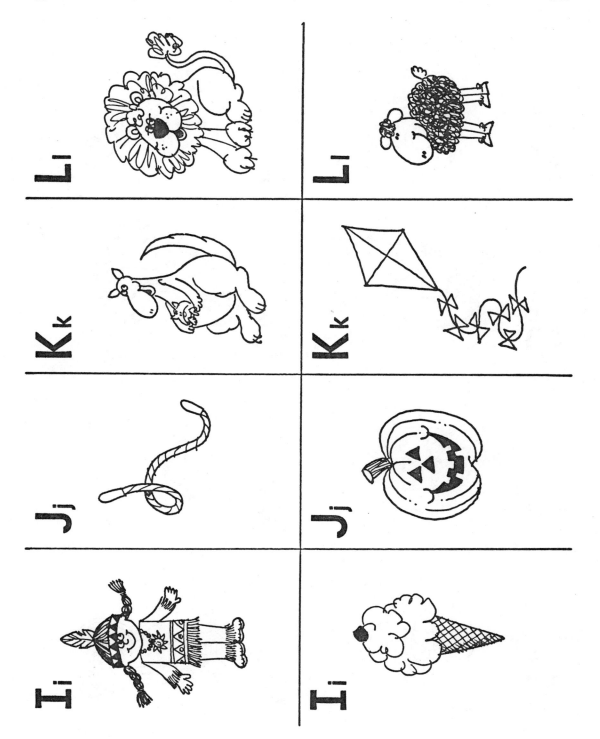

L l

L l

K k

K k

J j

J j

I i

I i

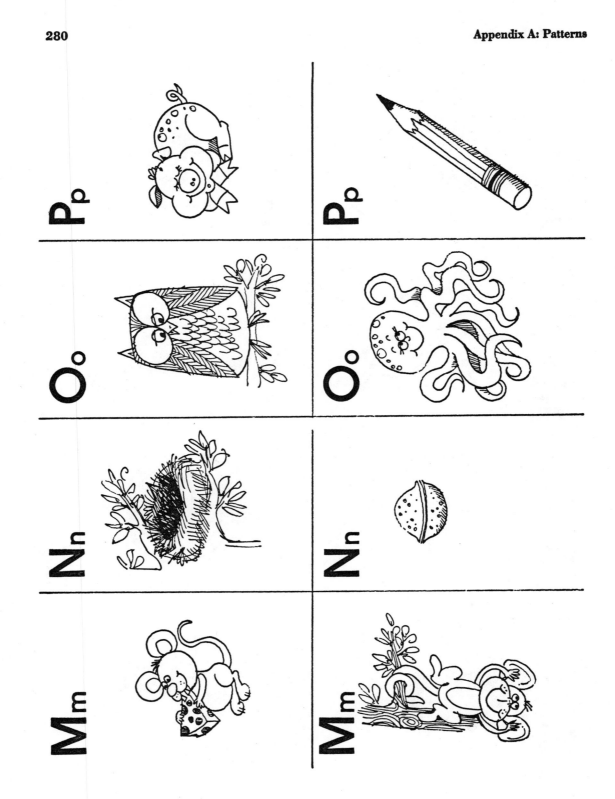

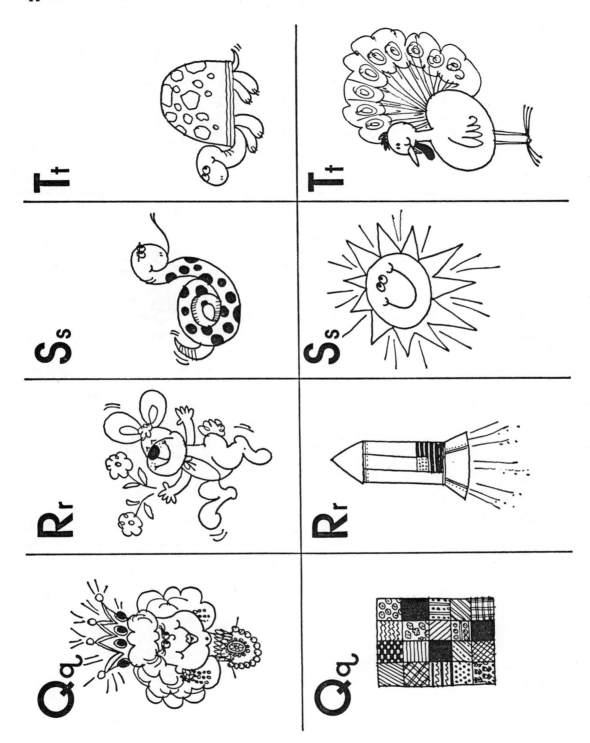

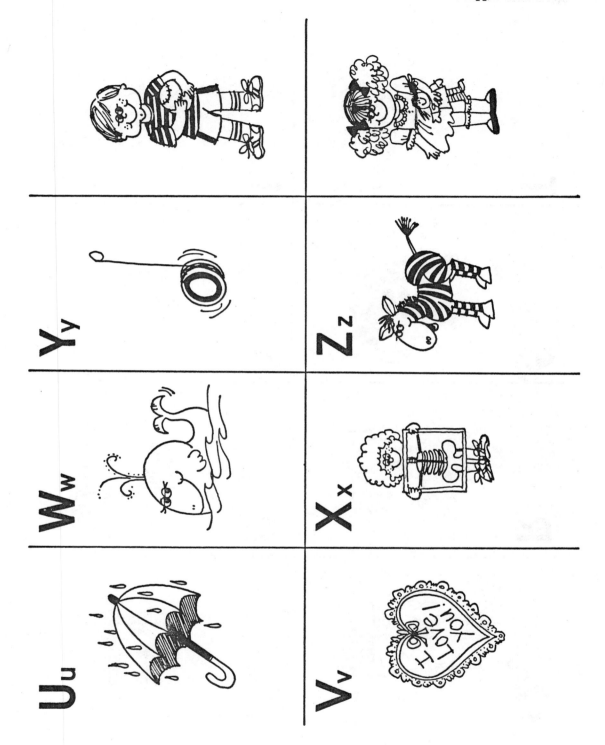

March

April

January

February

November

December

September

October

Appendix B

COMMERCIAL RESOURCES

COMMERCIAL RESOURCES

Most of these commercial suppliers will be happy to send you a catalog of their products.

ABC School Supply, Inc.
P. O. Box 4750
Norcross, GA 30091

American Guidance Service
Publisher's Building
Circle Pines, MN 55014

Angeles Toys, Inc.
9 Capper Drive
Pacific, MO 63069

Binney and Smith, Inc.
1100 Church Lane
Easton, PA 18044

Childcraft Education Corp.
20 Kilmer Road
Edison, NJ 08818

Community Playthings
Route 213
Rifton, NY 12471

Constructive Playthings
1227 East 119th Street
Grandview, MO 64030

T. S. Denison and Company
9601 Newton Avenue, S.
Minneapolis, MN 55431

DLM Teaching Resources
One DLM Park
Box 4000
Allen, TX 75002

Educational Teaching Aids
199 Carpenter Avenue
Wheeling, IL 60090

Environments, Inc.
Beaufort Industrial Park
P. O. Box 1348
Beaufort, SC 29901

Fearon Teacher Aids
500 Harbor Blvd.
Belmont, CA 94002

First Step Designs, Ltd./Hand in Hand
369 Congress Street
Boston, MA 02210

GameTime Inc.
101 Kingsberry Rd.
P. O. Box 121
Fort Payne, AL 35967

Good Apple Inc.
1204 Buchanan Street
Carthage, IL 62321

Gryphon House, Inc.
P. O. Box 275
Mt. Rainier, MD 20712

J. L. Hammett Company
P. O. Box 545, Hammett Place
Braintree, MA 02184

Judy/Instructo
4325 Hiawatha Avenue, S.
Minneapolis, MN 55406

Kaplan School Supply
P. O. Box 609
Lewisville, NC 27023

Kids-Play Inc.
P. O. Box 560
Falkville, AL 35622

Kimbo Educational
P. O. Box 477
Long Branch, NJ 07740

Lakeshore Curriculum Materials Co.
2695 E. Dominguez Street
P. O. Box 6261
Carson, CA 90278

Landscape Structures, Inc.
601 7th Street, S.
Delano, MN 55328

Lauri
P. O. Box F
Phillips-Avon, ME 04966

Lego Dacta
555 Taylor Road
Enfield, CT 06040

The Little Tikes Company
2180 Barlow Road
Hudson, OH 44236

Playdesigns
P. O. Box 427
New Berlin, PA 17855

Playscapes, Inc. Children's Environments
30 West Mifflin
Madison, WI 53703

Rainbow Play Systems
4480 Dakota Street, SE
Prior Lake, MN 55372

Scholastic, Inc.
730 Broadway
New York, NY 10003

Resources

Children

Allen, K., & Marotz, L. (1989). DEVELOPMENTAL PROFILES, BIRTH TO SIX. Albany, NY: Delmar.

Brazelton, T. (1974). TODDLERS AND PARENTS. New York: Dell.

Bredekamp, S. (1987). DEVELOPMENTALLY APPROPRIATE PRACTICE. Washington, DC: National Association for the Education of Young Children.

Briggs, D. (1970). YOUR CHILD'S SELF-ESTEEM. Garden City, NY: Doubleday.

Clemens, S. (1983). THE SUN'S NOT BROKEN: A CLOUD'S JUST IN THE WAY. Mt. Rainier, MD: Gryphon.

Elkind, D. (1982). THE HURRIED CHILD: GROWING UP TOO FAST, TOO SOON. Reading, MA: Addison-Wesley.

Gesell, A., Ames, L., & Ilg, F. (1979). THE GESELL INSTITUTE'S CHILD FROM ONE TO SIX. New York: Harper & Row.

Gordon, A., & Browne, K. (1989). BEGINNINGS AND BEYOND. Albany, NY: Delmar.

Hymes, J. (1981). TEACHING THE CHILD UNDER SIX. Columbus, OH: Charles E. Merrill.

Miller, K. (1985). AGES AND STAGES. Marshfield, MA: Telshare.

Salkind, N., & Ambron, S. (1987). CHILD DEVELOPMENT. New York: Holt, Rinehart, & Winston.

Spodek, B. (1972). TEACHING IN THE EARLY YEARS. Englewood Cliffs, NJ: Prentice Hall.

White, B. (1977). THE FIRST THREE YEARS OF LIFE. Englewood Cliffs, NJ: Prentice Hall.

Classroom Organization and Guidance

Cherry, C. (1983). PLEASE DON'T SIT ON THE KIDS: ALTERNATIVES TO PUNITIVE DISCIPLINE. Belmont, CA: David S. Lake.

Dreikurs, R., & Soltz, V. (1964). CHILDREN: THE CHALLENGE. New York: Hawthorne.

Faber, A., & Mazlish, E. (1982). HOW TO TALK SO KIDS WILL LISTEN AND LISTEN SO KIDS WILL TALK. New York: Avon.

Garber, S., Garber, M., & Spizman, R. (1987). GOOD BEHAVIOR. New York: Villard Books.

Ginott, H. (1975). TEACHER AND CHILD. New York: Avon.

Gordon, T. (1987). P.E.T. IN ACTION. New York: Bantam Books.

Mitchell, G. (1982). A VERY PRACTICAL GUIDE TO DISCIPLINE WITH YOUNG CHILDREN. Marshfield, MA: Telshare.

The Learning Environment

Beaty, J. (1988). SKILLS FOR PRESCHOOL TEACHERS. Columbus, OH: Merrill Publishing Company.

Carroll, J. (1983). LEARNING CENTERS FOR LITTLE KIDS. Carthage, IL: Good Apple.

Dodge, D. (1988). THE CREATIVE CURRICULUM FOR EARLY CHILDHOOD. Washington, DC: Teaching Strategies.

Flemming, B., Hamilton, D., & Hicks, J. (1977). RESOURCES FOR TEACHING IN EARLY CHILDHOOD EDUCATION. San Diego, CA: Harcourt Brace Jovanovich.

Miller, K. (1989). THE OUTSIDE PLAY AND LEARNING BOOK. Mt. Rainier, MD: Gryphon House.

Sanoff, H., & Sanoff, J. (1988). LEARNING ENVIRONMENTS FOR CHILDREN. Atlanta, GA: Humanics.

Curriculum

Beaty, J. (1985). SKILLS FOR PRESCHOOL TEACHERS. Columbus, OH: Merrill.

Croft, D., & Hess, R. (1985). AN ACTIVITIES HANDBOOK FOR TEACHERS OF YOUNG CHILDREN. Boston: Houghton Mifflin.

Flemming, B., Hamilton, D., & Hicks, J. (1977). RESOURCES FOR CREATIVE TEACHING IN EARLY CHILDHOOD. San Diego: Harcourt Brace Jovanovich.

Gordon, A., & Browne, K. (1989). BEGINNINGS AND BEYOND. Albany, NY: Delmar.

Miller, K. (1985). AGES AND STAGES. Marshfield, MA: Telshare.

Mitchell, G., & Chmela, H. (1987). I AM! I CAN! Marshfield, MA: Telshare.

Tarrow, N. & Lundsteen, S. (1981). ACTIVITIES AND RESOURCES FOR GUIDING YOUNG CHILDREN'S LEARNING. New York: McGraw-Hill.

Language Development and Reading Readiness

Baratta-Lorton, M. (1972). WORKJOBS. Menlo Park, CA: Addison-Wesley.

Barret, S. (1980). THE SOUND OF THE WEEK. Carthage, IL: Good Apple.

Beaty, J. (1984). SKILLS FOR PRESCHOOL TEACHERS. Columbus, OH: Charles Merrill.

Beckman, C., Simmons, R., & Thomas, N. (1982). EARLY CHILDHOOD ACTIVITY GUIDE FOR HOLIDAYS AND SEASONS. Colorado Springs, CO: Channels to Children.

Borba, M., & Ungaro, D. (1980). THE COMPLETE LETTER BOOK. Carthage, IL: Good Apple.

Commins, E. (1982). EARLY CHILDHOOD ACTIVITIES. Atlanta: Humanics.

Coudron, J. (1983). ALPHABET PUPPETS. Belmont, CA: David S. Lake.

Croft, D., & Hess, R. (1985). AN ACTIVITIES HANDBOOK FOR TEACHERS OF YOUNG CHILDREN. Boston: Houghton Mifflin.

Durkin, D. (1981). GETTING STARTED READING. Boston: Allyn and Bacon.

Eisenhart, C., & Bell, R. (1985). POCKETFUL OF MIRACLES. Livonia, MI: Partner Press.

Farnette, C., Forte, I., & Loss, B. (1975). KIDS' STUFF READING AND WRITING READINESS. Nashville, TN: Incentive Publications.

Flemming, B., & Hamilton, D. (1977). RESOURCES FOR CREATIVE TEACHING IN EARLY CHILDHOOD EDUCATION. San Diego: Harcourt Brace Jovanovich.

Gilbert, L. (1984). I CAN DO IT! I CAN DO IT! Mt. Rainier, MD: Gryphon House.

Gordon, I., Guinagh, B., & Jester, R. (1972). CHILD LEARNING THROUGH CHILD PLAY. New York: St. Martin's Press.

Hillerich, R. (1977). READING FUNDAMENTALS FOR PRESCHOOL AND PRIMARY CHILDREN. Columbus, OH: Charles Merrill.

Machado, J. (1985). EARLY CHILDHOOD EXPERIENCES IN LANGUAGE ARTS. Albany, NY: Delmar.

Mayesky, M., Neuman, D., & Wlodkowski, R. (1985). CREATIVE ACTIVITIES FOR YOUNG CHILDREN. Albany, NY: Delmar.

Miller, K. (1984). THINGS TO DO WITH TODDLERS AND TWOS. Marshfield, MA: Telshare.

Mitchell, G., & Chmela, H. (1987). I AM! I CAN! Marshfield, MA: Telshare.

Ramsey, M., & Bayless, K. (1980). KINDERGARTEN PROGRAMS AND PRACTICES. St. Louis: C. V. Mosby.

Stull, E., & Price, C. (1987). KINDERGARTEN TEACHER'S MONTH-BY-MONTH ACTIVITIES PROGRAM. West Nyack, NY: The Center for Applied Research in Education.

Tarrow, N. & Lundsteen, S. (1981). ACTIVITIES AND RESOURCES FOR GUIDING YOUNG CHILDREN'S LEARNING. New York: McGraw-Hill.

Zitlaw, J., & Frank, C. (1985). ALPHA-PETS. Carthage, IL: Good Apple.

Mathematics

Baratta-Lorton, M. (1976). MATHEMATICS THEIR WAY. Menlo Park, CA: Addison-Wesley.

Baratta-Lorton, M. (1979). WORKJOBS II. Menlo Park, CA: Addison-Wesley.

Beaty, J. (1984). SKILLS FOR PRESCHOOL TEACHERS. Columbus, OH: Charles E. Merrill.

Beckman, C., Simmons, R., & Thomas, N. (1982). EARLY CHILDHOOD ACTIVITY GUIDE FOR HOLIDAYS AND SEASONS. Colorado Springs, CO: Channels to Children.

Brown, S. (1982). ONE, TWO, BUCKLE MY SHOE. Mt. Rainier, MD: Gryphon House.

Commins, E. (1982). EARLY CHILDHOOD ACTIVITIES. Atlanta: Humanics.

Croft, D., & Hess, R. (1985). AN ACTIVITIES HANDBOOK FOR TEACHERS OF YOUNG CHILDREN. Boston: Houghton Mifflin.

Davidson, J. (1989). CHILDREN AND COMPUTERS TOGETHER IN THE EARLY CHILDHOOD CLASSROOM. Albany, NY: Delmar.

Indenbaum, V., & Shapiro, M. (1985). THE EVERYTHING BOOK FOR TEACHERS OF YOUNG CHILDREN. Mt. Rainier, MD: Gryphon House.

Schultz, K., Colarusso, R., & Strawderman, V. (1989). MATHEMATICS FOR EVERY YOUNG CHILD. Columbus, OH: Charles E. Merrill.

Tarrow, N., & Lundsteen, S. (1981). GUIDING YOUNG CHILDREN'S LEARNING. New York: McGraw-Hill.

Science

Allison, L., & Katz, D. (1985). GEE, WIZ! Canada: Little, Brown and Company.

Baratta-Lorton, M. (1972). WORKJOBS. Menlo Park, CA: Addison-Wesley.

Beckman, C., Simmons, R., & Thomas, N. (1982). EARLY CHILDHOOD ACTIVITY GUIDE FOR HOLIDAYS AND SEASONS. Colorado Springs, CO: Channels to Children.

Blackwelder, S. (1980). SCIENCE FOR ALL SEASONS. Englewood Cliffs, NJ: Prentice Hall.

Brown, S. (1981). BUBBLES, RAINBOWS, & WORMS. Mt. Rainier, MD: Gryphon House.

Cobb, V. (1972). SCIENCE EXPERIMENTS YOU CAN EAT. New York: J. B. Lippincott.

CONSERVATION SEEDS. (1984). Jefferson City, MO: Missouri Department of Conservation.

Forte, I. (1985). NATURE CRAFTS. Nashville, TN: Incentive Publications.

Nickelsburg, J. (1976). NATURE ACTIVITIES FOR EARLY CHILDHOOD. Menlo Park, CA: Addison-Wesley.

Rockwell, R., Sherwood, E., & Williams, A. (1986). HUG A TREE. Mt. Rainier, MD: Gryphon House.

Williams, R., Rockwell, R., Sherwood, E. (1987). MUDPIES TO MAGNETS. Mt. Rainier, MD: Gryphon House.

Storytime Magic

Anderson, P. S. (1963). STORYTELLING WITH THE FLANNEL BOARD. Minneapolis: T. S. Denison.

Breznau, C. (1980). THE REAL HAPPILY EVER AFTER BOOK. Nashville: Incentive Publications.

Daniels, J. (1982). FUN WITH ACTION STORIES. Minneapolis: T. S. Denison.

Dorian, M., & Gulland, F. (1974). TELLING STORIES THROUGH MOVEMENT. Belmont, CA: Fearon-Pitman.

Evans, J., & Moore, J. (1985). HOW TO MAKE BOOKS WITH CHILDREN. Carmel, CA: Evan-Moor.

Fagella, K., Hayes, M., & Leone, A. (1987). BUILDING ON BOOKS. Bridgeport, CT: First Teacher Press.

LaPenta, M., & Bielitz, J. (1982). STORYTELLING. New York: Macmillan Educational Company.

Olson, M. (1963). TELL AND DRAW STORIES. Minneapolis: Creative Storytime Press.

Schimmel, N. (1984). JUST ENOUGH TO MAKE A STORY. San Francisco: Sisters' Choice Press.

Strangl, S. (1984). PAPER STORIES. Belmont, CA: David S. Lake.

Taylor, F., & Vaughn, G. (1988). THE FLANNEL BOARD STORYBOOK. Atlanta, Humanics.

Trelease, J. (1987). THE READ-ALOUD HANDBOOK. New York: Penguin Books.

Warren, J. (1984). CUT AND TELL. Everett, WA: Totline Press.

Creative Arts

Bos, G. (1978). PLEASE DON'T MOVE THE MUFFIN TINS. Carmichael, CA: The Burton Gallery.

Brashears, D. (1985). DRIBBLE DRABBLE ART EXPERIENCES FOR YOUNG CHILDREN. Fort Collins, CO: DMC Publications.

Commins, E. (1982). EARLY CHILDHOOD ACTIVITIES. Atlanta: Humanics.

Croft, D., & Hess, R. (1985). AN ACTIVITIES HANDBOOK FOR TEACHERS OF YOUNG CHILDREN. Boston: Houghton Mifflin.

Frank, M. (1976). I CAN MAKE A RAINBOW. Nashville, TN: Incentive Publications.

Gilbert, L. (1984). I CAN DO IT! I CAN DO IT! Mt. Rainier, MD: Gryphon House.

Kohl, M. (1985). SCRIBBLE COOKIES. Bellingham, WA: Bright Ring.

Mayesky, M., Neuman, D., Wlodkowski, R. (1985). CREATIVE ACTIVITIES FOR YOUNG CHILDREN. Albany, NY: Delmar.

Mitchell, G., & Chemela, H. (1987). I AM! I CAN! Marshfield, MA: Telshare.

Schirrmacher, R. (1988). ART AND CREATIVE DEVELOPMENT FOR YOUNG CHILDREN. Albany, NY: Delmar.

Warren, J. (1988). 1-2-3 ART: OPEN-ENDED ART ACTIVITIES FOR YOUNG CHILDREN. Everett, WA: Warren Publishing.

Music and Movement

Andress, B. (1980). MUSIC EXPERIENCES IN EARLY CHILDHOOD. New York: Holt, Rinehart, & Winston.

Birkenshaw, L. (1977). MUSIC FOR FUN, MUSIC FOR LEARNING. Toronto: Holt, Rinehart, & Winston.

Croft, D., & Hess, R. (1985). AN ACTIVITIES HANDBOOK FOR TEACHERS OF YOUNG CHILDREN. Boston: Houghton Mifflin.

Fox, D., & Marks, C. (1987). GO IN AND OUT THE WINDOW. New York: Henry Holt and Company and the Metropolitan Museum of Art.

Glazer, T. (1980). DO YOUR EARS HANG LOW? New York: Doubleday.

Glazer, T. (1973). EYE WINKER, TOM TINKER, CHIN CHOPPER. New York: Doubleday.

Haines, B., & Gerber, L. (1988). LEADING YOUNG CHILDREN TO MUSIC. Columbus, OH: Merrill.

Meyer, C., & Pickens, K. (1989). SING AND LEARN. Carthage, IL: Good Apple.

Moomaw, S. (1984). DISCOVERING MUSIC IN EARLY CHILDHOOD. Boston: Allyn & Bacon.

Steinquest, J. (1982). PRACTICAL MUSIC ACTIVITIES FOR THE PRESCHOOL TEACHER. Ruston, LA: Louisiana Association for Children Under Six.

Trencher, B. (1976). CHILD'S PLAY: AN ACTIVITIES AND MATERIALS HANDBOOK. Atlanta: Humanics.

Warner, L., & Craycraft, K. (1987). FUN WITH FAMILIAR TUNES. Carthage, IL: Good Apple.

Warren, J. (1983). PIGGYBACK SONGS. Everett, WA: Totline Press.

Weller Pugmire, M. (1977). EXPERIENCES IN MUSIC FOR YOUNG CHILDREN. Albany, NY: Delmar.

Small Motor Skills

Baratta-Lorton, M. (1972). WORKJOBS. Menlo Park, CA: Addison-Wesley.

Beaty, J. (1984). SKILLS FOR PRESCHOOL TEACHERS. Columbus, OH: Merrill.

Commins, E. (1982). EARLY CHILDHOOD ACTIVITIES. Atlanta: Humanics.

Croft, D., & Hess, R. (1985). AN ACTIVITIES HANDBOOK FOR TEACHERS OF YOUNG CHILDREN. Boston: Houghton Mifflin.

Cryer, D., Harms, T., & Bourland, B. (1988). ACTIVE LEARNING FOR TWOS AND ACTIVE LEARNING FOR THREES. Menlo Park, CA: Addison-Wesley.

Gilbert, L. (1984). I CAN DO IT! I CAN DO IT! Mt. Rainier, MD: Gryphon House.

Miller, K. (1984). THINGS TO DO WITH TODDLERS AND TWOS. Marshfield, MA: Telshare.

Trister Dodge, D. (1988). THE CREATIVE CURRICULUM FOR EARLY CHILDHOOD. Washington, DC: Teaching Strategies.

Large Motor Skills

Beckman, C., Simmons, R., & Thomas, N. (1982). EARLY CHILDHOOD ACTIVITY GUIDE FOR HOLIDAYS AND SEASONS. Colorado Springs: Channels to Children.

Block, S. (1977). "ME AND I'M GREAT" PHYSICAL EDUCATION FOR CHILDREN THREE THROUGH EIGHT. Minneapolis: Burgess.

GET FIT. (1986). U.S. Department of Health and Human Services. Washington, D.C.: U.S. Government Printing Office.

Graham, T., & Camp, L. (1988). TEACHING TERRIFIC TWOS AND OTHER TODDLERS. Atlanta: Humanics.

Gregson, B. (1982). THE INCREDIBLE INDOOR GAMES BOOK. Belmont, CA: David S. Lake.

Gregson, B. (1982). THE OUTRAGEOUS OUTDOOR GAMES BOOK. Belmont, CA: David S. Lake.

Linderman, C. (1979). TEACHABLES FROM TRASHABLES. Mt. Rainier, MD: Gryphon House.

Torbert, M. (1980). FOLLOW ME, A HANDBOOK OF MOVEMENT ACTIVITIES FOR CHILDREN. Englewood Cliffs, NJ: Prentice Hall.

Warren, J. (1986). 1,2,3 GAMES. Everett, WA: Totline Press.

Werner, P., & Burton, E. (1979). LEARNING THROUGH MOVEMENT. St. Louis: C. V. Mosby.

Nutrition and Cooking

Baxter, K. (1980). COME AND GET IT. Ann Arbor, MI: Children First Press.

Beckman, C., Simmons, R., & Thomas, N. (1982). EARLY CHILDHOOD ACTIVITY GUIDE FOR HOLIDAYS AND SEASONS. Colorado Springs, CO: Channels to Children.

Christenberry, M., & Stevens, B. (1984). CAN PIAGET COOK? Atlanta, Humanics.

Cobb, V. (1972). SCIENCE EXPERIMENTS YOU CAN EAT. Philadelphia: J. B. Lippincott.

DIETARY GUIDELINES FOR AMERICANS. (1985). U.S. Department of Agriculture: U.S. Department of Health and Human Services. Home and Garden Bulletin No. 232.

DON'T LICK THE SPOON BEFORE YOU PUT IT IN THE POT. (1982). Ferguson, MO: Ferguson-Florissant School District.

FOOD...EARLY CHOICES. (1979). Rosemont, IL: National Dairy Council.

Johnson, B. (1980). CUP COOKING. Mt. Rainier, MD: Gryphon House.

Lansky, V. (1978). THE TAMING OF THE C.A.N.D.Y. MONSTER. Wayzata, MN: Meadowbrook Press.

Marotz, L., Rush, J., & Cross, M. (1985). HEALTH, SAFETY, AND NUTRITION FOR THE YOUNG CHILD. Albany, NY: Delmar.

Smith, L. (1985). FOODS FOR HEALTHY KIDS. New York: Berkley Books.

Stancil, R., & Wilkins, L. (1985). KIDS' SIMPLY SCRUMPTIOUS MICROWAVING. Atlanta: Kitchen Classics.

Veitch, B., & Harms, T. (1981). COOK AND LEARN. Menlo Park, CA: Addison-Wesley.

Wallace, M., & Wallace, J. (1978). SNACKERS: KICK THE JUNK FOOD HABIT. Seattle, WA: Madrona.

Wanamaker, N., Hearn, K., & Richarz, S. (1979). MORE THAN GRAHAM CRACKERS. Washington, DC: National Association for the Education of Young Children.

Warren, J. (1982). SUPER SNACKS. Everett, WA: Warren Publishing.

Putting It All Together with a Teaching Unit

Beckman, C., Simmons, R., & Thomas, N. (1982). EARLY CHILDHOOD ACTIVITY GUIDE FOR HOLIDAYS AND SEASONS. Colorado Springs, CO: Channels to Children.

Croft, D., & Hess, R. (1985). AN ACTIVITIES HANDBOOK FOR TEACHERS OF YOUNG CHILDREN. Boston: Houghton Mifflin.

Flemming, B., Hamilton, D., & Hicks, J. (1977). RESOURCES FOR CREATIVE TEACHING IN EARLY CHILDHOOD. San Diego: Harcourt Brace Jovanovich.

Mitchell, G., & Chemela, H. (1987). I AM! I CAN! Marshfield, MA: Telshare.

Moore, J., & Tryon, L. (1988). BEARS, BEARS, BEARS. Monterey, CA: Evan-Moor.

Steen, A., & Lane, M. (1986). TEDDY BEARS AT SCHOOL. Atlanta: Humanics.

The Professional Teacher

Beaty, J. (1988). SKILLS FOR PRESCHOOL TEACHERS. Columbus, OH: Merrill.

Endsley, R., & Bradbard, M. (1981). QUALITY DAY CARE. Englewood Cliffs, NJ: Prentice Hall.

Gestwicki, C. (1987). HOME, SCHOOL, AND COMMUNITY RELATIONS. Albany, NY: Delmar.

Hildebrand, V. (1981). INTRODUCTION TO EARLY CHILDHOOD EDUCATION. New York: Macmillan.

Hymes, J. (1975). EFFECTIVE HOME-SCHOOL RELATIONS. Carmel, CA: Hacienda Press.

Kuczen, B. (1982). CHILDHOOD STRESS: DON'T LET YOUR CHILD BE A VICTIM. New York: Delacorte.

Leeper, S., Witherspoon, R., & Day, B. (1984). GOOD SCHOOLS FOR GOOD CHILDREN. New York: Macmillan.

Stone, J. (1987). TEACHER-PARENT RELATIONSHIPS. Washington, DC: National Association for the Education of Young Children.

Swap, S. (1984). ENHANCING PARENT INVOLVEMENT. Boston, MA: Center for Parenting Studies.

Waitley, D. (1983). SEEDS OF GREATNESS. Old Tappan, NJ: Fleming H. Revell.